A Book Of

PRINCIPLES OF MARKETING

For
BBA & BBM (Semester - II)
As Per Pune University's Revised Syllabus
Effective from June 2013

Dr. Shaila Bootwala
M.Com., M.Phil, Ph.D. (Marketing)
Vice-Principal and Head, Dept. of Commerce,
Abeda Inamdar Senior College,
Pune

Advancement of knowledge

PRINCIPLES OF MARKETING　　　　　　　　　　　　　　ISBN 978-93-83750-07-8

First Edition : November 2013

© : Author

The text of this publication, or any part thereof, should not be reproduced or transmitted in any form or stored in any computer storage system or device for distribution including photocopy, recording, taping or information retrieval system or reproduced on any disc, tape, perforated media or other information storage device etc., without the written permission of Author with whom the rights are reserved. Breach of this condition is liable for legal action.

Every effort has been made to avoid errors or omissions in this publication. In spite of this, errors may have crept in. Any mistake, error or discrepancy so noted and shall be brought to our notice shall be taken care of in the next edition. It is notified that neither the publisher nor the author or seller shall be responsible for any damage or loss of action to any one, of any kind, in any manner, therefrom.

Published By :
NIRALI PRAKASHAN
Abhyudaya Pragati, 1312, Shivaji Nagar,
Off J.M. Road, PUNE – 411005
Tel - (020) 25512336/37/39, Fax - (020) 25511379
Email : niralipune@pragationline.com

Printed By :
Repro Knowledgecast Limited,
Thane

DISTRIBUTION CENTRES
PUNE

Nirali Prakashan
119, Budhwar Peth, Jogeshwari Mandir Lane
Pune 411002, Maharashtra
Tel : (020) 2445 2044, 66022708, Fax : (020) 2445 1538
Email : bookorder@pragationline.com

Nirali Prakashan
S. No. 28/27, Dhyari,
Near Pari Company, Pune 411041
Tel : (022) 24690371
Email : dhyari@pragationline.com
bookorder@pragationline.com

MUMBAI
Nirali Prakashan
385, S.V.P. Road, Rasdhara Co-op. Hsg. Society Ltd.,
Girgaum, Mumbai 400004, Maharashtra
Tel : (022) 2385 6339 / 2386 9976, Fax : (022) 2386 9976
Email : niralimumbai@pragationline.com

DISTRIBUTION BRANCHES

NAGPUR
Pratibha Book Distributors
Above Maratha Mandir, Shop No. 3, First Floor,
Rani Jhanshi Square, Sitabuldi, Nagpur 440012,
Maharashtra, Tel : (0712) 254 7129

BENGALURU
Pragati Book House
House No. 1, Sanjeevappa Lane, Avenue Road Cross,
Opp. Rice Church, Bengaluru – 560002.
Tel : (080) 64513344, 64513355,
Mob : 9880582331, 9845021552
Email:bharatsavla@yahoo.com

JALGAON
Nirali Prakashan
34, V. V. Golani Market, Navi Peth, Jalgaon 425001,
Maharashtra, Tel : (0257) 222 0395
Mob : 94234 91860

KOLHAPUR
Nirali Prakashan
New Mahadvar Road,
Kedar Plaza, 1st Floor Opp. IDBI Bank
Kolhapur 416 012, Maharashtra. Mob : 9855046155

CHENNAI
Pragati Books
9/1, Montieth Road, Behind Taas Mahal, Egmore,
Chennai 600008 Tamil Nadu, Tel : (044) 6518 3535,
Mob : 94440 01782 / 98450 21552 / 98805 82331, Email : bharatsavla@yahoo.com

RETAIL OUTLETS
PUNE

Pragati Book Centre
157, Budhwar Peth, Opp. Ratan Talkies,
Pune 411002, Maharashtra
Tel : (020) 2445 8887 / 6602 2707, Fax : (020) 2445 8887

Pragati Book Centre
Amber Chamber, 28/A, Budhwar Peth,
Appa Balwant Chowk, Pune : 411002, Maharashtra,
Tel : (020) 20240335 / 66281669
Email : pbcpune@pragationline.com

Pragati Book Centre
676/B, Budhwar Peth, Opp. Jogeshwari Mandir,
Pune 411002, Maharashtra
Tel : (020) 6601 7784 / 6602 0855

PBC Book Sellers & Stationers
152, Budhwar Peth, Pune 411002, Maharashtra
Tel : (020) 2445 2254 / 6609 2463

MUMBAI
Pragati Book Corner
Indira Niwas, 111 - A, Bhavani Shankar Road, Dadar (W), Mumbai 400028, Maharashtra
Tel : (022) 2422 3526 / 6662 5254, Email : pbcmumbai@pragationline.com

www.pragationline.com　　　　　　　　　　　　　　　　　　　　info@pragationline.com

Dedication ...

This book is for my son, "SAMEER MITHA".

Love you. May Allah always bless you.

Preface ...

This book has been written keeping in mind the new syllabus proposed by the Board of Studies in Marketing, University of Pune for BBA and BBM Semester II students adopted from June 2013. The subject, 'Marketing', as a separate body of knowledge, is introduced to undergraduate students at the first year itself. At the junior college level they do get a little insight into various aspects of Marketing. However, the study of Marketing, as a separate subject is introduced only at the first year level. As such this paper is titled as "Principles of Marketing" and deals with the various basic aspects of Marketing. All the chapters are written keeping in mind that the student is being newly introduced to the topic.

Marketing is a very dynamic and volatile subject. The success of any marketing endeavour depends upon its acceptance by the market or consumer. No marketing activity can be planned or implemented without the consumer being the key focus area. How a consumer will react to the marketing message will determine the success or failure of the marketing message/ strategy.

At the end of the book, I have included some marketing case studies. They are actually stories of how various products were introduced into the Indian Market, and how and why they succeeded or did not succeed. This chapter is not a part of the syllabus. It is just extra reading for the interested student. All case studies are old. The present status of no product is given. As such the interested student can take it up as a challenge to find out what happened to the products after the period of the case study given.

I have always been of the opinion that just as swimming cannot be learnt through a book without actually getting into the water, so also Marketing cannot be studied only through exposure to academic theories and knowledge. The study of any management subject should be related to real life business scenarios. I have therefore given some activities at the end of the book, which if performed by the student, will help the teacher understand how much of the practical application of the particular topic the student has understood. Performing these activities will make learning fun in the classroom.

I sincerely thank Shri. Dineshbhai Furia and Shri. Jignesh Furia, the publishers, for the confidence reposed in me and giving me this opportunity to reach out to the students of management studies.

I would also like to thank Nirja Sharma, Prasad Chintakindi, Prachi Mantri, Akbar Shaikh, Ravindra Walodare and Sachin Shinde of Nirali Prakashan for their help extended towards the preparation of this book.

Any suggestions towards the improvement of this book and sincere comments are most welcome on niralipune@pragationline.com.

AUTHOR

Syllabus ...

(New Syllabus w.e.f. June 2013)
B.B.A. : Semester – II (Course Code 202)

1. **Introduction and Functions of Marketing**
   1.1 Marketing – Definitions, Concept, Objectives, Importance and Functions of Marketing : On the basis of exchange, on the basis of physical supply and facilitating functions.
   1.2 Approaches to the study of marketing.
   1.3 Relevance of marketing in a developing economy.
   1.4 Changing profile and challenges faced by a marketing manager.

2. **Classification and Types of Markets**
   2.1 Traditional classification of marketing.
   2.2 Service Marketing : 7 P's of services marketing, importance of services marketing, importance of service sectors.
   2.3 Rural Marketing : Meaning, Features and Importance of rural marketing, Difficulties in rural marketing and suggestions for improvement of rural marketing.
   2.4 Retail Marketing
   2.5 Tele Marketing
   2.6 E-Marketing
   2.7 Digital Marketing : Meaning, importance of digital marketing.
   2.8 Green Marketing.

3. **Marketing Environment and Market Segmentation**
   3.1 Marketing Environment – Meaning, Internal and External factors influencing Marketing Environment : Political, Social, Economical, International, Technological Multi-cultural Environment.
   3.2 Market Segmentation : Meaning, Definition, Essentials of effective market segmentation, Types of segmentation.

4. **Marketing Mix**
   4.1 Product Mix and Price Mix
   Meaning, Scope and Importance of marketing mix.
   (a) Product Mix : Concept of a product, product characteristics : intrinsic and extrinsic, PLC, Product simplification, product elimination, product diversification, new product development.
   (b) Price Mix : Meaning, Elements, Importance of price mix, Factors influencing pricing, pricing methods and recent trends.
   4.2 Place Mix and Promotion Mix
   (a) Place Mix : Meaning and Concepts of channel of distribution, Types of channel of distribution or intermediaries, Factors influencing selection of channels, Types of distribution strategies : Intensive, selective and extensive, Recent changes in terms of logistics and supply chain management.

(b) Promotion Mix : Meaning, Elements of Promotion Mix : Advertising : Definitions, Importance and Limitations of advertising, Types of media, outdoor, indoor, print, press, Transit – Merits and demerits, Concept of media mix, Recent Trends in promotion.

5. **Marketing Planning, Marketing Information System, Marketing Research**

   5.1 Marketing Planning : Meaning, Scope, Importance, Essentials and Steps in marketing planning, Importance and Difficulties in marketing planning.

   5.2 Marketing Information System : Concept, Components and Importance of marketing information system.

   5.3 Marketing Research : Meaning, Definitions, Objectives and Scope of marketing research, Difference between market research and marketing research, Types and Techniques of marketing research, Use of marketing research in management.

B.B.M. : Semester – II (Course Code 204)

1. **Introduction**

   Marketing : Definitions, Concepts, Significance and Functions of Marketing, Approaches to the Study of Marketing, Relevance of Marketing in a Developing Economy, Role and Functions of Marketing Manager.

2. **Types of Marketing**

   Tele Marketing, E-Marketing, Services Marketing, Rural Marketing – Features, Importance, Suggestions for Improvement of Rural Marketing, Marketing Planning and Strategies.

3. **Marketing Mix (Product and Price)**

   Meaning – Scope, Utility – Product Mix, Product Concept, Product Life Cycle – Price Mix – Factors Affecting Pricing, Pricing Methods / Strategies, Importance of Pricing.

4. **Marketing Mix – Place and Promotion**

   Types of Channels, Factors influencing Channel Decisions, Role of Intermediaries, Elements of Promotion Mix, Recent Trends in Promotion, Advertising – Role of Advertising, Advertising Media, Sales Promotion Techniques – Dealers and Consumers.

5. **Market Segmentation**

   Meaning, Definition, Variables used to Segment Markets, Essentials of Effective Market Segmentation, Difference between Differential Marketing and Concentrated Marketing.

6. **Marketing Information System and Marketing Research**

   Concept and Components of Marketing Information System – Marketing Research – Meaning and Scope – Marketing Research Procedure – Types and Techniques of Marketing Research – Importance of Marketing Research.

Contents ...

1. Introduction and Functions of Marketing — 1.1 – 1.32

2. Classification and Types of Markets — 2.1 – 2.44

3. Marketing Environment and Market Segmentation — 3.1 – 3.24

4. Marketing Mix — 4.1 – 4.86

5. Marketing Planning, Marketing Information System, Marketing Research — 5.1 – 5.30

   Case Studies — C.1 – C.36

   Activities and Projects — A.1 – A.2

Chapter 1...

Introduction and Functions of Marketing

Contents ...
1.1 Meaning, Concept and Definition of Marketing
    1.1.1 Objectives of Marketing
    1.1.2 Elements of Marketing/Components of Marketing
    1.1.3 Functions of Marketing
1.2 The Traditional and Modern Concept of Marketing/Approaches to the Study of Marketing
1.3 Importance/Advantages/Benefits/Significance/Relevance of Marketing in a Developing Economy
1.4 Marketing Manager: Qualities, Duties, Responsibilities, Powers and Functions/ Changing Profile and Challenges faced by a Marketing Manager
- Points to Remember
- Questions for Discussion
- Questions from Previous Pune University Examinations

Learning Objectives ...
➢ To Develop an Understanding of the Concept of Marketing
➢ To Understand the Functions of Marketing
➢ To be able to Discuss the Various Approaches to Marketing

1.1 Meaning, Concept and Definition of Marketing

The concept of marketing has evolved from a simple exchange transaction to a complex and complicated one, involving a number of interconnected and interrelated variables. As the concept of marketing undergoes a change, numerous definitions have been put forward by different thinkers at different intervals.

These thinkers have given us definitions depending upon the existence of a particular concept of marketing that was prevalent when these definitions were put forward. Another reason for the variations in definitions lies in the fact that 'Marketing' has no recognised central theoretical base as exists for many other disciplines like physical sciences and some behavioural sciences.

The earlier definitions of marketing emphasised the flow of goods from the seller to the buyer. In this traditional sense, **"Marketing"** is said to consist of *such efforts as effect the transfer in ownership of goods and their physical distribution.*

"Marketing is the performance of a business activity that directs the flow of goods and services from the producer to the consumer". **- The American Marketing Association**

This emphasis was later shifted to an economic approach. Economists stressed upon the utilities and interpreted marketing as a creator of time, place and possession utilities.

"Marketing originates with the recognition of a need on the part of a consumer and terminates with the satisfaction of that need by the delivery of a usable product at the right time, at the right place and at an acceptable price."

Later, people became aware of the legal aspects of marketing, viz. the changes in the ownership and possession of goods and services.

"Marketing may be thought of as that phase of business activity through which human wants are satisfied by the exchange of goods and services on one hand and some valuable consideration usually money or its equivalent on the other hand. The transaction involves **'transfer of ownership'** *usually but not necessarily a* **'transfer of possession'** *and transportation of goods.* **- J. P. Pyle**

In the subsequent stages the emphasis was once again shifted to the customer.

"Marketing is the process of determining consumer demands for a product or service, motivating its sales and distributing it into ultimate consumption at a profit." **- E.F.L. Brech.**

Marketing today is so basic that it cannot be considered as a separate function. It is really the whole business as seen from the point of view of the final result i.e. from the point of view of the customer.

"Marketing is the creation and delivery of a standard of living to society." **- Paul Mazur**

1.1.1 Objectives of Marketing

The basic objective of marketing lies in the satisfaction of human wants at a reasonable profit to the company. Today, marketing has become consumer oriented. In fact, the latest trend in marketing is that it has become oriented to society in general. Hence, marketing can be said to have three fold objectives.

1. The objective of customer satisfaction.
2. The objective of reasonable profit to the company.
3. The objective of social good.

1. **Customer Objectives:** From the perspective of the customer, marketing will have the following objectives:

    (a) To locate the present and potential needs of the customers.

    (b) To create time, place and possession utilities in the goods to satisfy human wants.

    (c) To create satisfied customers.

2. **Company Objectives:** From the point of view of the company the objectives are:

   (a) To carry out the right kind of research activity so as to ensure production of need based products;

   (b) To make the right kind of goods available at the right time, in the right place, in the required quantities and at the right price;

   (c) To create satisfied customers so as to ensure their continued patronage to the company and its products.

3. **Social Objectives:** With social marketing taking root all over the world the objectives of marketing relating to the society cannot be overlooked. (The concept of Social Marketing is dealt with at a later stage in this chapter) From the view point of the society objectives of marketing will be as mentioned underneath:

   - To create consciousness in the customer about those needs, the satisfaction of which will give a benefit to the society at large.
   - To widely publicise and promote social causes and issues.

Thus, it can be said that marketing today has threefold objectives; that of satisfying customer needs at a profit to the company and benefit to the society.

1.1.2 Elements of Marketing/Components of Marketing

Marketing is a managerial function responsible for anticipation, identification, and satisfaction of consumer needs at a reasonable profit to the company. It is a multidisciplinary function having far reaching impact. In fact the best way to study its scope is by making a detailed study of its components/elements. Marketing can broadly be said to consist of four major components. They are the offer, the market, the system and the forces. The explanation of these elements is as follows:

1. **The Offer**

   An offer is a result of the marketing activities of the company. An offer is a proposal which is made by the company to individual and institutional buyers alike. This offer may or may not be accepted by the buyer. This offer does not include just the product or the service but it also includes every facet that is likely to encourage or discourage the transaction from taking place. Hence, when the purchaser accepts the offer he accepts not only the product or service but all allied conditions of the offer. More precisely, it includes the 'what', 'when', 'who', 'why' and 'through whom' of the purchase.

2. **The Market**

   Market comprises the total demand for a product or service by all the potential buyers of that product or service. Here, potential buyers would include all those people who need the product, want and desire the product, have the authority to buy and most importantly have the purchasing power to back up their want. Market can be a total market or it can be a segment of the total market. Thus, a small manufacturer of tyres, cannot even think of capturing the entire world market or even the entire local market for tyres but may be satisfied by capturing a small part of it, since he is not alone in the market but has to share it with other sellers of tyres. This is why market is equal to all the buyers and sellers' within a geographical area for a product and its close substitutes.

3. **The System**

   When we speak about the system as a component of marketing what we mean is the entire distribution system or the distribution network employed by a manufacturer or a firm in order to move its products from the place of manufacture to the ultimate consumer. Marketing is basically concerned with the flow of goods from the point of production to the point of ultimate consumption. Therefore to successfully carry out this object, a number of functions have to be performed. All these functions have to be systematically performed to ensure that the physical movements of the products of the company take place and reach the needy people. In order to ensure a proper physical movement of the goods many alternatives are available with the company manufacturers. The available options can be combined to ensure the fulfillment of the requirement of individual manufacturers. Selection of a channel or a combination of channels depends upon the nature of the product, the nature of the market segment to be approached, and the nature and quantum of efforts required for effective marketing. Thus, each manufacturer will have to adopt some system of distribution which will match with its product, target market as well as the philosophy of the company. For example, a manufacturer of high class "Rolex" watches will not choose a distribution network that includes all the small scale retailers, but will restrict its distribution network to the posh retailers of the high scale market areas.

4. **The Forces**

   The final component/element of marketing is the environment in which marketing takes place. The 'offer', the 'Market' and the 'System' are all affected even by a slightest change in the environment. Similarly, the changes in the other components also affect the environment. The environment is the most volatile of all the elements of marketing and is the one that is most subject to constant changes. The environment includes a number of factors like competitors' and buyers' likely reactions, buyers' psychology and behaviour, economic climate, legislation and government pressures etc. A change in any one will affect the environment, which in turn will affect the other components of marketing. Thus, this component has a vital impact value and hence, it should be studied with sagacity to understand the opportunities and counteract the threats associated with it.

1.1.3 Functions of Marketing

The Functions of Marketing are mainly divided into three groups:

(I) Functions of Exchange which include:

   (a)   Buying and assembling.

   (b)   Selling.

(II) Functions of Physical Supply which include:
(a) Transportation.
(b) Storage.

(III) Facilitating Functions which include:
(a) Standardisation and Grading.
(b) Branding, Packaging and Labelling.
(c) Insurance.
(d) Financing.
(e) Marketing Information.
(f) Risk bearing.
(g) Advertising.
(h) Market Research.

These functions of marketing are discussed below:

(I) Functions of Exchange

Exchange means the transfer of goods and services for money or moneys worth. It results in a change in the ownership of the product. When exchange takes place what happens is the product leaves the hands of the seller and goes into the hands of the buyer. Thus an exchange basically has a twofold effect one of buying and the other of selling. Both buying and selling automatically include assembling and hence when we talk of the exchange functions we mean the following three activities.

(a) Buying and Assembling

Buying: Buying is one of the important functions of marketing. It is the first step in the process of marketing. A manufacturer desirous of manufacturing any product will have to first buy the raw material of the required quality and quantity in order to efficiently operate his factory. A wholesaler has to buy the goods from the manufacturer or producer. Similarly a retailer has to first buy the goods from the wholesaler at reasonable prices so as to make a profit from the final sale to the consumer. Thus the buying function of marketing is concerned with taking important decisions relating to the selection of goods to be sold either to the ultimate consumer or to be used in the process of production.

According to **Pyle**, buying comprises *"All those activities involved in finding a suitable source of supply, selecting the desired quantity, quality, grade, style and size and coming to an agreement with reference to the price, delivery date and other conditions"*.

Elements/Sub-functions of Buying:

(i) **Estimating the demand:** Goods are bought for two reasons: one for consumption and second for resale. Estimating the demand for consumption is not very difficult, as a consumer is aware of his own requirement. However, a decision for purchase or resale is comparatively a difficult task. Basically, two factors help in this kind of demand estimation and they are past experiences and an estimation of future sales.

(ii) **Selection of consumer oriented goods:** It is said that goods well bought are half sold. Thus while purchasing the goods the seller must keep in mind the requirements of his final consumer. All the decisions must be made with the final consumer in mind, e.g., if sponge is being purchased for the manufacture of dusters, only that quality should be purchased and that price should be paid which will match the price and quality of the final product that is the duster.

(iii) **Selection of supplier:** The next step will be the selection of supplier. This step has to be carefully executed, for if the supplier is not a dependable one, all production activity may come to a standstill. Hence, that supplier who is able to supply required quantity of goods of the required quality at a competitive price regularly and reliably should be selected.

(iv) **Negotiation:** Once the suppliers are selected the buyers will have to negotiate and finalise the terms of purchase like quantity, quality, price, mode of payment, mode of transportation, risk coverage etc.

(v) **Entering into a contract:** When the terms and conditions of purchase are finalised the buyer and seller enter into a contract to buy and sell so that the ownership of the goods passes legally from the seller to the buyer.

Assembling: Assembling is an aid to the function of buying. Once the purchase contract is entered into with the various suppliers, purchases are made from them. All these purchases have to be collected in one central place under the control of the buyer. This is known as Assembling. Assembling is also called a "concentration function."

Assembling is required for all kinds of products, be they agricultural products, raw materials, industrial products and component parts or spare parts, or other manufactured products.

Assembling is required because of the following reasons:

1. To meet the demand of the buyers.
2. Provide adequate business to middlemen like retailers and wholesalers.
3. Aid the process of manufacture.
4. Makes transportation and storage economical.
5. Relieve manufacturers of the problems of material shortages.

(b) Selling

Selling is the second part of the exchange transaction. Efficiency in selling is the most important factor that affects the existence of a firm. The prime objective of an organisation, profit, can be achieved only through efficient selling.

Today with mass production being the call of the day and increasing competition being the order of the century, the importance of selling has increased many folds. Producing on a large scale is easy but selling on a large scale is very difficult. Thus, selling is a difficult aspect of the exchange transaction and must be given its proper importance.

The function of selling involves the following elements/ sub-functions:

1. **Product planning and development:** No marketing effort can be successful if the product itself is unsatisfactory. Hence it would not be wrong if we say that the success of any selling organisation depends upon the planning and development of the right type and kind of products. While planning the manufacture of the right kind of products, the manufacturer should take into account the requirements and needs of the final consumer in terms of quantity, quality, time, price, place etc . This information can be obtained through market research. **Karl H. Tietjen** defines product planning as *"The act of marketing out and supervising the search, screening, development and commercialisation of new products; the modification of existing lines; and the discontinuance of marginal and unprofitable items."* On the other hand, **product development** means *supplying or making available to the consumer only such goods as are needed and demanded by them*. Product development refers to activities of product research, engineering and design. The products developed and offered by a business enterprise may be industrial products, consumer products or agricultural products.

2. **Creation of demand:** Once the right product has been produced it will result in profit only if it is demanded. Thus an important aspect of selling is the creation of demand. The seller must inform the buyer about the availability of his products. He usually does this by resorting to activities like advertising and sales promotion. *All activities undertaken by a seller to keep his customers informed and updated about his products through the different means available to him* can be called as **demand creation**.

3. **Establishing contact with the buyers**: Buyers are many and scattered over a vast area. After creating a demand for the product it is essential to establish contact with the buyers. The marketing personnel have to find out the places where the buyers exist, establish contacts with them and maintain cordial relations with them. Establishing contacts with the buyers is an ongoing process and has to be undertaken continuously.

4. **Negotiations:** Once contact with the buyer is established the seller has to enter into discussions with the prospective buyers to finalise the terms relating to the quantity, quality, and price of the product, the time mode of transport, risk coverage etc. At this stage, offers and counter offers are made till a final agreement is reached. *This process of reaching some point of common understanding through offers and counter offers* can be called **negotiations**.

5. **Entering into a contract:** When the terms and conditions of sale are finalised the buyers and sellers enter in a contract to buy and sell so that the ownership of the goods passes legally from the seller to the buyer.

Even though buying and selling functions of marketing have been studied and analysed as two different functions, they are in actual practice complimentary to each other. After all, there cannot be selling without buying and buying without selling. They are the two sides of the exchange transaction and one cannot exist without the other.

II. Functions of Physical Supply

(a) Transportation

Transportation helps in the physical movement of goods from the places where they are made but not required to the places where they are required. Thus it creates place utility. In the very simplest form of marketing mechanisms where a consumer purchases directly from a local farm or a factory, here too transportation is involved and must be performed either by the buyer or the seller.

The revolution in the field of transportation has not only created new markets but has shrunk the size of the world. Long distances can be reached in a short span of time today. The speed and efficiency of the different modes of transportation have made available to the consumer different varieties of goods at a cheaper rate.

Modern systems of transportation have assisted marketing in various ways:
1. They have promoted the growth and distribution of wealth.
2. They have encouraged division of labour and specialisation.
3. They have created opportunities for better utilisation of labour and capital.
4. They have resulted in widening of existing markets, creation of new ones and thus the development of distant markets of the world.

Apart from aiding marketing in the above mentioned ways, transportation performs the following functions:

1. **Facilitates production:** The modern manufacturing and marketing units work smoothly and efficiently because of a well organised transportation system. Raw materials and component parts are carried to the units and the finished products to the markets and consumption centres only through a well established transportation system..
2. **Facilitates the growth of markets for perishable products:** Because of the existence of a well established and efficient transportation system it is possible to have a wide market for perishable products like milk, meat, vegetables, fruits, flowers etc.
3. **It creates place utility:** Industries are generally located away from consumption centres. It is transportation that moves the goods from production centres to consumption centres. Thus it moves goods from the place where they have little or no utility to the place where they possess maximum utility.

4. **Transportation raises the standard of living of the people:** Transportation makes available all those goods which are produced in different parts of the world. Thus with the availability of specialised goods manufactured with advanced technologies the standard of living of the people is raised.

5. **Transportation helps in equalising prices:** Transportation moves products from surplus to deficit areas and thus an adjustment in demand and supply is brought about and prices in different markets tend to be equalised.

6. **Provides employment opportunities:** The various modes of transportation used in a country provide employment opportunities to millions of people.

Modes of Transport

The various modes of transport used for the physical movement of goods are as under:

1. **Land Transport:** Land transport is divided into two categories:

    (a) Road Transport

    (b) Railway Transport

    (a) **Road Transport:** Road transport refers to all those means of transport that move on the ground. On the roads we have animals, carts, cars, buses trucks, rickshaws tankers etc. Road transport is the oldest type of transport. It plays a vital role in the expansion of internal trade.

    Road transport is less expensive and has a lesser maintenance cost as compared to other forms of transport. It is quick, convenient and flexible, and specially useful for the movement of perishable products. Though it has limited capacity and speed it can move products to places where other forms of transport cannot.

    (b) **Railway Transport:** Railways are a popular and important form of transport, and occupy an important place in our economy. In a vast country like India, it is the most effective form of bringing together the widely dispersed producers and consumers. Railways have some peculiar features like heavy capital expenditure and high operational costs. In most countries the railways are either nationalised, i.e., owned by the state or strictly controlled by the government in public interest. In India railways are nationalised public utilities.

    Railways have a huge carrying capacity and can transport goods at high speed with a high degree of punctuality. It is a speedy and dependable form of transportation.

2. **Water Transport:** Water transport is the cheapest form of transport available for carrying bulk goods. It makes use of natural water resources like rivers, canals, seas and oceans. Various vehicles like boats, ships, tankers etc. are used to carry people as well as goods over the various water ways of a country. Waterways are used for

foreign trade. It is a speedy and safe means of transport. However, water transport involves international restrictions and no water carrier can enter the waters of another country or make use of its harbour without prior permission.

3. **Air Transport:** Air transport is the latest mode of transport and is responsible for converting the entire world into one big market. It facilitates the marketing of perishable commodities like fruits vegetables and flowers to distant markets because of its high speed. Due to its high cost and limited capacity airways can be used only for specific commodities.

The selection of the mode of transport depends upon the type of product, type of market, type of organisation, time of delivery and finance available.

(b) Storage or Warehousing

Storage creates time utility. It preserves the goods at the point of consumption till that point of time when they are required. Production will bear fruit only if the produced commodities are available at the point of consumption at the right time. Storage becomes a necessary function because of the following reasons:

- The production of some commodities like food products are seasonal, but they are demanded throughout the year. Hence, they have to be stored.
- The demand for some goods like raincoats, umbrellas, sun coats etc. are only seasonal, but they are produced throughout the year. Such production has to be stored till it is demanded.
- Sometimes goods are stored in order to take advantage of an expected rise in the prices of goods in the future.
- In the case of some goods like wine, their quality improves if they are stored, and hence such goods require storage.
- In the case of almost all the products there exists a time gap between production and consumption and hence they need to be stored.

The function of storage is performed through warehousing. A warehouse is a place where the goods are stored. The important functions of storage are described below.

1. Storage ensures a continuous supply of goods and thus enables the customers to buy small quantities as and when required.
2. It helps producers to carry on production throughout the year by helping them maintain a stock of raw materials, finished products, etc.
3. Storage gives opportunity to the producers to maximise their profits, by taking advantage of the price fluctuations in the markets. Thus a producer can hold on to his goods during periods of low prices and sell them in the market when the prices of the goods rise.
4. Storage helps in equalising the prices over a period of time.
5. Storage improves the quality of certain products.

When the goods are stored in a warehouse the warehouse owner takes responsibility for the safe keeping of the products. Thus the risk of loss of goods due to deterioration in quality during the period of storage is borne by the warehouse keeper and hence the risk of the producer is shared and his burden is lightened. Further, the warehouse keeper gives the producer something known as a warehouse receipt for the goods kept in his warehouse. This receipt can be used by the producer to get easy finance from banks. Some warehouses also provide certain other services like packing the goods as per the instructions of the producers and dealers, breaking large parts into small lots, preparation of sample grading as per accepted standards.

Thus storage and warehousing are two sides of the same coin. However the above functions of warehousing come into existence when the warehouse is a hired one.

III. Facilitating Functions

To facilitate the easy availability of a product, it has to go through various stages like grading, branding etc. The facilitating functions can be explained as follows:

(a) Standardisation and Grading

   (i) **Standardisation:** A standard means an ideal or model product which provides a basis for comparison with other identical products. A standard specifies the minimum basic qualities which a product must possess. Standards are usually established by the Government Departments like Ministry of Agriculture, or Ministry of Trade and Commerce.

   When a product is standardised and a mark stating that this is a standard product (like ISI AGMARK) is put on it, it gives the consumer an assurance that this product has successfully passed the tests of quality assurance and possess, certain basic required qualities, and hence the consumer will not waste time in examining the product, but will accept it. Hence standardisation has been accepted as an ethical basis for marketing.

   (ii) **Grading:** Grading begins when standardisation ends. Grading is the process of sorting out the different types of commodities in accordance with the particular established standards and then classifying them into grades. Thus standard is a broad term and, generally established standards are known as grades.

   Grading enables one to have a comparison of quality and price. It is generally used for agricultural products and raw materials. Grading helps to have uniform prices for the same quality of a product in all the markets.

(b) Branding, Packaging and Labelling

   (i) **Branding:** Branding is an activity that includes giving a name and identification to a product. Branding includes activities like giving the product a brand name, a brand mark and also popularising the product.

Branding gives an identity to the product. Identity is essential to competition, because without a means of identification there is no way of making a choice. Branding definitely facilitates in making a choice.

(ii) **Brand:** A brand is a name, symbol, term or design or a combination of all these which is intended to identify the goods or services of one seller or a group of sellers and to differentiate them from those of the competitors, for example, pears soap, dove soap etc.

(iii) **Brand Name and Brand Mark:** Brand name is a part of the brand consisting of a word or a group of words or letters. A brand name is one which can be pronounced or vocalized, e.g. Wheel soap, Liril soap etc. Brand mark is a part of the brand that constitutes a symbol, mark or design. It is that part which can be recognised and not pronounced, e.g., the symbol of the Wheel on the Wheel soap bar, the symbol of Maharaja of Air India.

(iv) **Trade Mark:** When a brand name is registered and legalised it becomes a trade mark. Thus registered trade marks are brands. From this, we can come to the conclusion that all trade marks are brands but all brands are not trade marks. Trade mark is a legal term protecting the right of the manufacturer to use the brand name or brand mark.

(v) **Trade Name:** Trade name is the name of the business organisation. A trade name may also be used as a brand name. In such a case, it performs a dual function; it gives identification to the product as well as the manufacturer; e.g., Godrej is a trade name as well as a brand name for most of their products like Godrej refrigerator, Godrej cupboards, etc.

Functions of Branding

They can be enumerated as follows:
1. Branding helps in product identification and gives a distinction to a product.
2. It helps in price differentiation of products.
3. It eliminates imitation of products.
4. It gives a legal right on the product.
5. It denotes a certain quality or standard of the product.
6. It helps to create and sustain brand loyalty for a particular product.
7. It helps in advertising of the product.

Packaging

Package is the external wrapper or container of the product. It is the external wrapper or container of each individual product which is to be sold to the final consumer. Packaging may be defined as the general group of activities which involves designing and producing the container or wrapper for a product.

A good package protects the product, provides convenience to the customers, increases economy and communicates information about the product. A package protects the product against deterioration, preserves the freshness and flavour of the product, protects against changes due to climatic conditions, and loss due to evaporation. A good package makes the handling of the product easier for both the consumer as well as the dealers. From the consumers angle a good package makes it easy not only to handle but also to store the product, it also keeps the product clean and sanitary. From the dealers angle, apart from ease in handling, packaging saves time and money in selling, as an attractive package attracts the customers and makes store displays more attractive. Good packaging also helps in inventory control.

Kinds of Materials used for Packaging

1. **Earthenware:** Using earthenware for packaging is an old method for preserving products of liquid nature. Even today hot drinks such as liquors are kept in earthenware containers for improving their quality.
2. **China Jars:** China jars are used where the product is to be protected from light. They are also used for their beauty value.
3. **Wooden boxes:** Wooden boxes are very commonly used. They are used basically to prevent breakage due to rough handling.
4. **Cardboard containers:** Cardboard containers are used for packaging specialty goods which are not bulky.
5. **Straw baskets:** These are used for vegetables and fruits.
6. **Gunny bags:** Gunny bags are very popular especially for food grains.
7. **Glass:** Glass is used for packaging liquid products. Mostly, glass bottles are used.
8. **Tin containers:** Tin containers are quickly taking over glass, specially for liquid products.
9. **Tetra packs**: These are containers made out of foil and plastic and are quickly capturing the demand of the packaging industry.
10. **Plastic containers:** They are also very popular because of their low price, good appearance, convenience and ability for reuse.

Difference between Packing, Package and Packaging

When goods are put into containers for the purpose of transport or storage it is known as **'packing'**. Many goods need to be packed in order to be preserved or delivered to the buyer. Liquids are placed in barrels, bottles or cans. Bulky goods like cotton and jute are compressed into bales. Goods must be placed in boxes or bags for delivery to dealers. Retailers also pack goods and place them in bags or boxes for delivery to the ultimate consumer. Thus packing means the wrapping and crating of goods before transportation or storage.

'**Package**' is *the external container or wrapper of the product.* It is the individual wrapper or container of the individual units to be sole to the ultimate consumer.

Whereas '**packaging**' is all *the activities that are carried out in order to ensure that a product is given a good package.*

Labelling

A **label** is *a small slip placed on the product which gives information regarding the nature, contents, price, batch no., ownership etc. of the product.* A label is a medium through which the manufacturer gives necessary information to the consumer used of the product. The label is usually affixed on the package. A label plays an important role in making the packaging and branding function meaningful and hence these three functions are closely related.

Functions of Labelling

1. Labelling helps in the identification of the product.
2. It stresses the features of the product which are advertised.
3. It enables the manufacturer in giving proper instructions to understand the use of the product.
4. By mentioning the price of the product, labelling helps in curtailing defraudation of consumers by the retailers.
5. Labelling encourages the manufacture of quality products.

(c) Insurance

Insurance has been defined by **Koontz** and **Fulmer** as *"The process in which one party (the insurer) agrees for a sum of money (a premium) which is paid by a second party (the insured), to pay the insured a specified sum if he should suffer a particular loss."*

A business is full of uncertainties and risks. Insurance is a means to lessen the severity of unforeseen and unfavourable happenings. Insurance renders various services to the businessmen, manufacturers and marketers and thus its place in the business world remains unchallenged. Some of the benefits derived from Insurance are as under:

Importance of Insurance

1. **Transfer of Risk:** The risk of business losses can be transferred to the Insurance Companies against the payment of a small amount known as 'insurance premium'.
2. **Protection:** In the event of a business loss the insurance company makes good the loss. Thus the businessman is protected from the worry of loss or damage.
3. **Stable Prices:** Insurance affords a businessman avoidance of price fluctuations. If there is a loss it is absorbed by the insurance company. In the absence of insurance every time a businessman suffers a loss, he will increase the price of the product to make good his loss, thus resulting in drastic price fluctuations.

4. **Assured Profits:** It is insurance that assures normal profits to the businessmen; as losses are absorbed by the insurance company, even in the event of a loss the businessman can enjoy normal profits.

5. **Specialisation:** Insurance companies have the ability to shoulder the risk in a professional manner thus leaving the businessman free to carry out his duty of production and distribution of goods.

6. **Financial Assistance:** Insurance helps a businessman in raising finance as banks do not hesitate in giving loans against insured property.

7. **Minimising Risk:** There is no way to avoid risk completely. However, insurance spreads the risk between a number of parties and thus the individual risk is minimised.

8. **Industrial Development:** Insurance companies invest their funds in shares and debentures of companies. Thus, they help in the industrial development of a country.

Therefore, insurance is an important facilitating function to be performed.

(d) Financing

Finance is the life blood of commerce. In order to undertake any business activity finance is required. A business requires finance for a number of reasons right from the time it is born to its ultimate death/dissolution. One of the reasons for which finance is required is marketing. *The process of arranging finance for a business* is known as **'business finance'**, whereas *the process of arranging finance for marketing* is known as **'marketing finance'**. Thus marketing finance is a part of business finance. Just as a business requires both fixed as well as working capital, likewise the activities of marketing require both fixed as well as working capital. However, the requirement of fixed capital is comparatively low.

Fixed Capital: *The finance used for acquiring fixed assets like land, building, machinery etc.* is known as **'fixed capital'**. Fixed capital is invested in a business for a long duration of time and cannot be easily encashed. In fact, it has very little or no liquidity. Fixed capital is raised through the issue of shares, debentures or through long-term finance obtained from banks or other financial institutions.

In the case of marketing finance fixed capital is required for the provision of showrooms, service centres, warehouses, automobiles and other assets necessary for the distribution of products.

Working Capital: *Working capital is the capital that is required for meeting day-to-day expenses, or expenses of a recurring nature.* It is required for holding stocks of raw materials, stores, partly finished goods. It is also required for payment of salaries, wages, rent, electricity and advertisement bills etc.

Working capital is also known as **'circulating'** capital or **'revolving'** capital or **'floating' capital**. This is because the investment made in working capital is recovered and reinvested continuously. It is also known as **'liquid'** capital because it is held either in cash or in the form of assets which can be easily converted into cash. Working capital is required for short periods of time, and hence the requirement for this capital is met out of short-term loans from banks and financial institutions as cash credit, bank over draft etc.

Though the nature of fixed and working capital is different, an intimate relationship does exist between the two. They are complementary and supplementary to one another. Example, when an obsolete fixed capital is sold the proceeds become working capital and when profits are made a part of it, they may be used for acquiring fixed assets. Though different, fixed and working capital are related.

(e) Marketing Information

In the modern world, success of a business depends upon the manufacture and distribution of the products that are wanted by the consumers. For this at every point of time information about the needs and wants of the consumer is required in order that the right product decisions are taken. Thus marketing information is the basis on which the entire structure of a business stands. This function of marketing is studied in great depth in the next chapter.

(f) Risk Bearing

Marketing risk means the uncertainties, loss or damages arising out of unforeseen causes while undertaking the activities of marketing. However, this does not mean that risk arises only out of marketing activities. In fact assumption of risk is one of the functions to be shouldered while carrying out any business activity.

Marketing risks are mainly caused by changes in the attitude of the customers. This is referred to as "Changes in fashion". But changes in fashions is only one of the risks faced by marketers. Changes in incomes and standard of living of the people, appearance of substitute products, newer methods of sales promotion, etc., will make existing products obsolete.

Unless the seller is cautious, he will suffer losses. Basically the causes of marketing risks can be classified into the following five categories:

1. Economic risks
2. Physical risks
3. Political risks
4. Natural risks
5. Human risks

1. **Economic risks:** Economic factors are responsible for creating the below mentioned risks.

   (a) **Time risk:** Today production is in anticipation of demand and hence every producer is undertaking a 'time risk' when he undertakes production. The produced goods may not be in demand always. Fashions change and the product may go out of style. Similarly new technologies and substitute products may eat into the market share of your product.

   Changes in business cycles is another time risk which has to be shouldered by marketers as these changes cannot be predicted with any degree of accuracy. Storage of goods also carries a risk if the stored goods cannot be sold later on at a higher price.

   (b) **Place risk:** It is said that production bears fruit only when it reaches the consumer. Since the place of production and the place of consumption are away from each other, the manufacturer and marketer have to face a 'place risk'. After transporting the goods to the place of sale the trader may realise that the demand is not exactly what he thought it would be. Thus this risk has to be borne.

   (c) **Competition risk:** The business world today works on cut throat competition. In order to survive in this world, businessmen use various strategies. Sometimes the methods accepted by businessmen to counter the competition are not very fair. Price cutting is one of the methods generally adopted to establish a product in the market. Providing special guarantees for durable products is another method. To compete successfully in today's world, the manufacturer and marketer needs financial strength as well as an aptitude for foresight.

2. **Political risk:** These risks are losses arising out of intervention by the government. Imposition of various taxes, restriction on imports etc. are examples of intervention by the government leading to losses for the businessmen.

3. **Physical risk:** Physical risks are those risks that lead to a physical deterioration or destruction of the product. Examples of such risks are loss in transit, theft, deterioration in the quality of the product, loss due to improper handling, etc.

4. **Natural risk:** These are the risks arising out of natural causes which are beyond the control of man. Such risks include rains, earthquakes, floods, lightening etc. Due to such calamities the goods are destroyed or their quality is affected. Sometimes these calamities affect the demand for the product thus leading to losses.

5. **Human risk:** A business organisation may face a risk due to dishonesty, incompetence, carelessness, sickness or death of employees. Due to careless and dishonest employees an organisation may suffer a loss. Sickness or death of good employees also causes a loss to the organisation.

Dealing with the Risk

As mentioned earlier, a businessman has to face a variety of risks. Most of these risks arise out of ignorance and can be avoided by understanding the problems properly. Insurance companies shoulder many risks for the businessmen against the payment of a small amount known as premium. However, all the risks cannot be insured. The methods used to avoid or minimise the risks are as follows:

(a) **Avoiding risks:** By taking various preventive measures a large number of risks can be avoided. For example, loss by fire can be avoided by installing smoke alarms, keeping fire extinguisher devices handy, using fireproof bricks for the construction of godowns.

Risks due to changes in prices, fluctuations in demand, changes in fashions can be avoided by keeping production in tune with demand.

Risks can also be minimised by undertaking activities like market research which guide the manufacturers about the trends in market.

(b) **Absorption of risk:** Risks are inherent in any business. Where there are profits there are bound to be losses too. The losses can be adjusted with windfall profits. Thus it can be said to be absorbed by the business.

(c) **Shifting the risk:** Risks can be shifted to professional agencies. One of the major acceptor of risk is the insurance companies. Another way of shifting the risk is by entering into a 'hedging' transaction. Hedging is a transaction undertaken in the commodity exchanges. This type of transaction helps in transferring the risk of changes in price of commodities traded in the commodity exchanges. It involves entering into two transactions of equal and opposite nature, whereby the loss in one is offset by a gain in the other. Risks can also be shifted by 'subcontracting'. That is a part of the activity given to someone else to perform, thus shifting the risks associated with that part of the activity to the sub-contractor.

Thus risks can be handled in the above different ways.

(g) Advertising

The **American Marketing Association** has defined advertising as *"Any paid form of non-personal presentation and promotion of ideas, goods and services by an identified sponsor"*.

From the above definition the following points are clear:

1. Advertising is paid for and hence is a commercial transaction.
2. Advertising is non-personal. Whatever be the form of advertisement (visual, spoken, written) they are directed at a mass audience, and not directed at the individual as is the case in personal selling.
3. Advertisements are identifiable with the sponsors or originators.

Media of Advertising

Advertising media is a means through which advertisers communicate their message to prospects to influence them to purchase the product or services advertised.

Advertising media may be defined as *"The physical means whereby a manufacturer or supplier of goods utilities or services tells the consumer about his products or services."*

Brennan has defined advertising media as *"The term media embraces each and every method that the advertiser has at his command to carry his message to the public."*

There are various media of advertising that can be used like 'Press Media' which includes advertisements in newspapers and magazines, 'Broadcasting media' which includes television and radio advertising, 'Non Broadcasting media' which includes video, cable and cinema advertisements. You also have media like outdoor media which includes poster advertisements, advertisements on hoardings, neon signs and sky writing. Point of purchase media which includes advertisements at the place of final purchase of the product. This media takes the form of banners, stickers, hangings, packaging and painted displays.

(h) Market Research

While undertaking the various marketing activities, various decisions are to be undertaken. These decisions are taken on the basis of information collected through research. *This process of collecting information for the purpose of taking marketing decisions* is known as **'marketing research'**.

There are many ways and methods in which information can be collected. These ways and methods are known as the techniques of Marketing Research. The techniques generally used are as follows:

1. **Factual Survey:** Factual surveys are of three types,
    (a) House to House Enquiry or Personal Interviews.
    (b) Investigation through the post or mail survey.
    (c) Telephone Survey.
2. Observation Method.
3. Experimentation method.
4. The Panel Research.

1. Factual Survey

(a) House to House Enquiry or Personal Interview: In this kind of an enquiry, a printed questionnaire is made asking for various details. An interviewer is appointed who will meet the interviewee either at his residence or in his office. Usually an experienced person is appointed to conduct such an interview as he will be able to draw out all the required information. Such a person has to play an active part and many a times getting the right information depends upon the ability of the interviewer.

Merits: This method is superior to the telephone and mail method as data is received together with other observations like facial expressions, body language etc. Further clarifications can also be derived by asking supplementary questions. The interviewer can control the direction of the conversation and can guide the interviewee to get the required information.

Demerits: It is an expensive method as first and foremost you require an experienced person and hence the payment made to such a person will also be more. Secondly, this method involves a lot of time. Further the accuracy of the information depends upon the skills of the interviewer. The interviewer may not be very objective all the time and this may result in incorrect or inaccurate information.

(b) Investigation through the mail: As the name suggests, this technique refers to getting information from the respondents through the post. In this method there is no face-to-face contact with the respondent. A questionnaire is drafted in such a way that the answers to the questions can be given in a quick yes or no. This questionnaire is then posted to the respondent. A cover letter must be sent with this questionnaire, and this letter has to be so drafted that it motivates and induces the respondent to fill the questionnaire and send it back. Usually gifts and competitions are announced in order to motivate people to send back the questionnaire.

Merits: This method is economically less expensive, and a large number of people covering a large geographical area can be covered at little cost. The information is collected through standard questionnaires, and as there is no face-to-face contact, complete objectivity can be maintained. Further, as the information is collected from a large number of people accurate data can be collected.

Demerits: The main drawback of this method is that there is no way of ensuring that the respondents will surely fill the form and send it back. Many a times incomplete forms are sent back. It may also happen that no response is given at all. As there is no face-to-face contact there is no scope for the respondent to get any clarifications in case of misunderstanding or non-understanding.

(c) Telephone Interview: In this method, the interviewer contacts the respondents on the telephone. The questionnaire for this method will have to be drafted carefully as it cannot be lengthy and nor can it ask for any confidential information. The main hurdle of this method is building a rapport with the respondent so that he answers the questions completely and satisfactorily.

Merits: This is an economic and speedy method of collecting data. Normally people are more frank on the telephone than they are in person. They can talk freely without being influenced by anyone else. This method is specially suited for the upper classes of the society, as such people are very difficult to contact in person. They respond better to enquiries on the phone rather than to a strange person on their doorstep.

Demerits: This method can be employed only with those people who possess a telephone connection. Further nothing exceptionally complementary can be said about the Indian telecommunication network. Faulty telephone lines, dead phones and wrong numbers are very common. This may cause a breakdown in this method. Also, no information can be collected through personal observation.

2. Observation Method

Observation implies viewing or noting the act or occurrence. Under this method the observer silently views the behaviour of the respondent in an act. The respondent may or may not be aware that he/she is being observed.

Thus instead of asking questions, observation is used to get information. For example, if the researcher wants to know the popularity of a particular brand of shampoo he can get this information by observing the behaviour of various customers at the sales counter.

Observation can be done by humans as well as by machines. Observations undertaken by human beings are more comprehensive though less accurate; less convenient and uneconomical. Recently, many technical methods of observation have been introduced. Various devices for observation are available on a large scale. They include hidden cameras, audiometers, eye cameras etc. Use of machines for observation gives more accurate information.

3. Experimentation Method

Experimental method of research is the procedure of carrying out a small scale trial solution to a problem. The aim is to determine whether the tentative conclusions reached can be proved in actual conditions. The actual conditions are always changing and cannot be controlled by the researcher. However, a number of experiments can be conducted to find out the effect of the various variables. **Prof. Tull D.S.** and **Hawkins D.I.** have defined this method as "*The deliberate manipulation of one or more variables by the experimenter in such a way that its effect upon one or more variables can be measured.*" For example, a firm may try to determine whether the change in the design of the package of a particular product has an expected effect on sales. Thus three designs may be made and the different packages of the same product may be sold in three different markets in order to study which particular design is most acceptable.

4. The Panel Research

In this technique of market research the same group of respondents are interviewed on more than one occasion to find out whether there has been any change in their demand, tastes, preferences, likes, dislikes etc.

Thus, above are the various functions of marketing and each and every one of them is important and has to be performed in co-ordination with other functions, if the organisation as a whole has to be successful.

1.2 The Traditional and Modern Concept of Marketing/ Approaches to the Study of Marketing

Marketing philosophy has undergone a gradual but thorough change since the industrial revolution. This change in the philosophy of marketing can be compartmentalised into four stages or four different concepts of marketing. The first two are the traditional concepts and the last two are the new concepts of marketing.

1. Production Oriented Marketing,
2. Sales Oriented Marketing,
3. Consumer Oriented Marketing,
4. Socially Oriented Marketing, i.e., socially responsible marketing approach.

1. Production Oriented Concept

Till 1930, there was a feeling amongst the manufacturers that if a company manufactured a good product it would sell with little or no promotion effort. This concept of marketing i.e. if a product is really good and the price is reasonable, no special efforts are required to market the product is known as The Production Oriented Concept of Marketing. It is based on the following assumptions:

(a) A firm should manufacture only certain basic products.

(b) The most crucial task of management is to keep the cost of production relatively low.

(c) Anything that can be produced sells.

This concept of marketing can successfully exist only in a sellers' market, i.e., a market in which supply is limited and demand exceeds supply. Hence after 1930, when the market changed from a sellers' market to a buyers' market this concept was overthrown to be replaced by a new philosophy known as the "Sales Oriented Concept of Marketing."

2. Sales Oriented Concept

After 1930, certain social and economic changes took place which resulted in a shift from agriculture to industry. Transport and communication systems developed and mass production became the order of the day. This resulted in an increase in competition. As more and more competitors entered the area of manufacture, the market slowly turned into a buyer's market, i.e., the supply exceeded demand. It was no longer possible to sell everything that was manufactured. The problems of the manufacturer now focused on how to increase sales. This was mainly because for the same number of customers, now there were many sellers. The purchaser had a choice of products and hence the seller now had not only to manufacture a good product but also convince the purchaser that his product was better than the competitor's product. For this he had to have an effective sales organisation, choose the right channel of distribution, concentrate on advertising, sales promotion and other demand increasing activities. This phase continued till 1950. In fact, it still holds good to a certain extent even today; it is prevalent in the selling of consumer non-durables and consumer durables, especially products which have a status symbol.

3. Consumer Oriented Concept

This concept came into existence around the 1950's, when the manufacturers realised that no amount of aggressive selling would force people to buy a product they did not need. This era forced the manufacturers to rethink and realise that the basis of all their marketing efforts should revolve around the need of the customer. It was around this period of time that marketing research became an important function of marketing.

This concept concentrates on the consumer rather than the product. It is based on the following assumptions:

(a) The firm should produce only that product which is desired by the customer.

(b) Management should integrate all its activities in order to develop programmes to satisfy consumer wants.

(c) Management should be guided by long term profits rather than quick sales.

This philosophy of marketing brought about two major changes. Firstly, it placed the consumer at the crux of all marketing activities, and secondly, it replaced the age old **'caveat emptor'**, attitude with **'caveat venditor'**. This philosophy will continue so long as the customer continues to be the king of the market.

4. Socially-Oriented Marketing Concept

The philosophy of marketing was further refined during the 60's and 70's and a new concept of Social Marketing was coined and accepted by manufacturers all over the world. This concept focuses not only on customer satisfaction but also on customer welfare and social welfare as well. By customer and social welfare is meant a pollution free environment and good quality of human life. Thus, an automobile manufacturer must manufacture not only a good vehicle but one which will reduce pollution or a tobacco manufacturer must manufacture not only good quality tobacco but one which will do the least harm to the environment and health of the consumers. In fact, this concept of marketing goes a step further and says that it is the duty of the manufacturer to awaken those needs in the people, the satisfaction of which will lead to social good. Here the marketers concentrate on satisfying the needs of the society as a whole rather than on individual need satisfaction.

Social marketing is often concerned with a major change in 'attitudes' which is an uphill task. In India social marketing is undertaken by a variety of organisations and groups such as units of the UNO like WHO, UNICEF, international organisations like the Red Cross, and the Rotary Club, socially conscious companies, charitable societies and associations of individuals.

1.3 Importance / Advantages / Benefits / Significance / Relevance of Marketing in a Developing Economy

The evolution of marketing has brought about various other benefits along with it. These benefits can be categorised as follows:

1. Benefit accruing to the manufacturer/individual firm.
2. Benefit accruing to the society.

1. Benefit accruing to the Manufacturer / Individual Firm

- **Helpful in earning and increasing profits:** The basic reason for which any business organisation comes into existence is to make a profit. Marketing helps in increasing the profits of an organisation by reducing the selling costs on one hand and by increasing the demand for the product through advertising and sales promotion activities.

- **Marketing is helpful in business planning and decision making:** The major problems of every manufacturer are what, when, where, how, how much, and at what cost, the goods and services are to be made available to the consumers. The modern system of business has evolved in such a way that a manufacturer cannot answer all these questions by himself. If he wants the right answers he has to depend upon the marketing mechanism to feel the pulse of the market. It is marketing which is the stethoscope to measure these pulse beats. It is, marketing research that solves the consumers' and hence producers' problems in day-to-day operations. Thus, if a business organisation has to take the right decisions it has to depend upon the modern marketing system.

- **Marketing is a source of new ideas:** A business operates in a very dynamic and ever changing environment. Marketing is just a sub-system in this great environment. Every change in the environment affects marketing and thus a business unit has to keep changing its production, price, competition policies, depending upon the changes in the marketing environment. Thus, it can be said that it is this dynamic marketing environment which is the cause of changes and a source of new ideas to the businesses.

Marketing places the goods in the hands of the ultimate consumer: All business activity would come to a stop if the goods did not reach the consumers. It is marketing that bridges the gap between the producers and consumer and places the products in the hands of the final consumer.

2. Benefits accruing to the Society

- **Marketing is instrumental in improving the standard of living of the society:** Satisfaction of human wants being the main goal of marketing. It is for the satisfaction of human wants that products and services are created. This is why

Marketing Guru Paul Mazur said, "Marketing is the delivery of a standard of living to the society." Marketing creates and increases demand of the new and existing products and thus raises the standard of living of the people. It is through marketing that, yesterday's luxuries are converted into today's necessities.

- **It provides employment:** Marketing is a mammoth and complex mechanism involving a number of functions and sub-functions. Each function has countless job openings either direct or derived. In India, nearly 40% of the population is engaged in activities that have a direct or indirect impact on the activity of marketing. Thus, we can safely say that marketing creates employment opportunities for a large portion of the population of any country through its different marketing processes such as market research, wholesale and retail trade, transport, communication, storing, warehousing, publicity, promotion etc.

- **Marketing stabilises the economic conditions:** A stable economy is an efficient economy in which the economic activities are consistent and continuous. A stable economy implies the existence of near full employment, flexible prices and perfect balance between production and consumption or demand and supply of goods and services. Though economic stability is desirable it is not always achievable. Today production is one thing and distribution is another. There has to be a balance between the two. More production with less demand or less production with more demand, both situations are harmful for society. What is required is a balance between the two and this balance can be brought about by efficient marketing, as marketing is a vital link between production and distribution. It links production to distribution and solves the problems of imbalance between the two, thus bringing about a stable economy.

- **Marketing increases "National Income":** An efficient marketing system will not only maintain but increase the demand for goods and services. When demand increases, production activity is stimulated, which in turn increases the national income of a country.

Limitations, Disadvantages and Cost of Marketing

Along with benefits, several criticisms have been levelled against marketing. In general, they are related to unethical practices and inefficiencies. Some of them are as follows:

1. **Marketing increases the cost of goods and services:** It is said that nearly 50 paise of every rupee spent by a consumer on the purchase of a product is spent for making the product available to the customer at the right time, place and in the required quantities by the marketing system. Thus, marketing definitely adds to the cost of the product.

2. **Marketing misallocates scarce economic resources:** In a developing country like India, this assumes special significance. The manufacture of many luxury cars, T.V. sets, air conditioners and other luxury items and few schools, public hospitals, and roads are definitely a serious misallocation of national resources.

3. **Marketing creates needs:** The foundation of marketing is the identification of the needs of customers, and then creating products to satisfy these needs. Thus, marketing may at times create dissatisfaction amongst people by making them aware of new needs, the fulfilment of which is not available to them for the want of funds.

4. **Marketing makes human life very commercial:** The core of all businesses is marketing. In today's competitive world, there is cut throat competition and every business unit has to face a number of challenges. Every business concern tries to convert the maximum number of prospects into customers. A new way of doing this is relationship marketing. In this concept, a person becomes the distributor of the company by purchasing a product of the company. Thereafter, for every product that he sells he gets a commission. Not only this but he also gets a commission on every sale made by all the people who have become distributors of the company through him. Thus, a person by virtue of buying the product enters into a very viable business transaction through which he can make a lot of money. Thus, marketing makes human life commercial.

5. **Marketing involves too much competitive promotion:** In today's world of competition, each company has to spend a lot on competitive advertising. This competitive advertising expenditure has to be included by the companies just to maintain the competitive balance. No company gains anything concrete. It just results in increase in the cost of the product.

6. **Marketing ignores ethical and moral considerations:** Marketing creates materialistic and artificial values only to satisfy physical needs. Advertising and promotion which are a vital part of marketing are often offensive, misleading, and untruthful. Today's advertisements erodes the cultural value of the youth. Much of the advertising is unethical.

7. **Marketing adversely influences our environment:** Disposable packages have created a major problem in big cities. Paper napkins, plastic cups and glasses, disposable diapers, beverage cans have all polluted our cities and they add to the non-biodegradable garbage endangering our environment. Refineries, power plants, fertiliser factories, chemical factories and paper industries are all not only polluting our environment but also eroding the natural wealth of our Mother Earth.

Thus, even though marketing is the basic necessity of human life, it is a rose with thorns, and it is upto man how he handles it. It is mans greed that adds the thorns to the beautiful rose of marketing.

1.4 Marketing Manager: Qualities, Duties, Responsibilities, Powers and Functions/Changing Profile and Challenges faced by a Marketing Manager

[A] Qualities of a Marketing Manager

A Marketing Manager is a leader of a group of people who performs the various activities of marketing. He thus should have the below mentioned various qualities.

1. **Physical Qualities:** A Marketing manager should be a physically healthy person capable of putting in long hours at work. He should have an impressive personality that attracts people to follow him. A commanding voice would be an added asset.

2. **Mental Qualities:** The Marketing Manager should be intelligent enough to understand and grasp the entire marketing scenario. He should be able to juggle the various elements of the marketing mix and come up with a winning combination. He should have complete knowledge about all the different aspects of marketing. All this requires brain power.

3. **Political Qualities:** A marketing manager has to operate in an atmosphere of intense competition. He has to come up with winning marketing strategies and implement them in such a way so as to always be above the competition. In order to do this successfully a political bent of the mind together with intelligence would do wonders.

4. **Social Qualities:** The Marketing manager has to lead a group of people in the right direction. Thus he should have those social qualities that make him likeable and respectable to his subordinates. They should want to emulate him and look upon him as a role model. Thus he should have the ability to meet and convince various types of people about his point of views. He should be able to motivate people to give their best for the organisation.

5. **Moral Qualities:** It would not hurt the marketing manager to possess certain moral values and principles. A person with high moral values and principles is always respected and this would definitely add to his personality.

Thus the above mentioned are the desired qualities in a Marketing Manager and the possession of the same would go a long way in making him successful.

[B] Powers of a Marketing Manager

The power wielded by a marketing manager will depend on whether this marketing manager is operating in a buyer's market or a seller's market. If it is a sellers market the marketing functions to be performed are actually distribution functions and hence the importance of the role of the marketing manager is likely to be negligible. Thus his power will also be limited. But if it is a buyers market as it is today then his functions and consequently his powers will be quite different.

Today businessmen have to operate in a very competitive business environment. In this kind of a competitive market situation a lot of emphasis is placed on the marketing operations. As such the role of the marketing manager and consequently his powers are very much magnified. In such a situation the marketing manager will be given wide powers, authority as well as status in the organisation structure. He will be given the required necessary power and authority to take decisions without consulting the board in order to avoid delays in taking important decisions. When a company places such a lot of emphasis on its marketing manager they usually designate him as "Marketing Director". In this case, he can discuss with the other members of the board on an equal footing.

[C] Duties and Responsibilities and Role of a Marketing Manager

Whatever be the position of the marketing manager in the hierarchy of the organisation he is basically the leader of a group of people which performs the various functions of marketing. As such he is responsible for carrying out all of the marketing activities within the firm and of coordinating these with other company functions. Therefore his major duties and responsibilities are as under:

1. To be on the lookout for marketing opportunities
2. To determine marketing plans, policies and procedures in consultation with the managing director.
3. Evolving a marketing mix for each market segment.
4. Supervision and control over sales manager, advertising manager, product manager, distribution manager, and any other managers who are directly responsible for implementing and expanding the marketing programme of the company.
5. Developing and expanding existing markets.
6. Negotiating transactions with major suppliers and intermediaries.
7. Development of new products, new markets, new channels, new innovations etc. in the field of marketing.
8. Making modifications in the marketing plans, policies and procedures.
9. Controlling marketing costs.
10. Selection, management and control of the channels of distribution.
11. Formulation of marketing strategies.
12. Undertaking consumer and public relations.
13. Integrating all marketing activities.

[D] Functions of a Marketing Manager

The following are considered to be the basic functions of a marketing manager.

1. **Integrated Marketing:** The marketing manager has to take decisions on the various elements of the marketing mix in an integrated way. A customer does not purchase a product just because of its price or utility or appearance. While purchasing, a customer is influenced by all aspects such as the promotional and advertising strategy of the company, its channels of distribution, the actual product, after sale services etc. Thus the marketing manager has to integrate all the elements of the

marketing mix in such a way that the consumer finds the final deal very attractive. While doing this the marketing manager must never lose sight of the company's interests. He should try to reduce the cost of marketing the products and at the same time win the goodwill of the customers. He has to co-ordinate the activities of the various departments of marketing as well as co-ordinate between the marketing department and all other departments like production department, finance department etc.

2. **Determining Objectives:** It is the function of the marketing manager to determine the marketing objective of the company. The marketing objective must be fixed keeping in mind the overall objective of the firm. Not only does he have to fix the marketing objective, but he has to crystallise the product objective pricing objectives, promotion objectives and physical distribution objectives. He has to integrate and direct all these objectives towards the overall marketing objective.

3. **Product Policy:** The marketing manager must be very clear as to the type of customer who will use his product. He should be clear on whether his company wants to produce a single product or a line of products. Thus his product policy objective must be consumer oriented and in keeping with the overall marketing objective.

4. **Pricing Policy:** It is the duty of the marketing manager to fix the pricing policy in keeping with the marketing and overall company policy. The pricing policy and product policy are interrelated. The marketing executive should fix the price in such a way that it results in maximum profit for the company from the volume of sales secured at that particular price.

5. **Distribution Strategy:** The Marketing Manager has to decide upon the distribution strategy that he wants to adopt. Does he want a limited distribution or a widespread distribution, will have to be decided and then he will have to organise for the channels of distribution and will have to select the channel accordingly.

6. **Advertising and Sales Promotion:** The Marketing Executive has to decide upon the advertising and sales promotion policy. He will have to decide whether the advertising will be done by a separate department in his organisation or it would be better to entrust the work of advertising to the outside professionals, or to use a combination of both these methods.

7. **Proper Planning:** Planning is the steps to decide in advance what is to be done. All companies carry out planning. The marketing manager has to plan as to how the objectives that have been determined will be implemented. For proper planning the marketing manager has to carry out the following functions.
   - Marketing research,
   - Planning the sales policies,
   - Planning the long-term marketing programme,
   - Planning for product diversification.

8. **Selling:** The marketing manager has to perform the following functions in regard to selling:
   - To direct the sales manager to regulate sales,
   - To organise sales territories and fix sales quotas,
   - To select and train personnel for the sales department,
   - To motivate the sales personnel,
   - To organise and develop the channels of distribution.
9. **Service:** After sales service is regarded as an integral part of modern marketing management. In fact in today's competitive business world if a company has to survive, it has to be consumer oriented and has to take care to see maximum satisfaction is given to the customers. Thus a Marketing Manager must see to it that proper after sales services are given to the customers. Any complaints and problems of the customers are to be dealt with at once.

[E] Challenges Faced by a Marketing Manager

According to a survey conducted, creating growth (through the acquisition of new customers) and sustaining growth (through superior loyalty) are some of the challenges marketing managers' face in today's competitive world of marketing. 42% respondents suggested that acquiring new customers and 36% suggested driving loyalty and satisfaction were also some big challenges facing most marketing managers.

1. **Generating Awareness and Driving Traffic:** Marketing managers have to actually get the attention of their audience and get people interested in their business, product, or service. Many marketers face the challenge of not having a large enough volume of interested prospects, while some others just don't know which channels they should focus their efforts on for the highest return.
2. **Targeting Effectively:** Targeting is a key component of all aspects of marketing. To be more effective at targeting, one of the first things any marketer needs to do is identify their buyer personas to determine who it is they should be marketing to.
3. **Using Social Media to Generate Customers and Revenue:** The information technology boom and the growth of the social media, telecommunications, have had a major impact on the way marketing managers bring value to their customers. Most companies know there is real business value in social media marketing, but they don't know how to convert social engagement into rupees. It isn't enough to simply have a presence on social media, there is a science to targeting, engaging, and nurturing with social networks that will allow the marketing managers to build up a social following that they can use as a quality source of leads.
4. **Keeping up with Marketing Trends and Strategies:** Marketing has gone through many transformations, especially in the last decade. Marketing focus has shifted from print media to online media, and we have witnessed the decline of direct mail

and cold calling. This is due to technology introducing new tools that make communication with potential customers more efficient and effective. Social media has risen as a dominant platform for two-way communication and feedback collection. These are only a few of the recent changes marketing has gone through, and every day, we're seeing more and more changes, new technologies, different strategies are developed, new trends emerge.

5. **Increasing and Proving Return on Investment (ROI):** With more and more advanced analytics tools available, marketers are being held to a higher standard. It's no longer enough to simply do marketing, the marketing manager must be able to measure and understand the value all efforts in terms of leads, customers, and revenue. The marketing manager needs to prove that the return on investment is high enough to justify that effort, time, and money.

Points to Remember

- The concept of marketing has evolved from a simple exchange transaction to a complex and complicated one, involving a number of interconnected and interrelated variables.
- The earlier definitions of marketing emphasised the flow of goods from the seller to the buyer. In this traditional sense, "Marketing" is said to consist of such efforts as affect the transfer in ownership of goods and their physical distribution.
- The basic objective of marketing lies in the satisfaction of human wants at a reasonable profit to the company.
- Marketing can be said to have three fold objectives:
  1. The objective of customer satisfaction.
  2. The objective of reasonable profit to the company.
  3. The objective of social good.
- The philosophy of marketing can be compartmentalised into four stages or four different concepts of marketing. The first two are the traditional concepts and the last two are the new concepts of marketing.
  1. Production Oriented Marketing,
  2. Sales Oriented Marketing,
  3. Consumer Oriented Marketing,
  4. Socially Oriented Marketing, i.e., socially responsible marketing approach
- The evolution of marketing has brought about various other benefits along with it. These benefits can be categorised as follows:
  1. Benefit accruing to the manufacturer/individual firm.
  2. Benefit accruing to the society.
- A Marketing Manager is a leader of a group of people who performs the various activities of marketing.
- The power wielded by a marketing manager will depend on whether this marketing manager is operating in a buyer's market or a seller's market.

Questions for Discussion

1. What is Marketing? Explain its Evolution.
2. Explain the Objectives of Marketing.
3. Explain the Relevance of Marketing in a Developing Economy.
4. Discuss the Functions of Marketing.
5. Explain the Approaches to the Study of Marketing.
6. Explain the Roles and Functions of a Marketing Manager.
7. Write short notes on:
   (a) Elements of Marketing
   (b) Powers of Marketing Manager
   (c) Limitations of Marketing.

Questions from Previous Pune University Examinations

1. Define the Term Marketing. Explain Relevance of Marketing in a Developing Economy. **[April 2011]**
2. What is Marketing? Explain the Functions of Marketing. **[Oct. 2011]**
3. Explain the Approaches to the Study of Marketing. **[Oct. 2011]**
4. What is Marketing? Explain the advantages of Marketing in a Developing Economy. **[April 2012]**
5. Define Marketing. Explain Approaches to Study of Marketing. **[Oct. 2012]**
6. Define Marketing. Explain various Concepts of Marketing. **[April 2013]**
7. Write a Short Note on Functions of Marketing. **[Oct. 2006, 2007]**
8. What is Marketing? Explain Different Approaches to Marketing Giving Example. **[Oct. 2009]**
9. Define the term Marketing? Explain Approaches to Study of Marketing. **[April 2010]**
10. What is Marketing? Discuss the Various Approaches to the Study of Marketing. **[April 2008]**
11. Compare and Contrast: Marketing and Selling. **[April 2006]**

■■■

Chapter 2...

Classification and Types of Markets

Contents ...

2.1 Traditional Classification of Marketing

2.2 Service Marketing: 7P's of Services Marketing, Importance of Services Marketing, Importance of Service Sectors

2.3 Rural Marketing: Meaning, Features and Importance of Rural Marketing, Difficulties in Rural Marketing and Suggestions for Improvement of Rural Marketing

2.4 Retail Marketing

2.5 Tele Marketing

2.6 E-Marketing

2.7 Digital Marketing: Meaning, Importance of Digital Marketing

2.8 Green Marketing

- Points to Remember
- Questions for Discussion
- Questions from Previous Pune University Examinations

Learning Objectives ...

➤ To explain the concept of services marketing

➤ To discuss the classification of services

➤ To co-relate the concept of marketing mix with respect to services

➤ To elucidate the facts about services in the economy

➤ To understand the scope of service quality

➤ To discuss the importance of rural marketing

➤ To explain marketing mix suitability to the rural market

➤ To comprehend the challenges faced in the rural market

➤ To study meaning, characteristics, significance, functions, organised and unorganised retailing

➤ To discuss trends in retail formats

➤ To understand E-marketing, digital marketing and green marketing

2.1 Traditional Classification of Marketing

This topic is covered in Chapter one under the heading, 'The Traditional and Modern Concept of Marketing.'

2.2 Service Marketing: 7P's of Services Marketing, Importance of Services Marketing, Importance of Service Sectors

(A) Introduction to Services Marketing

Marketing thinking developed initially in connection with selling physical products such as toothpaste, soap, sugar, salt, bicycles, cars and so on. However, one of the major trends in recent years has been the phenomenal growth of services. In fact India in recent years has seen an explosion of service industries like banks, hotels, insurance, telecommunication and the like.

The rising affluence of people and more leisure time available has resulted in an increase in the demand for various services right from health to entertainment services. In fact the service sector today is the fastest growing one and service jobs are provided not just in service industries like banks, insurance, airlines and hotels but also within product based industries like trainers, consultants, lawyers, advertisers and medical staff.

Service industry has gained importance, not only because of rise of affluence of the general public but also due to the importance of professionalism. The choice of products is many in the market today, but what differentiates one supplier of goods from another is the kind of service he provides at the time of delivery and after sales.

For example, at the time of purchase of an Activa from the B.U Bhandari motors, the keys were handed over to the customer by the salesman of the showroom. No responsible person from the showroom thought it necessary to be with the customer to explain him the functions, servicing details etc. However, when an Alto car was purchased from a Maruti dealer, the sales person came for delivery and explained all functions and all details as if he was doing it for the very first customer with all his heart and soul in it! The difference in the 2 situations was not only the product but the personal touch given by the Maruti sales person.

(B) Meaning, Definition and Nature of Services

The **American Marketing Association** has defined services as, *"(1) activities, benefits or satisfactions which are offered for sale, or (2) are provided in connection with the sale of goods"*.

Phillip Kotler has defined services as, *"A service is any act or performance that one party can offer to another that is essentially intangible and does not result in the ownership of anything. Its production may or may not be tied to a physical product."*

Any offer made to a market place can range from being an offer of a pure good to a pure service with various combinations of good plus service in between. Usually an offer of a pure good also, has a service component. In fact every offer made to the market place has a service component. This service component can be a major or a minor component of the offer.

Phillip Kotler has distinguished the offers made to the market place into the following four categories:

1. **A Pure Tangible Good:** An offset of a pure tangible good such as toothpaste, soap, salt, sugar etc. The only service accompanying the sale of this product is the courtesy of the sales staff.

2. **A Tangible good with Accompanying Services:** Here the offer consists of a tangible good accompanied by one or more services to enhance its consumer appeal. For e.g. an automobile manufacturer sells an automobile with a warranty, service and maintenance instructions, and so on. In fact, the more technologically sophisticated the generic product, the more the sales are dependent on the quality and availability of its accompanying customer services like repairs, maintenance, installation advice, training etc. Maruti is probably as service intensive as manufacturing. Without its various service centres its sales would probably not be what they are.

3. **A Major Service with Accompanying Minor Goods and Services:** Here the offer consists of a major service along with some additional services and/or supporting goods. For example, airline passengers are buying transportation service. They arrive at their destination without anything tangible to show for their expenditure. However the trip includes some tangibles such as food and drinks, a ticket stub and an airline magazine. The service requires a capital-intensive good called an airplane for its realisation, but the primary item is a service.

4. **A Pure Service:** Here the offer consists primarily of a service. Examples include psychotherapy and massage. The Psychoanalysts give a pure service with the only tangible elements as an office and a couch. Similarly the masseuse gives a pure service with the only tangible elements being a room, couch and oil.

Thus a market offer today be it a good or a service has an element of the other. However, when we study services marketing, the reference in which it is meant is no. 3 and 4 above, i.e. a major service with accompanying minor goods and services or a pure service.

(C) Features or Characteristics of Services

Services have four major characteristics. These are as mentioned below:

1. **Intangibility:** Services are intangible. That is they cannot be seen, tasted, felt or smelled before they are bought. Thus a person on his first flight will have to buy the ticket and sit in the plane, and then only will he experience the "Feel" of flying.

Similarly a person going to a Psychiatrist's office cannot predict the outcome, unless he takes an appointment and attends some sittings. This is very unlike products, which you can touch; feel, smell and even taste both before and after you buy. A service by nature is an abstract phenomenon. It is not a physical object. It has a mental connotation.

2. **Inseparability:** Another characteristic of service is the inseparability of the client and provider of service. There has to be a provider of service as well as a user of service. Services are typically produced and consumed at the same time. Like products they cannot be manufactured, stored and then sold as and when there is a demand. Thus dentists, doctors, dancers and musicians create and offer services at the same time. A person who is the provider of service can sell his service only to a limited number of people in a day. However, an organisation that is a provider of service can appoint agents to sell the service. Example: insurance agents, travel agents etc.

3. **Variability:** Another characteristic of services is that they are highly variable. The quality of the service provided will differ depending upon who provides them and when and where are they provided. Even the same provider will give a different service from time to time depending upon the situation. For example, an entertainment programme of Lata Mangeshkar would be different from the one given by Sonu Nigam or Asha Bhosale. Similarly, an open-heart surgery done by a heart specialist will differ from patient to patient depending upon the energy level and mental makeup of the surgeon at the time of each surgery and also on the seriousness of the surgery.

4. **Perishability:** Services cannot be stored. Nor can they be carried forward. If a service is not used today, it is lost forever. They are highly perishable. Unutilised services render economic losses. A ship, plane or warehouse loaded to half its capacity, a hotel with rooms vacant, a theatre with empty seats during the airing of a movie, are all examples of services which have been lost forever. Thus services not utilised when they are produced, perish.

5. **Simultaneity:** Services are rendered and consumed during the same period of time. As soon as the service consumer has requested the service (delivery), the particular service must be generated from scratch without any delay and friction and the service consumer instantaneously consumes the rendered benefits for executing his upcoming activity or task.

Thus intangibility, inseparability, variability, simultaneity and perishability are the five main characteristic features of services.

Classification of Services - Marketing of Industrial Goods Services, Marketing of Consumer Goods and Services

Services can basically be classified according to the market in which they are sold. That is:
1. Services sold in the consumer market and
2. Services sold in the business or industrial market

However it must be remembered that many services like financial service, insurance, transportation and communication services are sold to both the markets. As such they have been included only in the consumer services and have not been repeated in the industrial services.

1. Consumer Services:

In the modern day world, dominated by effluence and a highly consumerist approach, where material things and comfort are on a high priority of people, the following are some of the services offered to the consumer market.

- **(a) Food Services:** Restaurants, hotels, cafeterias, dhabas, coffee shops, sandwich bars etc. offer food services to a consumer base that is growing everyday. All these provide food service. The service experience differs in each of these depending upon the ambience of each. Today, we also have fast food chains like Pizza Hut, Dominos, Mc Donald's and KFC open shop in India to cater to the growing demand of a different variety of food experience of Indians. We now have restaurants specialising in multi-cuisine to cater to the upper market adventurous consumer.

- **(b) Hotels and Motels:** With growing affluence comes the desire for entertainment and travel. Today, we see a large number of hotels right from the glamorous seven star hotels in the metropolitan cities to the smaller motels in the suburbs. The hotel industry offers not just a stay but a number of facilities like conference hall, health club, beauty salon, sports club etc. depending upon the level of the hotel.

- **(c) Personal Care Services:** These include the services offered by beauty parlours, naturopathy centres, massage parlours, health and fitness centres etc. Due to the increased standard of living and a growing self-awareness, people have become more health, beauty and physique conscious and this has led to an explosion of centres offering 'Personal Care Services' all over the country.

- **(d) Medical and Surgical Services:** As with all other professions, the medical profession too has seen a massive development in recent times. Many state of art medical centres that provide all kinds of services, right from consultation to diagnosis, operation to post operative care and rehabilitation have mushroomed. Specialisation is on the rise and we have specialists today on every small anatomical aspect of the human body.

- **(e) Educational Services:** Gone are the days when a 'Student' was merely someone who came to acquire knowledge. Today he is a customer to be satisfied by the education and educational facilities offered by the educational institution. With the growing number of foreign and private educational institutions, getting admission to an Institution of your choice is merely a matter of paying the right amount of money.

- **(f) Household Services:** With the increasing standard of living and affluence of people, we have an increasing number of household service providers. Organisations today provide maids, baby sitters, gardeners etc. for households.

(g) **Automobile Services (Garages):** Today we have a number of two-wheeler and four wheeler vehicle service centres. These centres today not only provide the service of repair and maintenance of the vehicle but also provide the service of pick and drop of the vehicle from the residence of the owner. They also remind the owner about when the next servicing is due.

(h) **Entertainment Services:** Rising purchasing power and more leisure time are responsible for the growing entertainment needs of the society. Today we have many amusement parks, water parks, theatres and multiplexes. Theme parties, fashion shows, dances and Gazal nights are also on a rise. Virtually every five star hotel today has a disco. Sports, entertainment and gaming parks too are on the rise. The number of entertainment options available is increasing day-by-day and so is the number of services being offered by them.

(i) **Transport Services:** Railways, roadways, airways and waterways provide transport facilities for the movement of both goods and people. Today we can see a massive improvement in the road and air facilities. The Golden Quadrilateral Project, linking the four major metropolitan cities in India is underway. A number of flyovers can be seen in the metropolitan cities. The BOLT (Build, Operate, Lease and Transfer) system has helped the Indian government in the development of its roads. Similarly the entrance of private airlines has led to a development of Indian airways. With the increase in competition, air travel has become cheaper and affordable to a growing number of people. A further reduction in air travel fares and increase in the number of people travelling by air will be seen in the near future.

(j) **Communication Services:** The greatest advancements have been seen in communication services. Especially with the advent of IT, traditional means of communication like mail and telephone have been replaced by mobile phones, e-mail, chat and sms (short message service). Through the satellite communication system, the whole world has become accessible within a matter of seconds and the click of/a few buttons.

(k) **Insurance Services:** Insurance gives us security and protection against risk to self and property. Today we have a number of private players in this sector and hence insurance services too are witnessing a high level of competition. This is very advantageous to the consumer as he benefits in the form of high level of service and lowering premium rates.

(l) **Financial Services:** Today we have a number of banks and financial agencies all willing to provide financial services to the consumers. Right from helping him invest funds to providing housing and car finance, to providing ATM and 24 hour banking services. Internet banking is the name of the game today and all banking transactions can be performed right from the consumer's office or residence.

(m) Personal Security Services: Today in India even though affluence and standard of living is increasing there is still a very strong divide between the haves and the have-nots. This has resulted in an increasing demand for personal security of the lives and possessions of the haves and as such has led to the establishment and growth of personal security services providers. This not only includes the providers of security guards and watchmen but also the providers of home security alarm systems.

2. **Industrial Services:**

   In the industrial market a number of services are offered that facilitate the production, finance, distribution and marketing of goods. Some of these are as under:

   (a) Engineering Services: Engineering firms undertake a variety of essential industrial services. These are specialised concerns that help businesses in the formulation and planning of new projects, designing and construction of plant and buildings, installation of special equipments and its maintenance.

   (b) Warehousing services: Warehousing services are essential to hold stocks from the time that they are manufactured to the time that they are consumed. Manufacturers and marketers should have their own warehousing facilities. However, there are various government and private warehouses that hire out their services to manufacturers and marketers requiring the same.

   (c) Advertising and Promotion Services: Advertising is a highly creative and capital intense line. Most manufacturers and marketers depend upon advertising agencies to promote their products. Advertising agencies are specialist institutions that plan, design and place advertisements in various media at the least cost with a professional touch.

   In other words they help marketers in the preparation of the promotion mix and the campaign for advertising and sales promotion. They also perform various other related services and act as market research agents for their principals.

   (d) Office Services: Every business today requires an office and office related services. There are many firms today that supply office related services like cyclostyling and duplicating services, supply of temporary office staff, cleaning services and security services.

   (e) Management Consultancy Services: Management consultancy services offer numerous services to business organisations. Such firms offer advice to organisations right from the stage of conception to inception of the firm. Such organisations further advice the top management on the handling of problem areas in all functional areas like production, marketing, finance, personnel, office administration etc. Management consultancy services are a boon to the small and medium firms as, due to the existence of these firms, specialised and professional advice is available to these firms, at a reasonable cost.

(f) **Marketing Research Services:** In today's scenario of a cut throat competitive environment, a competitive advantage plays a vital role in the success of a business. This is where market research gains importance. Knowledge about customers, consumers, competitors, suppliers etc. gives a competitive advantage to any firm. Market research firms perform the service of collecting, tabulating and analysing data about the various people and parties involved in a business and thereby help the business organisations to develop the right and correct marketing strategies.

(g) **Manpower Selection and Training:** The success of any business depends upon the productivity of its human resources. It is very essential to select the right candidate for the right job. Further, continuous training is a must to see that the human resource is working to its maximum capability. The more skilled and updated the human resource the better will be the performance of the company. Some business organisations prefer to outsource this important function of selection and training of human resources. As such you have firms that specialise only in recruitment and training and perform this service for various business houses that require the same, for a fee.

The above are some of the services that are offered to the industrial buyer. However services like food services, hotel and motels, financial, insurance, transportation, communication and entertainment are offered in both the markets. The above lists are by no means comprehensive they are only illustrative.

Marketing Mix for Services / Marketing Strategies for Services:

Phillip Kotler in his book "*Marketing Management - Analysis Planning and Control*" has defined marketing as "*Marketing is the analysis, planning, implementation and control of programmes designed to bring desired exchanges with target audiences for the purpose of personal and mutual gain. It relies heavily on the adaptation and co-ordination of Product, Price, Promotion and Place for achieving response*".

The **Cambridge International Dictionary** of English has explained strategy as "*A detailed plan for achieving success in situations such as war, politics, business, industry or sports, or the skill for planning such situations*".

Thus a marketing strategy is the planning and implementation of plans and programmes by an organisation to bring about the required exchanges with the target audience which results into benefits. That is, the consumer gains satisfaction from the use of the product/service and the marketer achieves success through a particular level of sales and profits. The plans and programmes required to bring about this result, rely heavily on the four P's of Marketing i.e. PRODUCT, PRICE, PLACE AND PROMOTION.

Therefore marketing strategy is the use of the four P's to bring about the required exchanges with the target market so as to lead to a success in business. However when we are focused on the marketing of services three more very important P's of marketing have to be taken into account. These are:

The Fifth P: People

People are the most important element of any service or experience. Services tend to be produced and consumed at the same moment, and aspects of the customer experience are altered to meet 'the 'individual needs' of the person consuming it. Most of us can think of a situation where the personal service offered by individuals has made or tainted a tour, vacation or restaurant meal. People buy from people that they like, so the attitude, skills and appearance of all staff needs to be first class. Here are some ways in which people add value to an experience, as part of the marketing mix - training, personal selling and customer service.

Training

All customer facing personnel need to be trained and developed to maintain a high quality of personal service. Training should begin as soon as the individual starts working for an organisation during an induction. The induction will involve the person in the organisation's culture for the first time, as well as briefing him or her on day-to-day policies and procedures. At this very early stage the training needs of the individual are identified. A training and development plan is constructed for the individual, which sets out personal goals that can be linked into future appraisals. In practice most training is either 'on-the-job' or 'off-the-job.' On-the-job training involves training whilst the job is being performed Off-the-job training sees learning taking place at a college, training centre or conference facility. Attention needs to be paid to Continuing Professional Development (CPD) where employees see their professional learning as a lifelong process of training and development. A well trained employee obviously adds value to the experience of the customer in his interaction with the employee.

Personal Selling

There are different kinds of salesperson. There is the product delivery salesperson. His or her main task is to deliver the product, and selling is of less importance, e.g. fast food, or mail. The second type is the order taker, and these may be either 'internal' or 'external'. The internal sales person would take an order by telephone, e-mail or over a counter. The external sales person would be working in the field. In both cases little selling is done. However, how they interact with the customer, while taking the order or delivering the product or talking on the phone will either add to the customer's experience or negatively impact the customer. Thus it is very important that sales people have a pleasing personality and interact in a good and polite fashion with the customer. The next sort of sales person is the missionary.

Here, as with those missionaries that promote faith, the salesperson builds goodwill with customers with the longer-term aim of generating orders. Again, actually closing the sale is not of great importance, at this early stage. The forth type is the technical salesperson, e.g. a technical sales engineer. Their in-depth knowledge supports them as they advise customers on the best purchase for their needs. Finally, there are creative sellers. Creative sellers work to persuade buyers to give them an order. This is tough selling, and tends to offer the biggest incentives. The skill is identifying the needs of a customer and persuading- them that they need to satisfy their previously unidentified need by giving an order.

All the different kinds of salespeople, whether they focus on sales or order taking, interact with the customer. The way they interact, their body language, their verbal and non verbal communication, all have an impact on the consumer. They all add to the feeling of either a good or a bad experience. The sales person is an ambassador of the organisation and a point of interaction with the consumer.

Customer Service

Many products, services and experiences are supported by customer services teams. Customer services provide expertise (e.g. on the selection of financial services), technical support (e.g. offering advice on IT and software) and coordinate the customer interface (e.g. controlling service engineers, or communicating with a salesman). The disposition and attitude of such people is vitally important to a company. The way in which a complaint is handled can mean the difference between retaining or losing a customer, or improving or ruining a company's reputation. Today, customer service can be face-to-face, over the telephone or using the Internet. People tend to buy from people that they like, and so effective customer service is vital. Customer services can add value by offering customers technical support and expertise and advice.

The Sixth P: Process

Process is the sixth element of the extended marketing mix, or 7P's. There are a number of perceptions of the concept of process within business and marketing literature. Some see processes as a means to achieve an outcome, for example - to achieve a 30% market share a company implements a marketing planning process.

Another view is that marketing has a number of processes that integrate together to create an overall marketing process, for example - telemarketing and Internet marketing can be integrated. A further view is that marketing processes are used to control the marketing mix, i.e. processes that measure the achievement of marketing objectives. All views are understandable, but not particularly customer focused.

For the purposes of the marketing mix, process is an element of service that sees the customer experiencing an organisation's offering. It's best viewed as something that the customer participates in at different points in time. Here are some examples to help build a picture of marketing process, from the customer's point of view.

Going on a cruise - from the moment that the customer arrives at the dockside, he/she is greeted; his/her baggage is taken to the room. The customer has two weeks of services from restaurants and evening entertainment, to casinos and shopping. Finally, the customer arrives at his/her destination, and the baggage is delivered to him/her. This is a highly focused marketing process.

Booking a flight on the Internet - the process begins with the customer visiting an airline's website. He/she enters details of the flights and books them. The ticket booking reference arrives by email or SMS. The customer catches the flight on time, and arrives refreshed at the destination. This is all part of the marketing process. At each stage of the process, marketers: deliver value through all elements of the marketing mix. Process, physical evidence and people enhanced services. Feedback can be taken and the mix can be altered. Customers are retained, and other services or products are extended and marketed to them. The process itself can be tailored to the needs of different individuals, experiencing a similar service at the same time. Processes essentially have inputs, throughputs and outputs (or outcomes). Marketing adds value to each of the stages.

The Seventh P: Physical Evidence

Physical evidence is the material part of a service. Strictly speaking there are no physical attributes to a service, so a consumer tends to rely on material cues. There are many examples of physical evidence, including some of the following:

- Packaging.
- Internet/Web pages.
- Paper Work (such as invoices, tickets and despatch notes).
- Brochures.
- Furnishings.
- Signage (such as those on aircraft and vehicles).
- Uniforms.
- Business cards: The building itself (such as prestigious offices or scenic headquarters).
- Mailboxes and many others.

Some organisations depend heavily upon physical evidence as a means of marketing communications, for example tourism attractions and resorts (e.g. Disney World), parcel and mail services (e.g. first flight courier), and large banks and insurance companies (e.g. ICICI Bank, HDFC Bank)

Marketing Strategy has to be used if business success is desired. Whether a marketer is marketing a product or a service, marketing strategy is a must. However, as a service has certain distinguishing characteristics and is much different from a product, the marketing strategy for marketing of services has to be different. The traditional approach to marketing cannot be used to market a service. What is required is the use of the Seven P's of marketing, with a focus on 'internal marketing' and 'interactive marketing'.

Internal Marketing: Internal Marketing describes the work done by the company to train and motivate its customer-contact employees so that all the employees work as a team to provide complete customer satisfaction.

Interactive Marketing: Interactive Marketing describes the employees' skills in handling customers.

Without internal marketing and interactive marketing, no marketing strategy for marketing of services will be complete as the experience of excellent service will be felt by the customer only when these two factors are hundred percent in place. In the marketing of services, the performance of the customer-contact people and their behaviour forms a major part of the service experience by the customer. Take the example of two finance companies. Company A and Company B. Both, providing zero percent finance for purchase of vehicles. The service of that company whose customer-contact staff is more customer service oriented will be thought of as the more efficient supplier of service.

Let us take the example of a bank and see how and why a bank has to use the four P's of marketing as well as internal marketing and interactive marketing in its marketing strategy. A bank performs various services. The basic reason why the marketing strategy for services is different is because services are intangible. That is, they cannot be seen, can only be experienced. Thus the major job of a marketer of services is to tangibilise the intangible. That is, he has to manage the evidence. Thus banks have to provide tangible images to tangibilise their services. This cannot be done by using only the four P's of Marketing. 'Internal Marketing' and 'Interactive Marketing' form a bulk of the marketing strategies for services.

Let us here see the various variables used by a bank to tangibilise its services. This is a part of its marketing strategy.

1. **Place:** The banks, buildings and offices should have a clean and spruced appearance. The location of the Head Office and branches speak volumes about its services. The layout within the bank is equally important. The way the customers are greeted and the shortest amount of waiting time for conducting any transaction are all ways and means of tangibilising the intangible. Soft background music can also be used to reinforce the impression of efficient service. Customer friendly bank personnel is another add on. Drinking water arrangement, seating arrangement for the customers are important.

2. **Price:** The banks pricing of its services, i.e. cheque clearance charges if any, ATM transaction charges if any, should be transparent to the customer, rather than he getting shocks later and they should be simple and clear.

3. **Marketing Communication:** The slogan promoting the bank should use words that give the impression of excellence. The bank should choose a name and symbol that once again imparts this impression. The name, slogan, logo of the bank should be eye catching in a subtle way. All communication from the bank should suggest efficiency. Pamphlets should have clean lines and avoid clutter. Illustrations for advertisements should be chosen carefully. Advertisements should communicate the banks positioning.

4. **Product and Equipment:** The equipments and computers used in the bank should be state of the art. Old and outdated computers will make a customer think about the level of efficiency of the bank.

5. **People:** The bank's personnel should be busy. They should wear appropriate clothing. They should be polite and courteous. They should do nothing from which any negative inferences can be understood.

Hence, it is clear from the earlier paragraphs that Place, Price, Marketing Communication, Product and Equipment form a part of the marketing mix. But the 'People' can be achieved only with 'Internal Marketing' and 'Interactive Marketing'. Thus the marketing strategy for services is very much different from the marketing strategy for products.

Services Marketing and the Economy - Scope of Services Marketing in Generation of Job Opportunity, Role of Services in Economy, Services Quality

The growth model of any economy, traditionally follows, the agriculture dominated to industry dominated, to services dominated, route. India, however has not followed this growth model. Economic development in India skipped the section of industry dominated growth and jumped straight from agriculture to services. India today is a services oriented economy.

The current situation in India is that the growth rate of services has overtaken both agriculture and industry and is now more than 50% of GDP. The contribution of service sector to GDP in the year 2012-13 was around 56%. The services sector has the highest growth rate and is the least volatile sector. Growth is particularly marked in public services, IT and financial services.

The services sector covers a wide array of activities ranging from services provided by the most sophisticated sectors like telecommunications, satellite mapping, and computer software to simple services like those performed by the hairdresser, the electrician, carpenter, and the plumber; highly capital-intensive activities like civil aviation and shipping to employment-oriented activities like tourism, real estate, and housing; infrastructure-related activities like railways, roadways, and ports to social sector related activities like health and education.

In India, The National Accounts classification of the services sector incorporates trade, hotels, and restaurants; transport, storage, and communication; financing, insurance, real estate, and business services; and community, social, and personal services. In the World Trade Organisation (WTO) list of services and the Reserve Bank of India (RBI) classification, construction is also included.

India's Services Sector

India's services sector has emerged as a major contributor to the national and state Income. The overall employment opportunities in India have increased many folds mainly because of the vast and ever growing service sector.

Services have dominated the economic growth all over the world and in India since the year 2000. The Indian service sector growth, like the rest of the world began at the level of 4-5% in the year 2000. However over the years the service sector growth in India has outpaced the service sector growth in the rest of the world. The Indian services sector growth has been responsible for the increasing overall growth rate of the Indian economy. In fact it is the growth of the service sector that has brought a great amount of stability to our economy.

One of the reasons for the growth of the service sector is that it has attracted a lot of foreign direct investment. According to the economic survey of India, the service sector has attracted nearly 47 per cent of the cumulative FDI equity inflows during the period April 2000- November 2012. This was possible because the government has taken many policy initiatives to liberalize the FDI policy for the services sector. These include liberalising the policy on foreign investment for companies operating in the broadcasting sector, like increasing the foreign investment limit from 49 per cent to 74 per cent in teleports (setting up up-linking HUBs/teleports) and direct to home (DTH) and cable networks, permitting FDI, up to 51 per cent, in multi brand retail trading, permitting foreign airlines to make foreign investment, up to 49 per cent in scheduled and non-scheduled air transport services.

A Government of Delhi Initiative

The Delhi Government, under its electronic monitoring service level agreement (e-SLA), has decided to integrate its online service with SMS facility. The new system, which is currently being tested, will enable Delhi citizens to check the status of their important documents like the driving license. Apart from that, they can also check the status of various other facilities such as electricity connections, water connections, ration card, freehold of Delhi Development Authority's flats, issuance of birth and death certificate, etc. The system is expected to be in place soon.

Services Employment in India

According to the economic survey of India the pattern of sectorial share of employment has changed over the last two decades. The share of agriculture and industry in employment has seen a downturn while the share of employment in the service sector has increased. The shares of the services and construction sectors in employment, increased from 19.70 per cent in 1993-94 to 25.30 percent in 2009-10 and from 3.12 per cent in 1993-94 to 9.60 in 2009-10 per cent respectively.

As per the National Sample Survey Office's (NSSO) report on Employment and Unemployment Situation in India 2009-10, for every 1000 people employed in rural India, 679 people are employed in the agriculture sector, 241 in the services sector (including construction), and 80 in the industrial sector. In urban India, 75 people are employed in the agriculture sector, 683 in the services sector (including construction) and 242 in the industrial sector. Construction; trade, hotels, and restaurants; and public administration, education, and community services are the three major employment-providing services sectors.

Some Recent Investments/ Developments in the Indian Service Sector / Indian Service Companies

- In a bid to enhance its presence in Asia Pacific and Middle-East regions, India's premier express courier company DTDC Courier and Cargo Ltd. has entered Australia and Kuwait through joint ventures (JV). The Australian venture, in which DTDC holds 34 per cent, will be handled jointly by DTDC and Fast World Express Pvt. Ltd., while the Kuwait venture will be handled by Kuwait Bayarek General Trading and Contracting Co. W.I.I. (who is the Master franchise). With this DTDC's global footprint has gone up to 16 countries providing services to over 240 international locations

- Accor, a European hotel operator, had first launched its property, Hotel Formule 1, in Gujarat. Now, the company is contemplating to have another property in the city. The group owns brands like Sofitel, Pullman, MGallery, Novotel, Suite Novotel, Mercure, Adagio, ibis, and Formule 1, which range from budget to luxury hotels, and the upcoming property could be any one of them. Accor has 19 hotels with 3780 rooms and two convention centers in India. Formule 1 is its low-cost brand. After opening a Formule1 in Greater Noida recently, it opened the second Formule 1 in Ahmedabad. It is all prepared to launch a third one in Pune and intends to have 15 Formule 1 hotels in India over the next few years

- Reliance Infra, or rather RInfra has introduced online chat service for Mumbai's 2.8 million electricity consumers. The facility will provide a service to consumers through which they would be able to resolve their issues on real-time basis by having an online chat with the company representatives. The consumers would also be provided with the guidance regarding application status, bill-related queries, payment options and other procedural information. Information regarding change of name requests, e-bills, SMS alerts, billing and payments, web-based services, etc, will also be made available

- Private telecom services provider Vodafone India has recently launched 'post-to-pre talk time transfer' service that enables its post-paid customer to immediately transfer talk-time (balance) to a pre-paid Vodafone customer. The first-of-its-kind service will be of special benefit for those post-paid customers who have family members, personal friends or office colleagues using a pre-paid connection and are in need of talk time (balance).

- Reliance Communications Ltd. has granted a US$ 1 billion-contract to Ericsson AB, the world's largest manufacturer of wireless networks, to manage the systems of the Indian phone operator. The contract is beneficial for Ericsson, as the company is trying to sell more services such as network management and maintenance and this contract will help it expand its services business in Asia. Reliance, which awarded a US$ 1 billion services contract to French phone-equipment maker Alcatel-Lucent SA also, is signing such deals to reduce the cost of running its networks.

Road Ahead

Needless to say, education is the thrust of development and hence, drives any industry and sector of the economy. Education in itself is one of the most crucial service industries and its growth comes prior to any other industry. A study named 'Indian Higher education Sector' by Deloitte has stated that the demand for higher education will continue to increase due to a booming economy, with a growing share of the knowledge-intensive services sector and growing middle class. The projection of increasing the Gross Enrolment Ratio from current levels to 30 per cent by 2020 would itself translate into 24 million additional enrolments.

Moreover, India currently has 80 million mobile internet users and the number is burgeoning with every passing year, according to an Internet and Mobile Association of India (IAMAI) and IMRB report. In order to cater to these users, digital entrepreneurs are evolving a plethora of mobile-based value-added services (VAS) for everything (from entertainment to payments and advertising). Industry experts believe that with passage of time, VAS would break out into separate verticals like entertainment, payments, social media and many more in the years to come.

Web courtesy:

- http://www.ibef.org/industry/services.aspx

2.3 Rural Marketing: Meaning, Features and Importance of Rural Marketing, Difficulties in Rural Marketing and Suggestions for Improvement of Rural Marketing

Rural Marketing

Meaning

In order to understand the term "Rural Marketing" we have to first understand the term 'Rural'. There is much confusion associated with the word rural as there is no accepted definition of the term. However there are different perceptions of the term and some of them are: To some, rural means a place with less than one lakh population; others consider the income level of the population to determine the rural segment. If the income levels are less than ₹ 11,000/- per annum then the segment is a rural segment. Yet to some others the term rural means smaller towns and mofussil areas having population of less than 10,000 persons.

Even the corporate sector faces this confusion about the term rural. In the absence of any clear concept of the rural area, there will not be a proper understanding of the rural problems and hence the marketing considerations and strategies might tend to go wrong.

In the absence of any standard definition of the term rural, let us understand it by studying the definition of the term 'Urban'. The Census Department of India defines the term

'Urban' as (a) *All places with Municipality, Corporation, Cantonment Board or Notified town area committee, (b) All the places with a minimum population of 5,000 persons, with at least 75% of the male working population engaged in non-agricultural activity and with a population of at least 400 persons per square kilometre or 1000 persons per square mile.* If we exclude the areas that come under the above definition, the remaining areas can be considered to be the rural areas.

When marketing activities are carried out in the rural markets it is known as 'Rural Marketing'.

Importance of Rural Marketing

Today, rural marketing is gaining importance especially in a country like India basically because 75 per cent of Indian population lives in the rural areas and 50 per cent % of the National Income is generated from these areas. It was all right for the marketers and manufacturers to ignore the rural markets in the 1960s. However in recent years, the Indian Market scene has undergone such a drastic change that the rural markets are outstripping the urban markets. Keeping this changing marketing environment in mind rural marketing can no longer be ignored. In fact it is growing in importance day after day. The reasons for the growth of the rural market and hence the increasing importance of rural marketing are as under:

1. **Increase in prosperity and purchasing power:** The rural market has achieved a rapid pace of material prosperity during the last decade due to the improvement in the productivity and output of agriculture. This has increased the purchasing power in the hands of the rural population.

2. **Flow of investment for rural development programmes:** Apart from the increase in agricultural productivity, prosperity has come to the rural areas through a flow of investments through many programmes such as Jawahar Rojgar Yojana, 20 point programmes, Programmes under IRDP, etc. Due to the inflow of this investment a large portion of the rural population has achieved agrarian prosperity levels.

3. **Shift of a segment of the Urban Population to the Rural areas:** The much improved transportation and communication facilities during the recent years on the one hand and the rapid rise in the cost of living in urban areas on the other hand has lead to the reverse flow of middle income classes of employees to move from urban to semi-urban and rural areas for residential purposes. As a result of this, products like washing and cleaning material, food and beverages, cosmetics, toiletries, televisions, refrigerators, fans and other appliances, ready-made garments etc. could penetrate into the rural market and gain substantial market acceptance.

Today each rural household is prosperous enough to acquire consumer durables such as TV sets, mopeds and pressure cookers. Thus it is a market growing at a very fast pace and no company can afford to neglect it.

4. **Awareness of modern technology due to penetration of media:** Due to penetration of popular media like Television, rural population has become aware of modern lifestyle. Also due to higher disposable income and increased awareness, scope for rural marketing has increased.

Features of Rural Market

There are certain unique features of rural markets and consumers in India. They are:

1. **It is a vast and scattered market:** India's rural market is vast comprising of 75% of India's huge population of around 1000 million. In terms of value it crosses more than 40,000 crores of which nearly 22,000 crores is for non-food and 18,000 crores for food items. The rural market is scattered and widespread over 76,500 villages unlike urban market confined to a handful of metros, cosmos and towns.

2. **The demand is seasonal:** Nearly 60% of the rural income comes from agricultural and related activities. Thus the demand for goods and services in the rural areas depends heavily on agriculture. Hence like agriculture the rural demand is also seasonal.

3. **Low standard of living:** The rural consumers have a low purchasing power, low per capita income, low literacy rate and therefore low standard of living. Added to that is social backwardness, traditions and religious pressures, cultural values and deep-rooted superstitions which force them to have simple living and high thinking and stop them from climbing the ladder of a better life style.

4. **Unity in diversity:** The rural population of India is marked by diverse cultures and languages. There is a great degree of diversity in the religions, languages, cultures and sub-cultures, social customs and traditions; even though they all together represent the rural population.

5. **The rural market is a steadily growing market:** The rural market of India today is a fast growing and expanding one. There is a huge rural demand today not only for agricultural inputs but for consumer goods both durable and non durable. Not only is there a demand in the rural market, but it is fast outstripping the urban market of India. This development of the rural market has been possible because of new employment income through rural development planning; and implementation, green and white revolutions and the revolution of 'rising expectation' of the rural masses.

Rural Marketing Mix - Importance, Elements and Scope

Meaning, Elements and Scope of Marketing Mix

The basic task of Marketing involves the identification of the needs of the customer and then the manufacturing and marketing of a product or service that satisfies this need.

In order to do this a marketing organisation has to concentrate on four important aspects known as the 4P's of marketing. The marketing manager has to combine these 4P's in such a way that the combination provides satisfaction to the customer and a profit to the manufacturer. When these elements (4P's) are combined together they are called as "The Marketing Mix".

The term "Marketing Mix", has been defined by **Phillip Kotler** in the following way: *"Marketing mix is a set of controllable variables and their levels that the firm uses to influence the target market."* Thus, according to this definition any variable under the control of the firm that can influence the customer demand is a marketing mix variable.

According to **Prof. Keeley** and **Prof. Lazor**, *"Marketing mix is composed of a large battery of devices which might be employed to induce consumers to buy a particular product".* In other words, marketing mix is the mixture of all the marketing efforts of a company revolving around the four ingredients namely product, price, promotion and place. These ingredients are interrelated and all revolve around potential consumer satisfaction as the focal point. It is the complex mixes relating to inputs and resources utilised in the marketing programme to attain the business objective.

The marketing mix of an organisation is made up of four elements namely PRODUCT, PRICE, PROMOTION AND PLACE. Each of these four elements or sub-mixes has a number of elements. The complete set of marketing mix, submixes and elements are given below:

The Marketing mix has four main sub mixes. They are:

1. The Product Mix
2. The Price Mix
3. The Place Mix or Physical distribution Mix
4. The Promotion Mix.

Each of the above four is the sub mixes of the marketing mix. They can also be called as marketing mix elements. Each of these elements has sub elements and they are as under:

1. **The Product mix:** The Product Mix includes:
   - Product Planning and Development,
   - Branding,
   - Packaging,
   - Labelling.

2. **The Price Mix:** The Price Mix includes:
   - Price policies,
   - Discounts,
   - Credit.

3. **Place Mix (Physical distribution mix):** The Place Mix includes:
   - Channels of Distribution,
   - Transportation,
   - Warehousing.

4. **Promotion Mix:** The Promotion Mix includes:
   - Advertising,
   - Personal Selling,
   - Sales Promotion,
   - Publicity.

Importance or Utility of Rural Marketing Mix

The Marketing mix whether for the rural or urban consumer can be used by marketers as a tool to assist in defining the marketing strategy. Marketing Managers use this method to attempt to generate the optimal response in the target market by blending a number of marketing mix elements in an optimum way. It is important to note that all the elements of the marketing mix are controllable variables. These elements can be adjusted on a frequent basis to meet the needs of the target market and the environment. Hence the Marketing mix is a very useful tool for targeting the market correctly and for achieving success with the target market.

The importance of marketing mix can be further understood as under:

1. **Attracting customers:** The 4P's are the tools of the marketing manager and he has to use these tools for attracting customers, for facing marketing competition and for promoting sales. With the help of the marketing mix, the marketing manager is able to best please the customer and this enables him to achieve his marketing objectives.

2. **Better use of resources:** Marketing mix promotes better utilisation of limited resources as it helps the marketing manager to understand his customer and invest in the areas in which the consumer is interested. It helps the marketing manager in focusing attention on: the needs of the consumer. With limited components at its disposal, it attempts to gain the best possible results.

3. **Precision:** Marketing mix provides precision to the study of marketing. It helps in, understanding the important tasks. Neil H. Borden has stated that "A chart which shows the elements of the mix and the forces that bear on the mix helps to bring understanding of what marketing is".

4. **Balanced approach:** Marketing mix is an effective tool for solving the problems. It keep the marketing manager to be on the right track. It reminds him that, on the one hand, he should be careful to consider the market forces and on the other hand think of a total marketing programme instead of relying on any one particular aspect.

5. **The significance of marketing mix lies in the mix or blend:** The components of marketing mix are individually important but their significance lies in the mix or blend. It is necessary to combine them properly so as to make them collectively effective in a dynamic marketing environment.

6. **Applicable to, business as well as non-business organisation:** The concept of marketing mix is applicable to business, as well as non-business organisations, such as clubs, colleges, associations etc.

Present Scenario of Rural Market - Problems and Challenges of Rural Market

Rural Marketing System, Problems and Solutions

Prima facie the rural markets appear to be virgin lands just waiting for the marketers to move in and cash on them. However getting into the rural market and capturing a sizeable share is not an easy task. It is indeed a lot of hard work. A lot many problems are encountered. These problems of rural marketing can be basically grouped under six different heads. They are:

1. Problems connected with 'Physical Distribution'.
2. Problems related to Channel of Distribution.
3. Problems associated with the Sales Force.
4. Problems of Marketing Communication.
5. Problems of Market Segmentation.
6. Problems related to Product Management.

1. Problems Connected with 'Physical Distribution':

While undertaking rural marketing a marketer faces three different problems connected with the Physical Distribution of goods. They are:

(a) **Problems of Transportation:** Not all villages in India are connected by railways and waterways. The only reliable means for transportation of goods are the road ways and they too are not all-weather. The transportation infrastructure of rural India is poor and inadequate to transport people and goods effectively.

(b) **Problems of Warehousing:** The facilities for storage in the rural areas, is even worse than the transportation facilities. Neither the Central nor the State Warehousing Corporation has been able to extend storage facilities to the rural areas. Though there are private warehouses in rural areas, they are meant for their exclusive use.

(c) **Problems of Communication:** The rural areas either do not have the basic minimum postal services like telephone and telegraphs, or if they are available they are very inadequate and not very effective. Communication is the basic requirement for marketing activities.

Due to lack of these infrastructural facilities, a marketer entering the rural market has to incur additional expenditure or compromise on the quality in either case it is the rural customer who suffers, in the form of higher prices and poor quality.

Solution: The solution to the problems of physical distribution lies in the fact that the government needs to set up Rural Warehousing Corporations exclusively to meet the needs of the rural market. Further, the responsibility for physical distribution can be shared with the stockists and stockists cum forwarding agents. A group of companies can come together to undertake common rural distribution.

2. **Problems related to Channel of Distribution**

   It is very obvious that the channel of distribution for rural marketing will be longer than the channel for urban marketing. This increased channel props up problems as mentioned below.

   (a) **Costly channel of Distribution:** A long channel automatically means a costly channel as a large no of middlemen are to be given their commission, furthermore, larger the channel, larger the number of administrative problems.

   (b) **Heavy dependence on intermediaries:** As far as rural marketing is concerned there is very little or no scope for the manufacturers to approach the customers directly. Thus they have no option but to depend upon the intermediaries.

   (c) **Feeble viability of retail outlets:** Rural markets are scattered, as such a large number of retail outlets are required to cover these markets. Moreover the rural areas are much more thinly populated as compared to urban areas. Thus these retail outlets are not commercially viable. Add to this a large number of intermediaries, the picture then is anything but rosy.

   (d) **Non-availability of dealers:** One of the major problems faced is the non availability of dealers in the rural market. The manufacturers have no choice but to make do with the available dealers.

   (e) **Non availability of banking and Credit facilities:** Retailers require credit facilities if they are to extend credit to their customers. If this facility is not available it will result in limited stock carrying and limited business. This basic facility is also not available in the rural areas.

Solution: The solution to the above mentioned problems lies in understanding the distribution system existing at the local village level. At this level there are the following available channels. They are private shops, cooperatives, fair price shops and village weekly markets popularly known as "village mandies". From all these, the manufacturer of consumer products has to rely on the private village shops, as the co-operatives are known for distribution of agricultural inputs, and the weekly mandies are meant for disposing off locally produced products. The fair price shops deal in items like wheat, sugar, atta, edible oil and sometimes cheap cloth. The village private shops are the most convenient and cheapest channel. Here the "Satellite distribution"; system works well. Under this system the manufacturer appoints stockists at fewer towns who bridge the gap between the manufacturers and the retail outlets in the villages.

3. Problems associated with the Sales Force

Rural marketing demands heavy doses of personal selling efforts. In this area too quite a number of problems are faced.

(a) **Getting salesmen to work in rural areas:** Those salesmen will be successful in the rural areas who will blend and mix with the rural population. Not only is this a very difficult task for the urban salesmen, but few urban salesmen are willing to move to the rural areas.

(b) **Matching with cultural differences:** The rural market itself is a diverse fold of different cultures. It is very difficult for any salesmen to master the different cultural heritages existing in the different rural areas.

(c) **Command over local languages:** In the vast rural areas of India a number of different languages are spoken. This also creates a problem for the salesman.

(d) **Greater creativity:** The job of a rural salesman becomes more difficult because many a times the products that he has to sell are totally new to the rural customer. Hence it requires a greater creativity on his part if he is to perform his function of creating needs, wants and desires.

Solution: The main solution to all these problems lies in proper recruitment, selection and training. Agreed, it is a herculean task but nothing is impossible. What can be done is that qualified people from the rural areas itself can be selected and proper training can be given to them in order to increase their efficiency.

4. Problems of Marketing Communication

Problems of marketing communication or sales promotion, in the rural areas also deserve attention. These problems arise out of the barriers to market communication. These barriers can be divided into two:

(a) **Barriers arising out of rural market structure:** The rural market structure is such that it is very diverse, scattered and full of people with different languages and cultures. Thus no advertising or promotional literature can be made available in any one language for the entire rural market. A number of local languages have to be used. Further the rate of illiteracy in the rural market is very high and thus the printed communication has little or no impact on the rural markets.

(b) **Barriers arising out of available media:** Even though media such as radio, TV, cinema, print and outdoor advertising are available in the rural areas, none of these has a total coverage of the entire rural area. Even though radio covers 90% of the rural areas its actual listenership is quite lower. TV covers 27%, cinema too has its share but not more than 35%, where as print media covers 20% of the rural population. Outdoor advertising has its potentialities. Thus the real problem here is that of selecting the right media mix.

Solution: The solution lies in combining media like radio, television, cinema, outdoor advertising and point of purchase. In addition to these formal media vehicles other non formal ones can also be used like musical shows, puppet shows, street plays, door to door campaigning etc. The advertising theme should be simple and straight forward stressing more on the product and its usage.

5. Problems of Market Segmentation

Market segmentation in rural marketing is more important than perhaps even in urban marketing. This is because there is a great amount of diversity in the various rural markets. They are by no means homogeneous. Further identifying and cultivating rural markets requires a huge amount of investment and hence due importance should be given to this aspect. There are various bases on which a rural market can be segmented.

Market segmentation can be done either on a primary basis like geographic and demographic, or on a secondary basis. The secondary basis for geographic segmentation would be level of irrigation, vicinity to fewer towns etc. The secondary basis for demographic segmentation would be age, sex, literacy levels. The major problem as far as market segmentation is concerned would be a choice of the basis of segmentation. However, much would depend upon the attitude and philosophy of the company on one hand and the resources available on the other hand.

6. Problems related to Product Management

Another problem faced in rural marketing is the decision of whether the same product, as is marketed in the urban area should be marketed in the rural areas also, or changes should be made. Taking into account the vastly different features of the rural markets certain changes in the colours, size and packaging will have to be made. However, as the rural consumer just like the urban consumer is a human being with the same desires and wants the basic product will be the same.

A rural customer like the urban customer wants quality at a lower price. Thus this aspect has to be borne in mind. However the rural customer has a low purchasing power and limited storage capacity and hence prefers to buy in small lots and small packages. Thus this aspect has to be given due attention. As the rural customer is poor it would pay the company to come out with cheaper products for this particular market. Even though the rural customer is by now used to branded products he is more carried away by the price factor. Further he gives more importance to regional or local brands. Thus while taking a decision to introduce a particular product in the rural market; these considerations should be paid attention to while deciding upon the changes to be made in the product.

Thus it can be concluded that rural marketing is both enchanting and challenging. However, they are fraught with challenges and problems which need to be overcome if the joys of profits are to be reaped.

Strategy for Rural Marketing

A marketing strategy is the total plan, shaped and designed specifically for attaining the marketing objective of the firm. A marketing objective tells us where we want to go and the marketing strategy provides us with the grand design for reaching there.

Usually a strategy is viewed as a system of building the defenses of a company against competitive forces. It stands for the competitive market actions taken by a firm either to counter competition or to evoke a response from the competition. Thus marketing strategies gain importance in rural marketing as rural markets are those virgin markets in which various companies are moving in, in order to capture the demand. Thus when we talk of marketing strategies for rural markets, we have to take into consideration the special characteristic features of the rural market.

Taking into account the great increase in exposure, fast changing expenditure pattern buying habits and increasing health care and consciousness of the rural consumer, a production driven marketing strategy will not hold for a long period of time. Thus a marketer will have to adopt either a Market driven strategy or a market driving strategy.

A market driving strategy aims at shaping the existing and potential demand in such a way that this demand matches the products offered by the company. Thus in this strategy the company has to make the buyer aware of new needs which can be fulfilled by consuming the products of the company. Or this strategy makes the consumer hunt for better products to satisfy their existing needs. Again this hunt for better products should end with the product of the particular company. Thus the demand driving strategy is more difficult than the demand driven one. A demand driven strategy would aim at providing those goods to the consumer that are needed, required and demanded by the consumer.

As far as the rural market is concerned, a market driving strategy would be more suitable as most companies enter the rural market in order to widen their markets. Thus their already existing products can be marketed with a little bit of variation. However for some products, a market driven strategy would also prove to be very useful because first and foremost it is easier and secondly taking into account the problems existing in the rural market it would be the best strategy.

However, the strategy adopted would depend upon the characteristics of the rural market and the extent and nature of the competition in existence.

2.4 Retail Marketing

Meaning and Characteristics of Retailing

The word retail is derived from the French word "Retaillier", which means "to cut a piece off" or to "break bulk". Thus, a retailer is a person who breaks up a big amount into small pieces, or buys in bulk and sells in small amounts. Retailing may be understood as the final step in the distribution of merchandise for consumption by the end consumers. Any firm that sells products to the final consumer is performing the function of retailing

According to **Philip Kotler**, *"Retailing includes all the activities involved in selling goods or services to the final consumer for personal, non-business use"*.

Thus retailing is a marketing activity involved in the sale of products to the final consumer. It consists of all activities involved in the marketing of goods and services directly to the consumers for their personal, family or household use.

Any organisation selling to the final consumers whether it is a manufacturer, wholesaler or retailer, is doing retailing. It does not matter how the goods or services are sold or where they are sold. The goods and services could be sold by person, mail, telephone, vending machine or internet. If they are sold to the final consumer it is retailing. The goods and services could be sold in a store, on a street or in the consumer's home. If they are sold to the final consumer it is retailing.

Characteristics of Retailing:

1. **Sale to the final consumer:** The most important characteristic of retailing is that it involves the sale of the product or service to the final consumer.
2. **Various channels:** In retailing the goods and services can be sold either in person, through mail, through telephone, through vending machines or the internet.
3. **Small order size:** The order size handled by a retailer is much smaller as compared to the wholesaler.
4. **Large number of orders:** The retailer handles a large number of orders.
5. **Wide variety of customers:** The retailer handles a wide variety of customers.
6. **Keeps a large assortment of goods:** The retailer keeps a wide variety of goods.

Significance and Functions of Retailing

Retailing occupies a key role in the world economy today. The importance of retail as an industry can be understood from the fact that the fortune 500 list of companies is headed not by a manufacturing firm but a retail major. The 2010 fortune 500 list of America's largest corporations is headed by the retail firm Wal Mart. And in the Global Fortune 500 list of 2009 Wal Mart has the 3rd place. In fact the fortune 500 list has about 50 retail organisations on its list. As an industry retailing not only contributes to the GDP, but it also employs a large number of people. In India retailing is believed to employ nearly 8% of the total workforce of the country.

Retailing is important to the national economy for the following reasons:

1. A big part of our personal income is spent on retail goods.
2. It is a major source of employment.
3. In the distribution system, retail is the link to the ultimate consumers.
4. The level of retail sales indicates the consumer's purchasing power, thus it becomes the basis for determining the economic status of the people of a country.

5. It adds value to the product because it creates time, place and possession utility.
6. It accounts for a major portion of marketing costs.
7. Taxes from retail store add income to our national treasury.

Functions of a Retailer:

The functions of a retailer are twofold.

1. The functions of a retailer with reference to the consumer.
2. The functions of a retailer with reference to the manufacturer or wholesaler.

Let us first understand the functions of a retailer with reference to the consumer. With reference to the consumer the retailer provides form, time, place and ownership utility to the consumer. This he does by providing the right kind of product, at the right time and place to the consumer.

1. **Provision of Form Utility:** The retailer provides the product to the consumer in the form that he can consume. The retailer does not offer raw material, but offers the consumer finished goods and services in a form that the consumer can consume. Further the retailer provides the consumer with an assortment of products in different categories.

2. **Provision of Time Utility:** The retailer provides time utility by keeping the store open, so that the consumer can shop at a time convenient to the consumer. Further the retailer stores the goods, and makes them available when the consumer wants them.

3. **Provision of Place Utility:** The retailer has his outlets i.e., places that are convenient for the consumer to visit. Thus retailing provides place utility to the consumer.

4. **Provision of Ownership Utility:** The retailer sells the product to the consumer thus transferring the title of ownership to the product from the retailer to the consumer and delivering ownership or possession utility to the consumer.

5. **Entertainment Utility:** Nowadays various organised retail outlets like malls have an inbuilt entertainment system. They organise programmes and contests to entertain the customers while they shop. Thus it is not only a shopping experience but an entertaining shopping experience.

6. **Environment:** Most big organised retail outlets take a lot of care of the retailing environment. They see to it that the environment is conducive to peaceful shopping. Huge shopping spaces, with temperatures controlled to very pleasing degrees by the use of air conditioning, well decorated retail outlets with pleasing aesthetics are the norm of the day. All these give the customer a very pleasant shopping experience and add to his level of satisfaction. Thus providing the customer with a pleasing shopping experience is also a function of retailing.

Thus, we may conclude that the function of retailing today is not just about delivering form, place, time and possession utility. Its function goes much beyond to entertaining the customer and ensuring such an atmosphere that the consumer is compelled to spend a lot of time and money in the shopping malls and outlets, and gains a high level of enjoyment and satisfaction by doing so.

The retailer serves the manufacturer by performing the function of distribution of goods to the end consumer, thus forming a channel of information and distribution leading to the final consumer. The retailer is the final link in the distribiution channel and a very vital one too. For several product categories where brand loyalty is not very strong, or for unbranded products the retailers recommendations, his placement of product in the store and his promotional schemes are very vital.

Organised and Unorganised Retailing

The Retail industry is divided into the organised and the unorganised sector.

Organised retailing refers to trading activities undertaken by licensed retailers, that is, those who are registered for sales tax, income tax, etc. These include the corporate-backed hypermarkets and retail chains, and also the privately owned large retail businesses. Unorganised retailing, on the other hand, refers to the traditional formats of low-cost retailing, for example, the local kirana shops, owner manned general stores, paan/beedi shops, convenience stores, hand cart and pavement vendors etc.

Unorganised retailing has dominated the Indian scenario for a number of centuries. It was only in the late 90's that organised retailing dared to crop its head on the Indian scenario. It faced stiff and organised protests from the unorganised sector.

According to the Census report of 2001 nearly 3 crore people in India, worked in wholesale and retail trade 1.1 crores in urban India and 1.9 crores in the rural areas of India.

India had well over 5 million retail outlets of all sizes and styles (or non-styles). However we sorely lacked anything that could resemble a retailing industry in the modern sense of the term.

In 2001, as much as 96 per cent of the 5 million-plus outlets were smaller than 500 square feet in area. This meant that India per capita retailing space was about 2 square feet (compared to 16 square feet in the United States). India's per capita retailing space was thus the lowest in the world *(source: KSA Technopak (I) Pvt Ltd, the India operation of the US-based Kurt Salmon Associates).*

In 2005, with over 12 million retail outlets, India had one of the highest densities of retail outlets in the world with one retail outlet for approx. 90 persons. India was the ninth largest retail market in the world with annual retail sales of approx. USD 215 Billion in 2005. However, the share of organised trade in India was very low, estimated at just ₹ 35,000 Cr. in 2005 (₹ 28,000 Cr. in 2004). This accounted for less than 4 per cent of the total retail trade in the country.

Till date most Indian shopping takes place in open markets and millions of independent grocery shops called kirana stores. Organised retail such as supermarkets accounted for just 5 per cent of the market as of 2008.

However McKinsey and Company, in a report 'The Great Indian Bazaar: Organised Retail Comes of Age in India', 2008 stated that 'organised retail was expected to grow from the current five percent of the total market to 14 - 18 per cent of total retail in 2015.

The report also states that of the 204 million households in the country, McKinsy expected only about 13 million households are comfortable and have the income to patronise organised retail. This relevant consumer segment would grow five fold from 13 million to 65 million households in the next eight years.

India's first true shopping mall, Crossroads – complete with food courts, recreation facilities and large car parking space, was inaugurated as late as in 1999 in Mumbai.

Thereafter there was no looking back.

The increase in the purchasing power of the Indian middle classes, the influx of foreign investments, change in the taste and attitude of the Indians, and the effects of gloabalisation have been responsible for encouraging the growth of retail companies in India.

The retail companies are found to be rising in India at a remarkable speed with the years and this has brought a revolutionary change in the shopping attitude of the Indian customers.

The growth of retail companies in India is most pronounced in the metro cities of India, however the smaller towns are also not lagging behind in this. The retail companies are not only targeting the four metros in India but also the second graded upcoming cities like Ahmedabad, Baroda, Chandigarh, Coimbatore, Cochin, Ludhiana, Pune, Trivandrum, Simla, Gurgaon, and others. The South Indian Zone has adopted the process of shopping in the supermarkets for their daily requirements and this has also been influencing other cities as well where many hypermarkets are coming up day to day. Few of the famous malls, supermarkets and hypermarkets that have taken roots in India are given below:

Lifestyle

Lifestyle in India was first founded in the year 1999, under the initiative of the retail chain of the company, Lifestyle International. The first Lifestyle store was introduced in Chennai. In the year 2004, the turnover of the retail store was ₹ 240 crores. There are Lifestyle stores in different parts of the country, both in the bigger metros like Delhi, Mumbai, Chennai, Kolkata, Hyderabad and also in the smaller towns. The Lifestyle India is originally a part of the Landmark Group based in Dubai in Middle East. It has a flourishing business out there, earning a revenue of nearly $600 million in the year 2004. However, the success of Lifestyle in India is not only a mere reflection of their track records in the Middle East, but the secret is that Lifestyle has understood the Indian market and changed their business model accordingly.

The Features of Lifestyle India

The features of the retail store Lifestyle in India is different from the original Lifestyle store in the Middle East where there are five separate stores for separate products like clothing, kids wear, household appliances and furniture, footwear, and health and beauty products. However, in Lifestyle India, one can find every core categories of Lifestyle under one roof. With the growing purchasing power of the Indians, the Indian consumers are able to afford more and more variety of products, making Lifestyle an epitome of success in the Indian retail sector.

Pantaloons

Pantaloons is the harbinger of the growth in the **Indian organised retail sector**. It is one of the largest among the latest format stores in India.

The largest retailer in the Indian organised retail sector, Pantaloons Retail (India) Limited is a chain of retail outlets all over the country. Pantaloons follows several formats of retail. Pantaloons engages in retail operations with 450 stores in 40 different locations in India. It is increasing its operations in India by opening more stores and employs around 18,000 people.

The retail formats followed by Pantaloons are **Food Bazaar, Big Bazaar, Pantaloons**, and **Central**. Pantaloons retail concentrates solely on apparels and accessories. Food Bazaar is an array of food products including fruits and vegetables, food grains, FMCGs, and packaged ready-to-cook products. Big Bazaar is a hyper mart which provides a variety of consumer goods at one place which include both apparel and non-apparel segments, while Central is a chain of stores that stocks music, books, global fashion brands, lifestyle and leisure accessories, restaurants and lounges.

Pantaloons is a fashion leader in India which follows international standards. It goes by its latest ideology of "Fresh feeling, Fresh attitude, Fresh fashion", according to which it provides fresh stock to its customers every week. This is a unique method of attracting customers. Previously modeled as a family store, Pantaloons went through a number of changes. Now it stands as a fashion depot, catering mainly to the younger generation.

There are a few additional formats which Pantaloons operates. They are Brand Factory, Fashion Station, Sitara, aLL, Shoe Factory, Depot, Top 10, mBazaar, Blue Sky and Star. Collection i focuses on the household furniture segment and the E-Zone on the eletronics segment. Pantaloons also has an online portal called the futurebazaar.com for catering to those who prefer to do their shopping online.

Pantaloons brought a revolution in the concept of shopping. The consumers' psyche was completely altered with the boom in the Indian retail sector which Pantaloons cashed in on. Today the consumer is aware of the power of money and has a desire to buy the best quality products.

Big Bazaar

Big Bazaar, a part of the **Pantaloon Group**. It is a hypermarket offering a huge array of goods of good quality for all, at affordable prices. Big Bazaar with over 50 outlets in different parts of India, is present in both the metro cities as well as in the small towns. Big Bazaar has no doubt made a big name in the retail industry of india, moreover shopping here is further made a memorable experience with the varied rates of discounts on products as well as discount vouchers available in a variety of amounts, like INR 2000, INR 3000, INR 4000, INR 5000 and INR 10000 on all Big Bazaar products and accessories.

The variety of product range in Big Bazaar

This large format store comprises of almost everything required by people from different income groups. It varies from clothing and accessories for all genders like men, women and children, playthings, stationary and toys, footwear, plastics, home utility products, cosmetics, crockery, home textiles, luggage, gift items, other novelties, and also food products and grocery. The added advantage for the customers shopping in Big Bazaar is that there are all time discounts and promotional offers going on in the Big Bazaar on its saleable products.

The significant features of Big Bazaar

Shopping in the Big Bazaar is a great experience as one can find almost everything under the same roof. It has different features which caters to all the needs of the shoppers. Some of the significant features of Big Bazaar are:

- The **Food Bazaar** or the grocery store with a department selling fruits and vegetables.
- There is a zone specially meant for the amusement of the kids.
- **Furniture Bazaar** or a large section dealing with furnitures.
- **Electronics Bazaar** or the section concerned with electronic goods and cellular phones.
- FutureBazaar.com or the online shopping portal which makes shopping easier as one can shop many products of Big Bazaar at the same price from home.
- Well regulated customer care telecalling services.

Landmark

The Landmark Group is a Dubai based US$ 500 million company. The Landmark Group has invested around ₹ 300 crores in India till date and still wishes to expand further in all metros and other semi-urban areas.

The Landmark Group entered the Indian market in 1999. Landmark operates in five cities and has eight stores. Landmark in India houses varied shops selling different types of essential commodities along with luxury items. The Landmark chains are mainly concentrated in urban areas and are now planning to operate in tier II cities also. Landmark stores typically have floor area of 17000 sq. feet each. Landmark in India typically has a heterogeneous mixture of large and small individual retailers. Most of these retail counters sell branded products of both, domestic and international manufacturers. Landmark in India offer products with different price bands for each and every sections of urban society. These stores generally sells clothing, footwear, and accessories of Indian and foreign make.

Giants

Giants is the **hypermarket**, situated in one of the biggest shopping mall of India, the InOrbit Mall, in Mumbai. It is the brainchild of the RPG Enterprises and one of the main reason for the birth of Giants is to aim at making the RPG Enterprises competitive on an international standard.

Giants: Overview

Giants is the hypermarket organised under the banner of the RPG Enterprises from the year 2004. Through these the customers can get connected with the brand owners and fulfil their requirements as per choice. The mother company, RPG Enterprises, had initially decided the revenue of Giants to be around ₹ 2,500 crores. The total area of this hypermarket is 50,000 sq. feet and of the expected format stores to be established by the RPG Enterprises, the Giants is the second in the list of 21 other hypermarkets in line. There are Giants hypermarket stores in different parts of India like in Delhi, Chennai, Vizag, Chandigarh, Jaipur, Kochi and Pune.

RPG Enterprises is responsible for important retail business and the hypermarket **Giants** always have been providing excellent quality products to their customers at the most convenient and affordable prices. The shopping experience at the Giants is so memorable that often the products of this hypermarket is referred to by the customers as beautiful, strong and cheap found within the same package. Moreover there are discounts and other promotional offers to attract more and more shoppers to shop in the Giants. The discount on the products of Giants might range from 4 to 40 %. Giants are in direct trade relation with the farmers, which definitely rules out the possibilities of any types of disintegration in the distribution system and waste of the products.

Inox India

The Inox group is a subsidiary of Gujarat Flurochemicals Ltd. Inox is the pioneer of multiplex theaters in India. Inox offers **world class multiplexes** that are unique movie theaters holding multiple shows at a time at different theaters within the same complex. Inox offers customers a world class viewing experience. Inox screens Indian cinemas and International cinemas too. Bollywood and Hollywood films are the most popular ones. **Regional films** are also screened, as are **animated films**. Inox owns 16 multiplexes with 57 screens in 14 Indian cities.

Inox offers:
- World class acoustics.
- State-of-the-art projector and its allied technology.
- Online ticket booking facility.
- Highly spacious area.
- Different classes of comfortable seating arrangements are offered.
- Snacks outlets serving Indian and international food items.
- Special meals and mini meals are on offer on weekends.
- Special discounts are offered on food items.
- Spacious parking lot.

Trends in Retail Formats/Classification of Retail Units

Retail units can be classified into the following different types/the following kinds of retail formats are found in India:

1. **Mom-and-Pop Stores:** These are generally family-owned businesses catering to small sections of society. They are small, individually run and handled retail outlets.

2. **Category Killers:** Category killers are also known as Multi Brand outlets. They offer several brands across a single product category. These are small speciaty stores which carry a deep assortment in a given category, and have a knowledgeable staff. These stores have expanded to offer a range of categories. They have widened their vision in terms of the number of categories. They are called category killers as they specialise in their fields, such as electronics (Best Buy) and sporting goods (Sport Authority). These usually do well in busy market places and metros.

3. **Department Stores:** These are the general merchandise retailers offering various kinds of quality products and services. Departmental stores carry several product lines, typically clothing, home furnishings and household goods. Each line is operated as a separate department managed by specialist merchandisers. Some departmental stores carry a selective product line. K Raheja's Shoppers Stop is a good example of department stores. Other examples are Lifestyle and Westside. These stores have further categories, such as home and décor, clothing, groceries, toys, etc.

4. **Malls:** These are the largest form of retail formats. They provide an ideal shopping experience by providing a mix of all kinds of products and services, food and entertainment under one roof. Examples, Intercity Mall, Kakde Mall, Ishanya Mall.

5. **Specialty Stores:** The retail chains, which deal in specific categories such as apparels, sporting goods, furniture, florists, bookstores, and provide deep assortment in them are specialty stores. A clothing store would be a single line

specialty store. A men's clothing store would be a limited line store and a men's custom shirt store would be a super specialty store. Examples are Music World, Crossword, The Body Shop, Chirag Din etc.

6. **Discount Stores:** These are the stores or factory outlets that provide discount on the MRP items. They focus on mass selling and reaching economies of scale or selling the stock left after the season is over.

7. **Hypermarkets/Supermarkets:** A relatively large, low cost, low-margin, high volume and self service operations designed to serve the consumers total needs for food and houlsehold products, These are generally large self-service outlets, offering a variety of categories with deep assortments. These stores contribute 30% of all food and grocery organised retail sales. Example: Big Bazaar

8. **Convenience Stores:** They are comparatively smaller stores located near residential areas. They are open for an extended period of the day, seven days a week and have a limited line of high turnover convenience products. Prices are slightly higher due to the convenience given to the customers.

9. **E-retailers:** These are retailers that provide online facility of buying and selling products and services via Internet. They provide a picture and description of the product. A lot of such retailers are booming in the industry, as this method provides convenience and a wide variety for customer. But it does not provide a feel of the product and is sometimes not authentic. Examples are Amazon.com, Ebay.com, etc.

10. **Vending Machines:** This kind of retailing is making inroads into the industry. Smaller products such as beverages, snacks, magazines are some of the items that can be bought through vending machines. At present, such machines can be seen at various major airports in India.

11. **Cash and Carry Shops:** Retail outlets of the Cash & Carry format are in many ways similar to discounters. The main focus of such shops is low prices. This format is different in the fact that it focuses on small-wholesale customers who pay in cash.

2.5 Tele Marketing

Telemarketing is basically the business or practice of marketing goods or services by telephone. It is the act of marketing goods or services to potential customers over the telephone. Telemarketing may either be carried out by telemarketers or by automated phone calls called "robocalls". Telemarketing is also called telesales or inside sales in some of the western countries.

It is a method of direct marketing in which a salesperson solicits prospective customers to buy products or services either over the phone or through recorded sales pitches programmed to be played over the phone via automatic dialing. Telemarketing is the most interactive marketing medium available. Telemarketing allows the marketer to answer prospects questions, address their concerns, and overcome their objections.

Telemarketing is the only marketing medium that allows marketers to adjust their strategy midstream and make any changes at any time necessary to increase results. With telemarketing, one can change both the offer and audience with just one phone call. Telemarketing scripts can be edited at a moment's notice. Further telemarketing calling hours can be adjusted.

Like email marketing, telemarketing tends to get a bad reputation, because, when it is done incorrectly or badly, it can be a great annoyance with which business owners risk driving prospective customers away and even alienating their existing consumers. In order to protect the population from the menace of telemarketing most countries have a national do not call (DNC) registry that give their residents the choice about whether to receive telemarketing calls or not at home. Consumers who are registered in the DNC database can file a complaint if they receive a call from a telemarketer, which could lead to a stiff fine and sanctions for the telemarketing firm. However, calls from charities, political organisations and telephone surveyors are permitted and would be received by a consumer, despite listing his or her phone number on the DNC registry. Also permitted are calls from businesses with whom the consumer has an existing relationship, as well as those businesses where consent to call has been provided in writing.

Despite the above Telemarketing is still used in marketing, because when done correctly, it can be incredibly effective. Given below are some of the advantages of telemarketing

Advantages of Telemarketing

1. **Turning opportunities into sales:**

While most people mistakenly believe that using telemarketers is limited to cold calling, telemarketing can be used in a number of other ways to turn opportunities into sales.

Appointment setting is one. Generating new business always has, and always will, rely on getting in front of the right decision maker. Follow-up calls are an equally effective way to make the most of other marketing initiatives.

A time-tested use of telemarketing is market research, which is a highly cost-effective method of conducting large-scale market research and can cover vast geographical locations from a single base. Similarly, the telephone is a vital tool in keeping databases up to date. By using telemarketers to work through your data, you can correct, delete or amend the details of your existing customers, leads or prospects. By making sure that your data is up to date and accurate, you can increase the rate at which your sales staff can make sales.

2. **Enhance value gained:**

Telemarketing can also be used to enhance the value gained out of events. In addition to doing follow-ups with attendees after an event, telemarketing can provide a constructive way to conduct profiling and ensure that the right people attend your events. This applies equally to new market initiatives.

Getting to the right people is important in any marketing or sales project. Whether you're entering a new market, or wanting to showcase your products and solutions in an event platform, you don't want to waste time talking to the wrong people. Getting your message to the right audience is half the battle won.

Choose the right telemarketing partner with care, and a focus on building lasting relationships with customers. Set out clear goals before you start. Ask yourself whether you want to drive repeat business, just remind them about special offers so that you can stay fresh in their minds, or encourage word of mouth products. If you do it correctly, you may just manage to accomplish all those goals.

Building information can become a powerful tool if managed and utilised effectively. There is no methodology existing today which can communicate to more customers in a better way than through the use of the personal touch, relationships, market research and reinforced marketing programmes.

Telemarketers are the thread that brings these elements together, making the sales cycle simpler.

(**Web courtesy :** http://www.bizcommunity.com/Article/196/423/102003.html)

Tips on How to be a good Telemarketer:

A telemarketer is a person who is responsible for selling a product or service over the phone. Telemarketers may work in a private office, from a call center or from home. It is often the case that telemarketers never meet their customers face to face, so good telemarketing skills are of utmost importance to achieve success as a telemarketer. Follow these suggestions for how to be a good telemarketer.

1. **Prepare for telemarketing.**

   - **Learn as much as you can about what you are selling:** You should have a thorough understanding of what it is, how it works and how it may be useful to potential customers. Additionally, you should have genuine confidence in what you are selling, and in its value to the people you will be calling.

   - **Learn about the company you work for:** A good telemarketer not only sells a product or service, but also sells the company. You should be able to tell potential customers why they should choose you over your competitors. Study the company's history, philosophy, customer reviews/testimonials and industry ratings in order to be able to provide customers with a complete and favourable picture of who they are dealing with.

   - **Make sure you understand the sales process:** Once you convince a customer to invest in what you are selling, good telemarketing skills require that you are able to explain the sales process from start to finish. This includes closing paperwork, billing, shipping, refund/return policies, customer support and any necessary follow-up.

- **Compile contact information for your customers:** You should have the business name, mailing address, phone number(s), email address, website, your manager's relevant information (especially if you work in a call center) and any other pertinent contact information that your customers may ask for over the telephone.
- **Practice your script:** Read it aloud until you are comfortable that you can deliver it without any prompts.
  1. **Express confidence:** A good telemarketer speaks with a tone of authority that puts customers' minds at ease. If you are amply prepared, then you should be able to talk about the reason for your call and your company with confidence.
  2. **Practice effective communications skills:**
     - Speak slowly, loudly and clearly enough that customers can easily understand you. Do not mumble.
     - Be considerate of the people you are calling. Introduce yourself and explain the purpose of your call as soon as possible in the conversation. Pause and take time to listen to responses as you go.
     - Find the right balance between saying too much and not saying enough. Dead air during a telephone conversation can be uncomfortable. On the other hand, you can overwhelm and confuse a potential customer by saying too much, too fast.
     - Avoid distracting conversation spacers such as, "um" and "ah."
  3. **Try not to sound rehearsed:** Scripts are common in telemarketing, especially in a call center atmosphere, but it is possible to deliver a script without sounding like you are reading from a piece of paper. Take some slow breaths and relax before making your calls, then focus on the message behind what you are saying rather than the words themselves.
  4. **Maintain a positive mental attitude:** Remember that some (or many) of the people you call may not be expecting your call and, additionally, may not be receptive to your call. It is not unusual for even a good telemarketer to be rejected by several potential customers in a row before reaching one interested customer. Don't take rejections personally but, rather, take them as opportunities to develop your telemarketing skills.
  5. **Stay resilient:** Telemarketing is a numbers game, and it takes time and persistence to develop good telemarketing skills. Commit to making a certain number of calls each day and see those calls through.
  6. **Recognise when it is time to move on to the next call:** If a contact is expressly not interested in what you have to say, then politely end the call and move on to the next call.

(**Web Courtesy:** http://www.wikihow.com/Be-a-Good-Telemarketer)

2.6 E-Marketing

E-Marketing or electronic marketing refers to the application of marketing principles and techniques through electronic media and more specifically the Internet. The terms E-Marketing, Internet marketing and online marketing, are frequently used interchangeably, and are often considered to be synonymous.

E-Marketing is the process of marketing a brand using the Internet. It includes both direct response marketing and indirect marketing elements and uses a range of technologies to help connect businesses to their customers.

Thus E-Marketing encompasses all the activities a business conducts via the worldwide web with the aim of attracting new business, retaining current business and developing its brand identity.

The benefits of E-Marketing

E-marketing gives businesses of any size access to the mass market at an affordable price. Unlike the traditional media of advertising like TV or print advertising, E-Marketing provides for a truly personalised marketing system. Some specific benefits of E-Marketing are as under:

- **Global reach:** Through e-marketing, an organisation can reach anyone in the world who has internet access. This allows the organisation to identify new markets and compete globally for only a small investment.
- **24-hour marketing:** When an organisation has a website, the customers can find out about its products and services, round the clock.
- **Better conversion rate:** if you have a website, then your customers are only a few clicks away from completing a purchase. Unlike other media which require people to get up and make a phone call, post a letter or go to a shop, e-marketing is seamless.
- **Lower cost:** A properly planned and effectively targeted e-marketing campaign can help an organisation to reach the right customers at a much lower cost as compared to the traditional methods of marketing.
- **Ability to track and measurable results:** E-marketing techniques like marketing via email or banner advertising makes it easier to understand how effective the campaign has been. You can also obtain detailed information about the customers' responses to your advertisement.
- **Personalisation:** If your customer database is linked to your website, then whenever someone visits the site, you can greet them with targeted offers. The more they buy from you, the more you can refine your customer profile and market effectively to them.

- **One-to-one marketing:** E-marketing lets you reach your target audience at every point in time. Many people take mobile phones wherever they go. Combine this with the personalized aspect of e-marketing, and you have very powerful, targeted campaigns.
- **Interactive campaigns:** E-marketing gives you the advantage of creating interactive campaigns using videos, pictures and music.

Together, all of these aspects of e-marketing have the potential to add up to more sales.

2.7 Digital Marketing: Meaning, Importance of Digital Marketing

The promotion of products or brands using one or more forms of electronic media, is called Digital Marketing. Thus an organisation may use a variety of advertising mediums as a part of its digital marketing strategy like the Internet, social media, mobile phones and electronic billboards. It could also use digital and television and radio channels.

Thus Digital marketing makes use of electronic devices such as computers, tablets, smart phones, cell phones, digital billboards, and game consoles to engage with their customers. Internet Marketing is a major component of digital marketing. However digital marketing expands beyond internet marketing by including other channels that do not require the use of the Internet. Due to non-dependence on the Internet, the field of digital marketing includes a whole lot of elements such as mobile phones or cell phones, display / banner advertisements, sms /mms, digital outdoor, and many more.

The following are the various Medium used by Digital Marketing:

1. **On line Marketing:** This would include: Website Optimisation, Search Engine Marketing, Video Search Engine Optimisation, Blogs and Forums, Online Display Advertising, e mails etc
2. **Mobile Marketing:** This would include : Messaging , mobile internet, mobile apps and app advertising
3. **Radio Marketing:** This would include: Radio Advertising, Podcasts, Interview and Sponsorships
4. **T.V. Advertising:** This would include: TV Advertising, sponsorship, Product placements and interviews
5. **E. Media Marketing:** This would include: Video , audio and content delivered through electronic devices, and digital bill boards.

According to **Dave Chaffey**, author of five best selling books on digital marketing: Digital Marketing is *"Achieving marketing objectives through applying digital technologies."*

According to Dave Chaffey: the six main types of digital media communication channels for every business to consider as a part of their digital marketing strategy are given below:

Principles of Marketing   Classification and Types of Markets

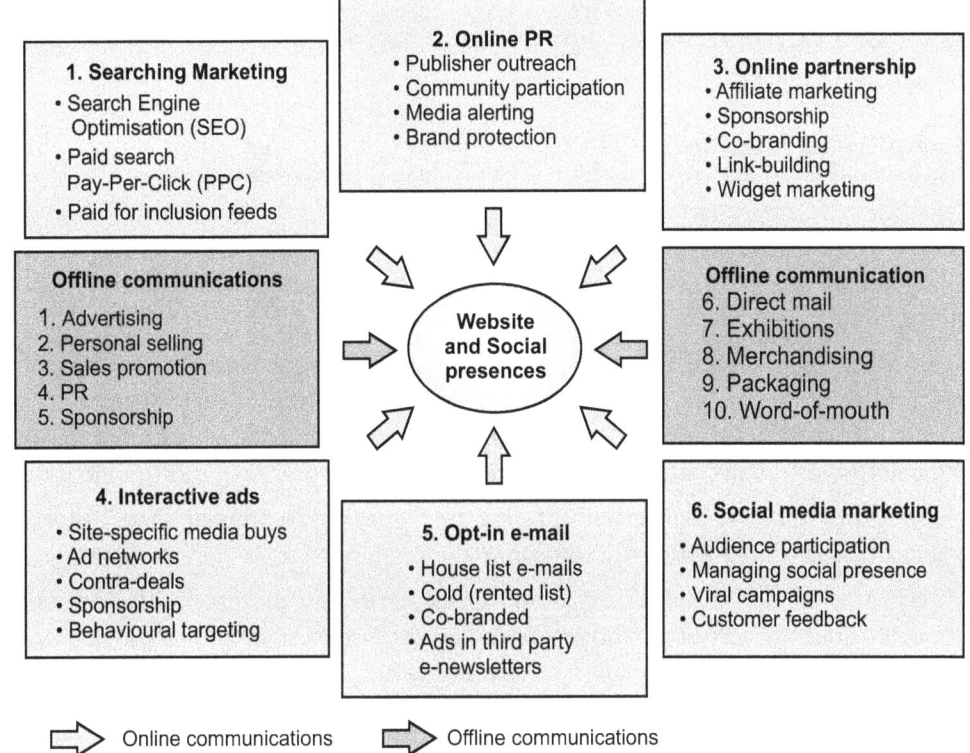

(**Web Courtesy:**http://www.smartinsights.com/digital-marketing-strategy/online-marketing-mix/definitions-of-emarketing-vs-internet-vs-digital-marketing/)

Importance of Digital Marketing:

Digital Marketing delivers the same advantages as delivered by traditional means of promotion and advertising. However it is important due to the changing world scenario.

Digital marketing is the marketing of the future. Today the world is getting more and more connected on-line, every day. This is leading to an increase in digital strategies. As more consumers begin to adapt to technological devices, they expect businesses to do the same.

Digital marketing methods allow small businesses to reach out like never before and empower them to interact with the audiences they want to target.

Digital Media makes it possible for consumers to see examples, hear videos and opinions about how products helped solve their problems.

New organisations that have yet to establish a solid reputation within their industry or attract a loyal customer base may find that taking an online approach to be especially helpful. Competition, coupled with the recent economic recession, has made digital marketing strategies more vital than ever before.

It is a good marketing medium for small new businesses as it allows such businesses to access a relatively larger audience at a smaller cost. It is progressively been used by organisations to stay ahead of the competition.

2.8 Green Marketing

According to the **American Marketing Association**, *"Marketing is the performance of business activity that directs the flow of business from the producer to the consumer."* When this business activity is carried out in such a fashion that it causes the least damage to the environment it is known as green marketing.

Green Marketing is also known as environmental marketing or sustainable marketing. It refers to all activities that facilitate any exchange intended to satisfy human needs and wants in such a way that the satisfaction of the said needs and wants occurs with the minimum detrimental impact on the natural environment.

It refers to organisations efforts at designing, pricing, promoting and distributing products that will not harm the environment.

Green Marketing is a holistic marketing concept wherein the production, promotion, distribution, consumption and disposal of products and services takes place in such a way that the least damage is inflicted upon the environment.

According to the **American Marketing Association**, *"green marketing is the marketing of products that are presumed to be environmentally safe"*.

Green marketing focuses on the green marketing efforts companies use, including corporate social responsibility plans and sustainability efforts. Many consumers are environmentally conscious, seeking eco-friendly products and services from organisations that are socially responsible.

Green marketing companies seek to go above and beyond traditional marketing by promoting environmental core values in the hope that consumers will associate these values with their company or brand. Engaging in these sustainable activities can lead to creating a new product line that caters to a new target market.

Green Marketing incorporates broad range of activities including product modification, changes to the production process, packaging changes, and modifying advertising. Green marketing focuses on satisfaction of customer needs and wants with no or minimum harm to the natural environment.

Why is Green Marketing Important?

It is a well known fact that increasing production and business activities are polluting the environment. Damage to people, crops, and wildlife is being seen in different parts of the world. As resources are limited and human wants are unlimited, it is essential for marketers to use resources efficiently, so that organisational objectives are achieved without waste of resources. So green marketing is unavoidable. There is growing awareness among people around the world regarding protection of natural environment. People are getting more disturbed for the environment and changing their behaviour for the protection of environment. As a result of this, the term "Green Marketing" has emerged. Hence, marketers are feeling their responsibility towards environment and giving importance to green marketing.

Not only marketers but consumers are also concerned about the environment, and consumers are also changing their behaviour pattern. Now, individual as well as industrial consumers are becoming more concerned about environment-friendly products.

Points to Remember

1. **Phillip Kotler has defined services as,** *"A service is any act or performance that one party can offer to another that is essentially intangible and does not result in the ownership of anything. Its production may or may not be tied to a physical product."*

2. **Characteristics of services:** Intangibility, inseparability, variability, simultaneity and perishability are the five main characteristic features of services.

3. **Marketing Strategies for Services:** Planning and implementation of plans and programmes by an organisation to bring about the required exchanges with the target audience which results into benefits.

4. **Three more, important P's from the marketing mix for the services sector:**

    (a) **People:** Training, Personal selling and Customer service.

    (b) **Process:** Process is an element of service that sees the customer experiencing an organisation's offering.

    (c) **Physical evidence:** Physical evidence is the material part of a service.

5. **Definition of Rural Marketing:** When marketing activities are carried out in the rural markets it is known as 'Rural Marketing'

6. **Importance of rural marketing:**

    (a) Increase in prosperity and purchasing power

    (b) Flow of investment for rural development programmes

    (c) Shift of a segment of the Urban Population to the Rural areas

7. **Features of Rural Market:**

    (a) It is a vast and scattered market

    (b) The demand is seasonal

    (c) Low standard of living

    (d) Unity in diversity

    (e) The rural market is a steadily growing market

8. **Problems faced during rural marketing:**
   (a) Problems connected with Physical Distribution.
   (b) Problems related to Channel of Distribution
   (c) Problems associated with the Sales Force
   (d) Problems of Marketing Communication
   (e) Problems of Market Segmentation
   (f) Problems related to Product Management
9. **Retailing** includes all the activities involved in selling goods or services to the final consumer for personal, non-business use.
10. **Retailing** is a marketing activity involved in the sale of products to the final consumer. It consists of all activities involved in the marketing of goods and services directly to the consumers for their personal, family or household use.
11. **Telemarketing** is basically the business or practice of marketing goods or services by **telephone**. It is the act of Marketing goods or services to potential customers over the telephone.
12. **E-Marketing** or electronic marketing refers to the application of marketing principles and **techniques** through electronic media and more specifically the Internet.
13. The promotion of products or brands using one or more forms of electronic media, is called **Digital Marketing**.
14. **Green Marketing** is also known as environmental marketing or sustainable marketing. It refers to all activities that facilitate any exchange intended to satisfy human needs and wants in such a way that the satisfaction of the said needs and wants occurs with the minimum detrimental impact on the natural environment.

Questions for Discussion

1. Define services. What are the features of services?
2. Elaborate the different services offered in the consumer market.
3. Write a detail note on industrial services.
4. Write a note on services marketing and the economy.
5. Give classification of services.
6. Define Rural Marketing. State the importance of Rural Market.
7. Explain the importance of Rural Marketing.
8. Explain the Factors of Rural Marketing.
9. Discuss the various problems of Rural Marketing. Explain its Remedial Measures.

10. What do you understand by the term 'Retailing'? Bring out the characteristics of "retailing".
11. Why is Retailing an important economic activity?
12. Write a note on the different retail formats which can be seen in India.
13. Write a note on the functions of Retailing.
14. What is Digital Marketing? State its importance.
15. Write short notes on:
    (a) Telemarketing
    (b) E-marketing
    (c) Green marketing

Questions from Previous Pune University Examinations

1. What is Rural Marketing? Explain the Factors and Importance of Rural Marketing.
   [Oct. 2011, April 2013]
2. What is Service Marketing? Explain the Classification of Services. **[April 2012]**
3. What is Rural Marketing? Explain Problems of Rural Marketing in Detail. **[Oct. 2012]**
4. Write Short Notes:
   (A) Rural Marketing. **[April 2009, 2011]**
   (B) E-marketing. **[Oct. 2009, 2011, April 2012, 2013]**
   (C) Rural Marketing and its Importance. **[April 2012]**
   (D) Telemarketing. **[April 2009, Oct. 2012]**
   (E) Service Marketing. **[Oct. 2009, 2010, 2012]**
   (F) Suggestions for Improvement of Rural Marketing. **[Oct. 2009]**
   (G) Problems of Rural Marketing. **[Oct. 2010]**
5. What is Rural Marketing? Explain Importance of Rural Marketing. **[April 2010]**

Chapter **3**...

Marketing Environment and Market Segmentation

Contents ...

3.1 Marketing Environment
    3.1.1 What is Environment?
    3.1.2 Factors Constituting the Marketing Environment / Nature and Scope of Environment
    3.1.3 Micro and Macro Environment
    3.1.4 Impact of Marketing Environment on Marketing Decisions
3.2 Market Segmentation
    3.2.1 Introduction - Meaning, Importance and Benefits of Market Segmentation
    3.2.2 Types of Market Segmentation
    3.2.3 Patterns and Procedures of Market Segmentation / Bases of Segmentation
    3.2.4 Criteria and Approaches of Segmenting a Market
    3.2.5 Essentials of Effective Market Segmentation / Qualities of Good Segmentation
    3.2.6 Differentiated / Differential Marketing and Concentrated Marketing
- Points to Remember
- Questions for Discussion
- Questions from Previous Pune University Examinations

Learning Objectives ...

➢ To Understand the Definition and Nature of Marketing Environment
➢ To Describe the Factors which Constitute the Marketing Environment
➢ To Explain the Micro and Macro Environment
➢ To Discuss the Impact of Marketing Environment on Marketing Decisions
➢ To Elucidate the Meaning and Importance of Market Segmentation
➢ To Discuss the Qualities of Good Market Segmentation

3.1 Marketing Environment

Introduction

Every company big or small operates in an environment. The environment is made up of several distinct components, political, economic, cultural, social and technological and others. As the business organisation operates in an environment which is made up of various components, it is naturally affected by the changes in these components. These components interact with each other and have an effect not only on each other but also on the business organisations. The business organisation in its turn, also affects the environment to some extent.

The environment is always changing. Some components of the environment change at a faster pace as compared to others. For e.g. technology may change at a faster pace as compared to cultural changes. Similarly the environment of a particular industry changes faster than the environment of another industry. But change in the environment at a slow or fast pace is inevitable and hence a business needs to constantly adapt itself to its environment.

For this, a business has to constantly study and monitor its environment so that the required necessary changes can be made by the business in time, in keeping with the changes in the environment. Thus these changes in the environment constantly create opportunities for the business enterprise and at the same time pose threats for it. Hence the study of the business environment forms an integral part of business or corporate planning.

3.1.1 What is Environment?

Environment is something that surrounds an enterprise. It is the sum total of all factors within which the enterprise operates. These environmental factors may be controllable and uncontrollable. They may be economic, political, legal, technological etc. Some factors may be static and some dynamic. Some may be qualitative others quantitative. Environment is therefore a complex phenomenon.

It is a collectivity of all the factors within the control of the business and beyond the control of the individual business. Environmental factors which are within the control of the individual business are known as controllable factors where as factors beyond the control of the individual business are known as uncontrollable factors.

According to **Phillip Kotler**, "*A company's marketing environment consists of the external factors and forces that affect the company's ability to develop and maintain successful transactions and relationships with its target consumers.*" In other words environment represents those factors which affect the successful marketing operations of the company.

These factors or forces can be divided into two groups:
- Internal factors having a direct impact on the marketing operations of the company,
- External factors having a direct bearing upon the marketing operations.

Before we take a look at the various internal and external environmental factors let us first understand the nature and scope of environment.

3.1.2 Factors Constituting the Marketing Environment/Nature and Scope of Environment

An organisation's environment is anything and everything that is external to it. But it is difficult to demarcate an organisation's boundary i.e. where the organisation ends and the environment begins. An organisation has its own internal environment. This environment is made up of the people that work in the organisation, their work ethos and culture. The major participants in the organisation share a set of attitudes towards what they want to accomplish and what they think of, is of value.

The organisation's culture may be favourable or unfavourable to the overall total development. All this constitutes the organisational environment. This internal environment interacts with the external environment which consists of several components like social, political, technological etc.

However between the internal and external environment there exists something known as a task specific environment. A task specific environment is an environment for an individual business. It consists of those forces outside the organisation which are directly relevant to the decision making and transformation process of the individual organisation.

Business organisations basically are resource converters and use inputs from the environment to convert them into product and services for the customers. These products and services are carried to the market either directly or through a chain of marketing intermediaries. A typical organisation thus achieves its objectives by operating through its task environment. Thus an organisation is surrounded in three layers of environment, the internal environment, the task environment and the external government.

The internal environment is made up of factors like people, their culture and work ethos and their attitudes and values. The task environment is made up of suppliers, marketing intermediaries and customers whereas the external environment is made up of factors like political, economic, social, cultural, ecological etc. The factors of the internal environment are controllable by the organisation.

The task environment includes factors that are external to the organisation but controllable to quite an extent and the external environment includes those factors that are external to the organisation and uncontrollable by the organisation.

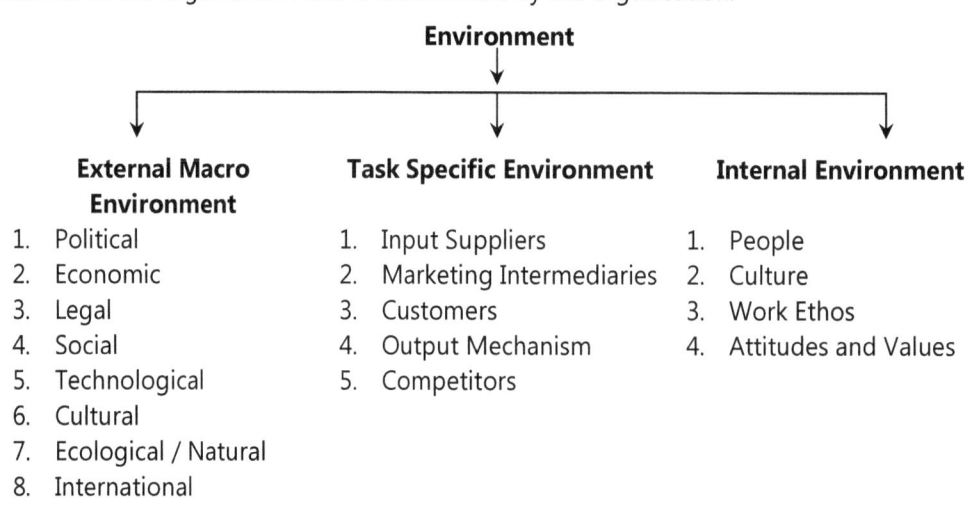

Environment

External Macro Environment	Task Specific Environment	Internal Environment
1. Political	1. Input Suppliers	1. People
2. Economic	2. Marketing Intermediaries	2. Culture
3. Legal	3. Customers	3. Work Ethos
4. Social	4. Output Mechanism	4. Attitudes and Values
5. Technological	5. Competitors	
6. Cultural		
7. Ecological / Natural		
8. International		

3.1.3 Micro and Macro Environment

Internal Controllable Factors / Micro Environmental Factors

The internal factors that affect the marketing environment can be controlled by the company, and hence are known as internal controllable factors. These factors are within the total system of the organisation and the management can adjust them as and when required. These internal controllable factors are:

1. **The Company**

   The marketing organisation of a company is only a part of the entire business organisation. The business organisation consists of other departments like production, finance, personnel etc., as well. In addition a company includes a top management which lays down the policies and procedures to be followed by the various departments. All these have a direct impact on the success of the marketing operations. Understanding of the marketing plans by these forces as well as proper co-ordination at different levels by the marketing manager is a must for success.

2. **Marketing Intermediaries**

   This factor includes marketing agents, distributors, wholesalers, retailers etc. who aid the company in the distribution of its products and services. They are considered as internal factor as they aid the business of the company. In fact, without them the distribution of the product will not take place and hence business itself will come to a standstill. Their success depends upon the success of the firm and as such they can most definitely be treated as internal to the firm. Hence clear understanding and communication with them on all matters related to their activity is very essential.

3. **The Staff**

   The employees are the most important factors which contribute to the success of any plan. The management should make a continuous study about the attitude and willingness of the employees in achieving the goals of the organisation.

   When you talk about the staff as a controllable internal factor what is referred to is the staff of the entire company and not just the staff of the marketing department. A well-motivated staff with the right kind of attitude will definitely add to the success of the firm and take it along the correct path. However dissent amongst the employees and non-cooperation even from one section or department, may lead to a major upset in the working of the organisation. The burden of ensuring a proper motivational environment to the staff lies with the management and the management's policy on recruitment, training and development of the staff. With proper control, right attitude and correct policies, the management can definitely control this very major factor.

External Controllable Factor

The marketing environment of a business organisation is affected not only by internal factors but also by external one. These external factors can be divided into two. Those factors which the organisation or management can control to a certain extent and those which are totally uncontrollable. Let us review the external controllable factors first.

1. Customers

Different kinds of customers exist for different products. Depending upon the market in which they operate, customers can be classified as:

- **Customers operating in the consumer market:** These are basically individual customers and institutional customers, who buy products for consumption. The institutions include schools, colleges, hospitals, temples and other organisations.

- **Customers operating in the industrial market:** These include those individuals, companies and organisations, who purchase products and services needed to manufacture other products and services.

- **Customers operating in a resellers market:** These customers are those who buy the goods and services for resale at a profit.

- **Customers operating in the international market:** Today with globalisation, liberalisation and privatisation being the norm, markets have widened and we have more and more business taking place across the borders of the nation. Thus we have customers that purchase goods and services for export. We also have customers who import from other countries.

Customers can also be classified on the basis of their gender, age and characteristics. However, any way in which you classify customers, the fact remains that this is a very dynamic factor as no two human beings behave in the same way, even in the same given set of circumstances. This is a very important external factor, as the success of an organisation depends upon the number of people that patronise its products. With the right kind of approach this very volatile and dynamic factor can be controlled to quite an extent.

2. Competitors

In India not so long ago we followed a system of a protected economy. The fall out of this system was that a number of products enjoyed a monopoly in the market. For example, Bajaj Scooters had a virtual monopoly in the market for a number of years. However with the opening up of the economy this situation has undergone a drastic change and now a number of two wheelers are vying with each other for attention of the customers. Today in the two wheeler market itself you have a number of companies like Hero-Honda, Yamaha, Suzuki, Kinetic Honda etc. The same is the state for many other products. Be it a consumer product, an industrial product or a consumer durable or non-durable product. It cannot escape competition. Not only does competition exist, but it is of a cut-throat nature. (Thus the business scenario today is such that if a business has to survive and prosper it has to keep a tab on what its competition is doing. The competition has to be constantly monitored, so that the business and marketing strategies can be altered at the right time and markets can be successfully captured and loyal customers maintained.

Just as one company monitors its competitors so also the competitors monitor the other companies in the same industry. Thus, there is a constant scenario of keeping check on each other. Here a company may instigate an action which will compel the competition to come up with a corresponding action of its own. In this way one competitor can catch the reaction of another competitor in a particular way. And hence it is said that competition is an external factor that may be controllable, at least to some extent. For e.g. a price cut policy adopted by Pepsi will result in a similar or comparable price cut by Coca-Cola.

3. Public/Public Image

When we talk of external environmental factors we cannot ignore the Public at large. The public in the case of a company is any individual or group that has some relationship/impact on the ability of the company to achieve its objectives. The public actions and reactions to the activities of the company are important, as the company operates in a society, and the public has got the ability or potential to facilitate or hinder the working of the company/organisation. It is because of this that today almost all organisations have a public relations officer, exclusively for building up relations with the public at large, and seeing to it that the company enjoys a good public image.

4. Suppliers

Suppliers include all those individual and firms that supply the raw materials and other goods required in the manufacturing process by a company/organisation/firm. The marketing managers should keep a constant watch over the price trend and availability of the products needed. They should locate suppliers well known for their good quality and reliability and establish and maintain good relations with them. In addition to this it is always beneficial to maintain multiple sources of supply as it is not good to keep all your eggs in one basket.

Suppliers are external factor, which if good relations are maintained will result in a smooth flow of inputs required for production. However a breakdown of relations with them or a break down in the supply will result in a halt in the production process and hence definite efforts have to be made to see that this does not happen.

Thus, even though the above mentioned factors or forces form a part of the external environment to the company, with the right kind of policy, strategy, attitude and human relation techniques they can be made to operate in a way that is beneficial for our organisation and hence it is said that they are controllable, to a certain extent at least.

External Uncontrollable Factors/Macro Environmental Factors

The following are the factors of the external environment that are uncontrollable by the firm and the management.

Demographic Environment/Demographic Factor

Demographics are the quantity and characteristics of the people, especially in relation to their age, where they live, how much money they have and what they spend it on. Thus demographic factors relate to the characteristics of the population of a country. Various characteristics such as age distribution, sex distribution, racial, caste, ethnic, religious and class distribution, density of population, urban rural population characteristics etc., determine the demand of the population for various goods and services. Thus the demographic factors have to be taken into account by a company while planning its marketing strategies so as to capture a large market share. If a demographic analysis reveals that in a particular society the women outnumber men then the demand for ladies products will be more and the company will have to formulate its strategies accordingly. In India, today if you look around, you will see more and more working women. This has resulted in the introduction of time saving appliances like washing machines, vacuum cleaners, microwave ovens etc. Similarly in a society where the birth rate and death rate are low, such a society will have a large section of old people and this segment of population is attracted more by safety than any other feature. Thus, the company will have to take this into account when deciding upon features of its products. This will have to be borne in mind by the manufacturer. A society in which the birth rate is high will concentrate on baby products.

An understanding of the demographic factors helps a manufacturer in deciding upon, an optimum marketing mix. It also helps him to decide whether to enter a particular market segment or not., For example, today 85% of the Indian market is a young market consisting of people up to the age of 44 years. Thus if you look around most of the products are targeted at the youth. You see the mushrooming of fast food joints, long queues in front of Pizza hut and McDonalds. Fancy bikes and readymade clothes are the motto of the day.

Demographic factors differ from country to country and from time to time. As these factors determine the nature and extent of demand they need to be carefully studied and analysed.

Economic, Political, Social, Cultural Environment / Factors

Basically all these factors are interrelated. The economic environment affects the sociological environment and vice versa. The work culture of Japan, a part of its social environment results in high productivity, a part of the economic environment. Similarly political and economic environment are also related. Political stability makes a way for business expansion and growth, also allows entrepreneurs to take risks and invest money. The cultural environment also affects the sociological and economic environment. For e.g. a culture that stresses on education will lead to the formation of a society of enlightened people willing to work hard and will result in the economic development of the society. However an educationally backward society, like the gulf countries had to import man power from other countries in order to progress. Thus all these factors are interrelated and a change in one affects the others.

Economic Environment

The economic growth of a company increases the real income available to the people. This results in more purchasing power in the hands of the people which is a boon to marketing. However the purchasing power differs from region to region and is a function of current income, inflation rate, saving habit, credit facility and prices. Factors such as inflation, shortages etc. will result into a price rise and less savings by the people. This will result into a lesser purchasing power and higher debts.

The marketing manager has to analyse and keep constant watch over the economic scene of the country, the real income of the people, the additional employment opportunities, the consumer expenditure trends, the consumption pattern, the life styles etc. Changes in the major economic variables have a direct impact on the marketing scene, and hence the marketing manager should be aware of these changes as and when they take place. Information about these changes are available from various sources in a country like India and the marketing manager or the company itself need not carry out economic forecasting themselves.

Political Environment

The political environment of a country affects its marketing system to a great extent. It is the government that regulates the business activity as it is the custodian of the nation. A democratic form of government will lead to a less controlled marketing system where as, an autocratic or Marxist based political system will lead to a marketing system which is controlled and dictated by the state. A government or political system that follows the formula of a mixed economy will lead to marketing system that is partially controlled by the state or government.

Whatever be the political system in which the marketer operates, all marketing decisions are to be based on the policies that are determined by the government, and within the legal framework provided by the ruling political party. In fact, what is to be produced, how much, of what quality, for whom, when and at what cost and at what price are to be determined by the policies of the government. The producers and marketers have to work within the concessions and limits set by the political forces. Thus government policies have to be studied and interpreted before having individual policies and strategies in case of marketing units.

Social and Cultural Environment/Factors

The social and cultural environment plays a major role in deciding or at least influencing the wants and needs of the people. This is because the consumers being social and rational animals their life-style is deeply influenced by the social and cultural make up. The social and cultural traditions influence the taste of the consumer, because their attitude to life and their life style patterns depend upon these. The social and cultural, influences shape the beliefs and values of people. The attitude, faith belief and psyche of a person is influenced and moulded by family as well as society's social and cultural considerations. The core cultural and social values which are got from the family and reinforced in school are formed on solid considerations and do not change with time and place, whereas other cultural and social values which are not so important, and are not hard formed, but form a part of the total environment tend to fluctuate occasionally.

It goes without saying that the alert marketer cannot afford to neglect or underestimate these aspects. The needs, wants, desires, hopes and aspirations of the consumers can be understood in totality only if the marketer has a thorough knowledge of the sociological and cultural influences on his customers.

Technological Environment/Factors

Science and technology is always changing. This changing face of science and technology has an impact on the marketing environment. New technology means new ideas, new products, new manufacturing systems and processes and new marketing efforts. In the last 20 years technological changes have been taking place at a faster pace than earlier on. Be it the field of science, medicine, entertainment, communication, travel or office equipment all these have witnessed great changes brought about by new, and different technology. Be it any field one can see the changes in the products and services offered and these changes have changed the life style of the consumers.

A point to be understood here is that technological developments may affect the firm's raw material, packaging, products and services. For example, technological changes in packaging and plastic industry have brought in new packages in the form of tetrapacks, pet bottles, cellophane etc. This has definitely reduced the cost of packaging, besides making the package attractive and easier to carry and transport. Likewise containerised movement of goods, deep freezers, trawlers fitted with deep freezers etc. have affected the operations of all firms including those involved in the seafood industry. Today perishable goods too can be transported in a safe manner. Developments in Information Technology have also affected the firms competitive position.

However technological change has its own cost and investment in research and development. A lot of expenditure has to be incurred and this is the major reason why the pace of technological development is slow in developing countries,

It should also be borne in mind that technological changes have brought about an artificial demand and a quicker or faster obsolescence of products. Technological changes lead to a shortening of the product life cycle and create a new set of customer expectations as well. What happens is that products shoot to meteoric growth and then quickly slip into their decline phase. Electronics is one such product group. However not all sectors of the economy are equally susceptible to technological changes. Some like the electronic sector experience more volatile changes while others like coal, textiles and primary ferrous metals are much more stable industries in any economy.

Advance indicators of technological developments are available through trade journals and other industry magazines. The marketers should definitely keep updated with the technological changes taking place in order to maintain the competitive strength of their organisation.

Ecological Environment/Factors

In recent years there is increasing concern as to whether the natural resources are being irrevocably damaged by industrial activity. It has been pointed out that industrial activity is not only polluting the water and earth but is depleting the forests. In fact because of industrial - activity the earth is in danger from bio-non degradable material like plastic. This has led to the formation of various groups of environmentalists.

No government can afford to remain a silent spectator to environmental degradation and pollution. The governments are trying to monitor environmentally damaging activity and take corrective actions as and when they can. However the efforts of the government to protect the environment often run counter to the attempts to generate more employment opportunities and increased economic growth. The marketers and managers must be alert and open to all those regulatory developments that are aimed at conserving the environment and preventing the earth from environmental degradation.

In a nut shell it can be said that changes in all the above factors/forces keep taking place every moment of time and the marketer cannot afford to miss these minute yet far-reaching influences while designing and implementing the marketing strategy for the success of his firm and the benefit and prosperity of society at large. This is because the enterprise is an open adoptive system that works in the environment. It does not exist independent of the environment. It has an interaction and interdependence with the various environmental forces. The marketing strategy hovers around the four P's namely Product, Price, Promotion and Place. All these four aspects are governed by the above forces. As these forces continue to develop and change they determine the changing requirements for the efficient and effective marketing plans, strategies and policies. Hence whatever the modern marketer has to decide he has to do so taking into account these changing forces and act accordingly. He has control over the four P's but not over these external forces. And hence if he has to be successful he has to be on red alert so as to adapt to these forces as and when required.

3.1.4 Impact of Marketing Environment on Marketing Decisions

According to **Mary Strain of Demand Media, USA,** The marketing environment is everything a company must take into consideration when developing and presenting a new product. The elements of a marketing environment include, but are not limited to, the changing preferences of customers, the competition, the legal, political and regulatory environment, the company's resources and budget, current trends and the overall economy. All these elements affect the marketing decisions or at least they should, because all of them influence the company's prospects.

Tastes and Trends

All marketing decisions should take into account the consumer preferences and current market trends. For example, many large retailers have decided to adapt to consumers' increasing enthusiasm for social media by establishing corporate Twitter accounts and opening online storefronts on Facebook. Consumers no longer need to visit a retailer's main website to buy; some platforms allow them to make the purchase without ever leaving Facebook. Companies that fail to take major trends into account may find their sales lagging behind the competitors that are in sync with the current trends.

Demographics

Demographics give marketers details about who is buying or should be buying their services and products. Ethnicity, age, lifestyle, housing, household composition, income and education are just a few demographic points that marketers track, and take into account while taking marketing decisions. For example, a demographic trend of increasing money power in the hands of the rural population will give rise to a shift in marketing policy focused only at the cities to shift towards the rural areas.

Budget

Your corporate budget or the amount of finance available to you will definitely impact your marketing decisions. For example your advertising budget will determine exactly which media you will use to grab the attention of the consumer.

The Current Economic Scenario

Economic trends can be local, regional or even global, and may cause marketers to increase or decrease spending depending on the buying power in each marketplace.

The overall current existing economic scenario is thus a major factor influencing the marketing decisions. If the overall economic scenario is one of depression or on a decline then the consumers by and large will have less finance at their disposal to buy your products and services. In such a scenario the company's pricing decisions will usually be that of pricing below the competition.

Competitors

All prudent marketing decisions must take into account the competitors. A good marketer will have complete information on who is the competitor, where they are and how good the competing product is. Further a good marketer will be in complete sync with the marketing strategy of the competition as it directly affects his own marketing decisions. If for example your competitor is charging a particular amount for a particular size or package of the product you may decide to price either over, below or with the competition depending on the status of the other environmental factors.

Legal and Political

The changes in the political and legal environment too affects the marketing activities. For example the passing of the legislature of allowing FDI in single brand retail by the Indian Government had a high level of impact on all single brand retail organisations that geared up to open their outlets in India. In a similar move the Passing of the legislature for allowing FDI in multi brand retail too has had its impact on the marketing decisions to be taken not just by the brands gearing up to enter India but the other Indian big and small retailers who foresee these giant multi brand retail outfits as their competitors.

3.2 Market Segmentation

3.2.1 Introduction – Meaning, Importance and Benefits of Market Segmentation

It is a known fact all over the world that no two human beings will behave and react in a similar fashion even in the same given set of circumstances. Human behaviour differs from person to person and from situation to situation. Similarly, the demand of different human beings for different products is also different. Their reactions to prices, various promotional schemes etc., is also different. Marketers have realised this, thus giving rise to Market Segmentation.

Market segmentation gives formal recognition to the fact that wants and desires of consumers are diverse and we can formulate a specific marketing offering (product/ service) to meet the needs of a specific category or segment of the market so that supply can best be co-related to demand.

Market segmentation is the process of grouping buyers into different categories on the basis of their common needs or desires, or on the basis of the differences in their needs, desires and requirements. It is a strategy of subdividing the target market into sub-groups of consumers with definable, distinct and homogeneous characteristics so that a different marketing programme can be set up for each group. This will result in an enhancement in the satisfaction to the consumers and profit to the marketer.

Market segmentation has been defined in different ways by different experts.

Some of the common definitions are as under:

- According to **Professor Phillip Kotler** *"Market Segmentation is the sub-dividing of a market into homogeneous sub-sects of customers where any sub-sect may conceivably be selected as a market target to be reached with a distinct marketing mix"*.

- According to **Professor William Stanton** *"Marketing Segmentation consists of taking the total heterogeneous market for a product and dividing it into several sub-markets or segments each of which tends to be homogeneous in all significant aspects"*.

- **Segmentation** has also been defined as *"Divisions of a market into sub-groups, with similar motivations"*.

- Another accepted definition of **Segmentation** is *"Segmentation means nothing more than dividing a market or a consumer base, into pieces and understanding the dynamics of each category"*.

Thus, market segmentation is basically a method of achieving maximum market response by dividing the market into various groups on the basis of certain common characteristic, common need, desire, common response etc. In a sense it is a strategy of 'divide and conquer' i.e., divide the market in order to conquer the demand.

Market segmentation enables the marketers to give better attention to a selection of customers and offer an appropriate marketing mix for each chosen segment, or group of buyers having homogeneous demand. Each sub division or segment can be selected as a target market to be reached with a distinct marketing mix.

Thus, market segmentation is a twofold process. Namely:

1. Identifying the viable segments or pockets of consumers and
2. Designing separate marketing programmes for each segment of the market, so as to achieve maximum consumer satisfaction and profit to the organisation.

3.2.2 Types of Market Segmentation

There are many ways in which a market can be segmented. However, basically, there are two approaches to segmenting a market:

1. People-Oriented Approach
2. Product-Oriented Approach

1. **People-Oriented Approach:** It is also called as customer personal characteristic approach. Under this approach a consumer can be classified based on various consumer dimensions such as geographic location, demography, socio-economic characteristics and psychographic characteristics. (All these characteristics are analysed in detail in the later sections of this chapter).

All the above mentioned variables are independent of any product service or situation in which the buyer makes the purchase decision. These variables relate only to the buyer himself. They help in finding out the type of consumer who will buy our product.

2. **Product-Oriented Approach:** This approach is also known as the consumer response approach. Under this approach to market segmentation the response or behaviour of the buyer is studied in relation to the product benefits, product usage, sections patronage and brand loyalty. (All these criteria are analysed in detail at a later stage in this chapter). This approach segments the market on the basis of why consumers purchase a particular product or service. Buyer behaviour involves psychological factors such as buying motives, attitudes, perceptions and preferences.

3.2.3 Patterns and Procedure of Market Segmentation / Bases of Segmentation

As we have read above, market segmentation is the act of breaking or dividing the entire market into small sub-markets or sub-zones whose customer characteristics have some similarity or homogeneous character and a single marketing strategy can be applied to each such sub-market. The basic idea of market segmentation is not to serve the entire market but preferably only an effective section of the market more effectively for the best mutual benefit of the consumer and the seller. Hence, the question arises: What is the criteria on which the customers should be grouped together? Or on what basis should segmentation be done? Unfortunately, there is no one best way of segmenting the markets. That is why; marketing managers are expected to examine a variety of segmentation criteria so as to identify those that will be most effective for defining their market.

Basically the following are the criteria which are studied by marketers in order to identify their markets. Also following are the basis on which market segmentation is done. The below mentioned criteria are usually applied for segmenting the market for consumer products.

(a) **Geographic Characteristics:** Geographic location is the usual and popular basis for market segmentation. It is a well known fact that people coming from different areas have not only different characteristics but also different product preferences. Thus, the sellers distinguish carefully among the regions in which they operate and select those where they have a comparative advantage. Usually, when segmentation is done based on geographic characteristics, a common base used is the rural Vs. urban markets. Another common base is the metro Vs. non-metro markets. Thus, if a seller's product has reached the saturation point in the urban areas he may decide to venture into the rural areas. If a new product is to be introduced it should be borne in mind that the city people are more adventurous and willing to try out novel products as compared to people living in rural areas. However this is not so any more. With the advent of T.V., Video and now the satellite T.V., the rural customer is far more aware and wants to buy (in fact he actually buys) the same branded products which his urban counterpart buys. In fact, as the satellite T.V's popularity increases and the rural markets get developed, one will soon see the homogenisation of the rural and urban needs. Also, in future, geographical segmentation will help the marketer only in planning his distribution function.

(b) **Demographic and Socio-economic Characteristics:** The next commonly used basis for segmentation is the demographic and socio-economic characteristics of the market. Demography is the study of the human population. Demographic characteristics are gender, age, marital status, number and age of children, place of residence and mobility of household. Socio-economic characteristics are income, education, occupation, social class, religion and culture. These demographic and socio-economic factors are used, or in a combination to segment the market. Usually, in the case of frequently bought consumer goods example, tea, coffee, toothpaste, soap, detergents etc., we use these demographic and socio-economic variables.

It has been widely observed that consumer needs are influenced by demographic and socio-economic characteristics of consumers. It is also observed that fine tuning of marketing decisions and strategies could be done with market segmentation on the basis of these variables. However the use of these variables for segmenting the market can lead to marketing operations on unexpected levels for example, Maggie noodles was launched for the target market of children however it is liked even by adults. Some women's magazines like Femina, Eile, Cosmopolitan etc. are also read by men. Sometimes some cheap but useful item is also purchased by the relatively rich class of society.

Demographic and socio-economic characteristics are important variables in segmentation. They are widely used to give a broad picture of market segmentation. They influence buyer behaviour indirectly. They have an influence on buyer behaviour and buyer decisions only through psychological factors such as motives, attitudes, perceptions, preferences etc.

(c) Psychographic Characteristics: Psychographics is a recent approach to market segmentation which has emerged as a major alternative to the traditional approaches. (Geographic, demographic and socio-economic segmentation are the traditional approaches). In this segmentation the market is subdivided on the lines of *lifestyle* or *personality traits*. Consumers in the same demographic group can exhibit or respond in a very different way depending upon their life styles or personality.

For example, Park Avenue, Pierre Cardin, Van Hussein, or Louise Phillips garments are sported by fashionable or affluent consumers in a wide section of the age group belonging to fashionable or westernised lifestyles.

Products like cigarettes, cosmetics, soaps, shoes, garments, pan masala etc. are often marketed on the basis of lifestyle market segmentation. Marketing companies are increasingly targeting products to suit lifestyle groups.

Personality variables are also found useful in segmenting the market. Products are designed in such a way so as to match a particular personality. Products or brands are shown to be associated with a film personality or sports personality.

There are two short-comings the marketer must be aware of while using psychographics:

1. Data collection and analysis for segmenting the market on this basis can be problematic because survey instrument may have many questions.
2. Psychographic segmentation studies are very costly demanding even ₹ 15 to 20 lakhs for a complete research package.

(d) Behaviouristic Characteristics: In this the consumers are divided on the basis of consumer behaviour by focussing on their background which influences their purchase decision like knowledge, attitude, belief, faith, family and analytical attitude towards a product or service. The knowledge of the personal characteristics of the consumers include points like who are the buyers of product, where they live and how they think, also what is their response or behaviour towards the product. The behaviour of different people is different towards a product, or a store selling a product. Many times, purchase behaviour is directed either because of usage expected from the product or because of loyalty to a particular brand, or after sale services promised by a company. Thus, market segmentation can also be undertaken on the basis of behaviour of the consumers. Some of the characteristics used for market segmentation on the basis of behaviour of the consumers are: Benefits expected, usage response, loyalty response-brand loyalty and store patronage. Let us study these briefly.

- **Use Pattern:** On the basis of the use pattern of the consumer, the consumers can be divided as heavy users, medium users, light users and non users. In case a company can segment the market and identify the heavy users, it can chalk out its advertising strategy in such a way that it can maintain the patronage of the heavy users. Usage information is generally combined with other characteristics of consumers like age income level, level of education so as to understand the customer better.
- **Benefit Pattern:** Different consumers buy the same product. But each of these consumers expects a different benefit from the product. Some of the benefits which consumers expect from the purchase of a particular product are economy, performance, style, durability, status product appearance, taste, flavour etc. Thus, one of the ways in which market segmentation is carried out by a marketing company is by dividing its consumers on the basis of the benefits they expect from the use of the product. Thus, all consumers who expect economy as a benefit to be derived from the use of the product will be grouped together, whereas all those who purchase the product for its appearance will be grouped together. Once consumers are grouped or segmented on the basis of the benefits that they expect from the use of the product then each segment can be further analysed on the basis of demographic, socio-economic characteristics so as to secure a better understanding of each segment.
- **Brand/Store Loyalty:** Customer loyalty may be used as a basis for market segmentation. A segmentation of the population based on loyalty will enable the marketer to come up with such promotional schemes as will retain the loyal consumers, attract new consumers from competing brands, or convert non-loyal into loyal buyers. However brand/store loyalty is not easy to measure. In fact the meaning of brand loyalty itself is not very clear as a consumer may purchase a particular product because of economy, or habit and not because of loyalty.

Thus, the above are the different basis on which segmentation can be done by a company marketing consumer products.

However when the industrial market is to be segmented, a slightly different basis of segmentation is used. Of course geographic segmentation is common to both consumer and industrial markets. Even demographic and socio-economic variables are used to segment the market for certain industrial products. Apart from these the following variables are used to segment the industrial market.

1. **Operating Variables:** These include variables such as customers, technology used, products suitability, user/non-user status like heavy user, medium user or non user. Customers' requirements for other services, requirement of the product urgently for immediate use, companies using the product for specific application only.

2. **Purchasing Variables:** Usually, the purchasing system of industrial consumers vary from consumer to consumer. Thus, we can group companies on their system of purchase like companies following the centralised system of purchase can be one segment, others following the decentralised can be another segment. Further tender buyers can fall into another category. Further industrial buyers may be segmented on the basis of the scale on which they purchase, their purchasing policies, requirement of after sale services etc.

3. **Personal Attitude:** Under this segmentation fall the following criteria; loyalty to the suppliers, ability to take risks, reciprocity etc.

Benefits of Market Segmentation

The Strategy of Marketing Segmentation benefits both the marketing organisation as well as the consumer. Following are the specific benefits that accrue from Market Segmentation to the Marketing Organisation:

1. **A more precise definition of the market:** Market segmentation enables an organisation to understand why consumers do or do not buy certain products or services. In other words, it provides an understanding of how best to meet the changing market demands. Thus, the firm would be in a better position to locate and compare marketing opportunities.

2. **A more effective marketing programme:** When customer needs are fully understood, marketers can effectively formulate and implement marketing programmes which will be in tune with the demands of the market.

3. **Better assessment of the competition:** Market segmentation helps in assessing the strengths and weaknesses of the competitors and taking action in the light of these. If a particular competing product appears to be in a very dominating position in a particular market segment but in a vulnerable position in another segment it would be better for company to try to capture the vulnerable segment instead of the wasting energies on the competitors dominant segment. Thus, resources are utilised profitably by catering to customer demand which is not being met by rivals.

4. **Better allocation of resources:** Once the target segment is clearly defined and identified, the limited resources at the command of the company can be channelled for best results. Thus, promotional campaigns can be co-ordinated effectively so that the consumers would recognise the promotional appeal quickly and the marketers would minimise the losses resulting from excess exposure.

Marketing segmentation helps the consumer as well. Some of the benefits of segmentation that accrue to the customers are as follows:

(a) **Availability of right product at right place and right price:** It helps the customer to get the right product at the right place and at a price which he can afford. This is because the marketing programme is prepared keeping in mind the specific characteristics of the particular market segment.

(b) **Saving of time:** As Market segmentation caters to the specific needs of each consumer segment it results in the creation of loyal customers. Thus, when new competing products are introduced the consumers do not feel the need to try these new products. Thus, this saves the time of the consumers which would otherwise have been lost in the hunt for alternative products.

(c) **Improves the standard of living:** The marketing programme for a particular segment tries to arouse the hidden needs of the customers and persuades them to buy different products. It thus raises their standard of living.

Limitations/Costs of Market Segmentation

As we have seen above, market segmentation benefits both the organisation as well as the consumers. However we cannot forget that these benefits do not accrue for free. Certain costs have to be borne. It may also sometimes so happen that the costs of segmentation outweigh its benefits. This would render the entire exercise of segmentation as futile.

The costs of segmentation are as under:

1. **Product Cost:** In order to take care of the specific needs of each market segment the firm usually develops a separate product for each segment. This difference in product for each segment may range from a difference in label or package right to a totally different product. If a different product for each different segment is to be created a lot of expenditure on research and development has to be undertaken.

2. **Production Cost:** In order to enjoy economies of scale a certain number of units of a particular product have to be produced. In case a company divides its market for a particular product into many segments, and manufactures different products for each section it may not be able to sell enough number of each product so as to enjoy economies of scale and this would increase the production cost.

3. **Promotion Cost:** Every organisation has to come up with a promotion strategy that will attract its customers from the varied segments. For this a large amount of expenditure in terms of human and financial resources has to be undertaken as various different advertisements have to be designed and placed in various different media. This results in mounting promotion costs.

4. **Inventory Costs:** The more the number of segments that a company wants to serve the more will be the inventory cost. The inventory costs will work out higher because of the following two basic reasons.
   - Larger selection of products will force the firm to maintain more and more records covering location and quantity of merchandise.
   - The company will have to maintain increased buffer stock for normal demand and increased safety stock for unpredicted demand levels.

5. **Management Costs:** Designing the different marketing programmes to be implemented for the different market segments involves a lot of expenditure in the valuable time of the management. Usually a company appoints a product or market manager whose main responsibility is to develop and monitor the different marketing programmes.

Thus, market segmentation has both its benefits as well as costs. However, for segmentation to be effective, following three areas should be investigated:
- The segments should be measurable, i.e. data collection should be possible for analysing, planning and control.
- In markets where great use is made of advertising, there may be only a little match between segment population definition and media audience definition.
- Each segment should be large enough to warrant specialised attention.

3.2.4 Criteria and Approaches of Segmenting a Market

As market segmentation involves the grouping or dividing of consumers on the basis of similarity of need or response to a product of the company, it can be said that the possibilities of segmentation are so many that each consumer can be a segment as no two consumers are exactly similar. Thus to have an optimum segmentation of the market the following requisites of sound segmentation should be borne in mind. These have been put forward by **Prof. Martin L. Bell of Washington University, USA.**

1. **A market segment should be identifiable and measurable:** Firstly the group of buyers or the segment should be clearly defined. The questions like, who is in the segment? who is outside the segment? should be clearly answered. After this demographic, socio-economic and cultural information on the segment members should be collected. This data will help in identifying the size and importance of the segment as a potential project for marketing strategy. Unfortunately, obtaining segment data is seldom easy especially when the segment is defined in terms of behavioural features.

2. **The market segment should show an adequate market potential:** A particular group of buyers together should be identified as a segment only if the purchasing power vested with them is large enough to justify a separate marketing programme. A separate marketing strategy is worked out for each segment. The segment should be large enough to justify this separate strategy. It is purchasing power that represents a meaningful marketing opportunity that is likely to stem either from income, savings or credit as the case may be. Thus, if a market segment of only five consumers with a need for the product and a huge purchasing power is identified it is an effective segment. However, a number of buyers with a need but no backing of purchasing power will not be an effective market segment.

3. **The market segment should be economically assessable:** A market segment should be such that a company can identify and reach a group of buyers in the same segment economically. For example, segment members could be concentrated

geographically. That is buying at the same store or ordering that same magazine. This kind of segment is economic in identifying and reaching. On the other hand if you want to segment the market on a physiographic basis like the basis of segmentation for a toothpaste undertaken on the basis of people who wish to enhance their sex appeal, this will not be as economic to identify. T.V. as a media of advertising to reach this segment will have to be used; however it is a comparatively expensive media. Further it reaches both the identified segment as well as others. The cost per segment member is much higher in case of T.V. advertising.

4. **A market segment should react uniquely to marketing efforts:** A market segment should respond differently to a marketing programme as compared to a different market segment. Different segments unless they respond differently to particular marketing efforts hardly justify the use of a separate marketing programme.

5. **The market segment should be stable over a period of time:** The basic purpose for which segmentation is undertaken is that a separate marketing strategy can be formulated for each segment so as to best serve the customers at a profit to the organisation. Marketing strategies are long range plans and cover a period of 3 to 5 years into the future. Therefore market segments should be such as will remain stable over a period of time. Segments that emerge rapidly and disappear just as quickly do not offer a good marketing opportunity to the firm. Only highly innovative entrepreneurs can, at considerable amount of risk, attempt to serve these segments.

6. **Market segments are dynamic:** Once a firm identifies a market segment it does not mean that the segment will remain static. The market is constantly changing. Technology, competition, perceptions and attitudes are all dynamic and changing. Because of these changes the marketers should constantly monitor the market and change their strategies to adapt to these changes. This is nothing but dynamic segmentation.

3.2.5 Essentials of Effective Market Segmentation / Qualities of Good Segmentation

In order to arrive at an accurate segmentation of the market what is required is good quantitative and qualitative information about the product as well as the market. However the following are the logical steps that should be followed in order to effectively segment the market:

1. Assess the difference between one customer group and others in terms of their needs and their likely responses to the products offered by the company.

2. Find out what are the factors that influence in grouping certain customers into a particular segment.

3. After studying the above aspects, group the customers into certain segments.

4. Study and confirm that certain marketing programmes and marketing mixes can be formulated for different segments.

5. Find out which segments would accept the product/services of the company and can be considered as natural targets of the company.

6. Estimate the likely purchases of the products of the company by each segment.

7. Select those segment which offer higher potential and which would be suitable to the product/services offered by the company.

3.2.6 Differentiated / Differential Marketing and Concentrated Marketing

1. Differentiated / Differential Marketing

Market strategy whereby a company attempts to appeal to two or more clearly defined market segments with a specific product and distinctive marketing strategy adapted to each separate segment. It is called multi-segment marketing.

A differentiated marketing strategy is when a company creates campaigns that appeal to at least two market segments or target groups. For example, a store can promote a sale that appeals to people in at least two cities or locations, or a company can market a product that appeals to women in at least two age groups. Differentiated marketing strategies can target many more than two segments; shoe companies often create campaigns that appeal to both men and women in a variety of age groups. Differentiated marketing strategies can also use different messages in the same campaign for different segments. For example, a retailer might market low cost to a budget-conscious segment and product quality to an affluent market segment.

2. Concentrated Marketing

Market strategy whereby a product is developed and marketed for a very well-defined, specific segment of the consumer population. The marketing plan will be a highly specialised one catering to the needs of that specific consumer segment. Concentrated marketing is particularly useful for small companies with limited resources because it facilitates the company to achieve a strong market position in the specific market segment it serves without mass production, mass distribution, or mass advertising.

A concentrated marketing strategy is targeted to one specific market segment or audience. For example, a company might market a product specifically for women, or a retailer might market his business to residents in a specific town. Concentrated marketing strategies are often geared for smaller groups of people, because they are designed to appeal to a specific segment.

Distinction between Differentiated/Differential Marketing and Concentrated Marketing

Points of Difference	Differentiated Marketing	Concentrated Marketing
(a) **Meaning:**	Differentiated marketing is a market coverage and market segmentation strategy in which the product is aimed at two or more specific segments in the market.	Concentrated marketing is a market coverage and market segmentation strategy in which the product and marketing message is aimed at a few well defined segments of the consumer population in a market.
(b) **Suitability:**	Differentiated marketing is suitable for medium and big scale marketing organisations.	Concentrated marketing is suitable for small scale marketing organisations.
(c) **Cost:**	It involves high marketing cost.	It is comparatively less costly proposition.

Points to Remember

1. **Definition:** According to **Phillip Kotler**, "*A company's marketing environment consists of the external factors and forces that affect the company's ability to develop and maintain successful transactions and relationships with its target consumers.*" In other words environment represents those factors which affect the successful marketing operations of the company.

2. **Factors constituting the Marketing Environment:**
   (a) External Macro Environment - political, economic, legal, social, cultural, ecological, technological, international
   (b) Task Specific Environment - Internal suppliers, Marketing intermediaries, Customers, Output Mechanism, Competitors.
   (c) Internal Environment
       (i) People
       (ii) Culture
       (iii) Work ethos
       (iv) Attitudes and Values

3. **Impact of Marketing Environment on Marketing Decisions** - All the below elements affect the marketing decisions:
   (a) Tastes and Trends
   (b) Demographics
   (c) Budget
   (d) Current economic scene
   (e) Competitors
   (f) Legal and political scene

4. **Definition of Market segmentation:** According to Professor **Phillip Kotler,** "*Market Segmentation is the sub-dividing of a market into homogeneous sub-sects of customers where any sub-sect may conceivably be selected as a market target to be reached with a distinct marketing mix*".

5. **Types of Market Segmentation:** There are two approaches to segment a market:
   (a) People-Oriented Approach
   (b) Product-Oriented Approach

6. **Criteria for Market Segmentation:**
   (a) A market segment should be identifiable and measurable.
   (b) The market segment should show an adequate market potential.
   (c) The market segment should be economically assessable.
   (d) A market segment should react uniquely to marketing efforts.
   (e) The market segment should be stable over a period of time.
   (f) Market segments are dynamic.

7. **Benefits of Market Segmentation for Marketer:**
   (a) Market segments are dynamic.
   (b) A more effective marketing programme can be made.
   (c) Better assessment of the competition.
   (d) Better allocation of resources.

8. **Benefits of Market Segmentation for Consumer:**
   (a) Availability of right product at right place and right price.
   (b) Saving of time.
   (c) Improves the standard of living.

9. **Limitations of Market Segmentation:**
   (a) Increase in Product Cost.
   (b) Increase in Production Cost.
   (c) Increase in Promotion Cost.
   (d) Increase in Inventory Costs.
   (e) Increase in Management Costs.

Questions for Discussion

1. Explain the Nature and Scope of Marketing Environment.
2. Explain the Various Internal Controllable Factors affecting Marketing Environment.
3. Explain the effect of the Demographic Environment on Marketing Decisions.
4. How does the Technological Environment affect Marketing?
5. Describe the various External Controllable factors affecting Marketing.

6. Discus the Economic, Political, Social and Cultural Environment affecting Marketing.
7. What is the requirements for effective market segmentation?
8. Give any five benefits of market segmentation.
9. How can a market be segmented?
10. What are the elements of market segmentation?
11. What are the features of market segmentation?
12. Describe segmentation of industrial market and consumer market.
13. Explain basic principles governing market segmentation.
14. Why and how are markets segmented?
15. State the importance of market segmentation in modern marketing.
16. Distinguish between product differentiation and market segmentation.
17. What should be the nature of the marketer's approach in segmented consumer market for achieving success in marketing? Explain with examples the alternative open to him.
18. Explain the techniques and principles governing market segmentation.
19. Assess the benefits and limitations of market segmentation. Give examples.
20. What is the importance of market segmentation in marketing strategy?
21. What do you mean by "market segmentation" and what are the elements of market segmentation?

Questions from Previous Pune University Examinations

1. What is Market Segmentation? Explain the Procedure for Market Segmentation and also write the Significance of Market Segmentation. **[April 2012]**
2. Define Market Segmentation. What are the Benefits and Limitations of Market Segmentation? **[April 2013]**
3. Write Short Notes:
   (A) Types of Market Segmentations. **[April 2011]**
   (B) Market Segmentation. **[Oct. 2012]**
4. What is Market Segmentation? Explain Essentials of Effective Market Segmentation.
   [April 2009, 2010]
5. Define Market Segmentation. **[Oct. 2007]**

Chapter 4...

Marketing Mix

Contents ...

4.1 Product Mix and Price Mix
4.2 New Product Development Strategy
4.3 Meaning and Definition of Product Planning
4.4 Role of Product Manager
4.5 Product Life Cycle
4.6 Price Mix
4.7 Need and Importance of Pricing
4.8 Pricing Methods/Pricing Strategies
4.9 Supply Chain Management
4.10 Types of Distribution Intermediaries and their Characteristics
4.11 Designing Distribution Channel/Factors Influencing Selection of Channel
4.12 Promotion Mix: Meaning, Elements of Promotion Mix
4.13 Advertising: Meaning, Definition, Importance and Limitations of Advertising
4.14 Types of Media: Outdoor, Indoor, Print, Press, Transit - Merits and Demerits, Concept of Media Mix, Recent Trends in Promotion
- Points to Remember
- Questions for Discussion
- Questions from Previous Pune University Examinations

Learning Objectives ...

- To understand the Meaning of Marketing Mix
- To understand its Importance
- To elucidate the Factors affecting Pricing Decision
- To describe the Pricing Objectives
- To understand the Concept of Logistics
- To explain the Channel Structure
- To discuss the designing of Distribution Channels
- To elucidate the factors which affect the Marketing Promotion Mix
- To discuss the definition, importance and the methods of Advertisement and Sales Promotion
- To debate the goals of Advertising and Media

Introduction: Meaning, Scope and Importance of Marketing Mix

The basic task of Marketing involves the identification of the needs of the customer and then the manufacturing and marketing of a product or service that satisfies this need. In order to do this a marketing organisation has to concentrate on four important aspects known as the 4P's of marketing.

The marketing manager has to combine these 4P's in such a way that the combination provides satisfaction to the customer and a profit to the manufacturer. When these elements (4P's) are combined together they are called as "The Marketing Mix".

The term "Marketing Mix" was first coined by the American Marketing expert James Culliton. The description of the "Marketing Mix" as four P's was given by the well known American Professor Jerome Mc Carthy. Since then the terms "Marketing Mix" and "the four P's" have been used synonymously. Thus if you say that the Marketing mix of an organisation is nothing but a right mix of the four P's of Marketing i.e. product, price, place (physical distribution) and promotion, the interpretation is absolutely right. This term has been defined by **Philip Kotler** in the following way: *"Marketing mix is a set of controllable variables and their levels that the firm uses to influence the target market."* Thus according to this definition, any variable under the control of the firm that can influence the customer demand is a marketing mix variable.

According to **Prof Keeley** *and* **Prof. Lazor** *"Marketing mix is composed of a large battery of devices which might be employed to induce consumers to buy a particular product".* In other words, marketing mix is the mixture of all the marketing efforts of a company revolving around the four ingredients namely product, price, promotion and place. These ingredients are interrelated and all revolve around potential consumer satisfaction as the focal point. It is the complex mixes relating to inputs and resources utilised in the marketing programme to attain the business objective.

The marketing mix of an organisation is made up of four elements namely PRODUCT, PRICE, PROMOTION AND PLACE. Each of these four elements or sub-mixes has a number of elements. The complete set of marketing mix, submixes and elements are given below:

The Marketing mix has four main sub mixes. They are:
1. The Product Mix
2. The Price Mix
3. The Place Mix or Physical Distribution Mix
4. The Promotion Mix.

Each of the above four is the sub mix of the marketing mix. They can also be called as marketing mix elements. Each of these elements has sub elements and they are as under:

1. **The Product mix:** The Product Mix includes:
   - Product Planning and Development,
   - Branding,
   - Packaging,
   - Labelling.
2. **The Price Mix:** The Price Mix includes:
   - Price policies,
   - Discounts,
   - Credit.
3. **Place Mix (Physical Distribution Mix):** The Place Mix includes:
   - Channels of Distribution,
   - Transportation,
   - Warehousing.
4. **Promotion Mix:** The Promotion Mix includes:
   - Advertising,
   - Personal Selling,
   - Sales Promotion,
   - Publicity.

Importance of Marketing Mix

The Marketing mix can be used by marketers as a tool to assist in defining the marketing strategy. Marketing Managers use this method to attempt to generate the optimal response in the target market by blending a number of marketing mix elements in an optimum way. It is important to note that all the elements of the marketing mix are controllable variables. These elements can be adjusted on a frequent basis to meet the needs of the target market and the environment. Hence the Marketing mix is a very useful tool for targeting the market correctly and for achieving success with the target market. The importance of marketing mix can be further understood as under:

1. **Attracting customers:** The 4P's are the tools of the marketing manager and he has to use these tools for attracting customers, for facing marketing competition and for

promoting sales. With the help of the marketing mix, the marketing manager is able to best please the customer and this enables him to achieve his marketing objectives.

2. **Better use of resources:** Marketing mix promotes better utilisation of limited resources as it helps the marketing manager to understand his customer and invest in the areas in which the consumer is interested. It helps the marketing manager in focusing attention on the needs of the consumer. With limited components at its disposal, it attempts to gain the best possible results.

3. **Precision:** Marketing mix provides precision to the study of marketing. It helps in understanding the important tasks. Neil H. Borden has stated that "A chart which shows the elements of the mix and the forces that bear on the mix helps to bring understanding of what marketing is".

4. **Balanced approach:** Marketing mix is an effective tool for solving the problems. It keeps the marketing manager to be on the right track. It reminds him that, on the one hand, he -should be careful to consider the market forces and on the other hand think of a total marketing programme instead of relying on anyone particular aspect.

5. **The significance of marketing mix lies in the mix or blend:** The components of marketing mix are individually important but their significance lies in the mix or blend. It is necessary to combine them properly so as to make them collectively effective in a dynamic marketing environment.

6. **Applicable to business as well as non business organisations:** The concept of marketing mix is applicable to business, as well as non-business organisations, such as clubs, colleges, associations etc.

4.1 Product Mix and Price Mix

Product Mix

What is a Product ?

A product is anything that can be offered to a market to satisfy a want or need. Products that are marketed include physical goods, services, events, people, ideas, information, places, properties and organisations.

Products are tangible, intangible or both. Products of manufacturing units like pens; cameras, phones, cosmetics etc are tangible products whereas products of the service industry are intangible. An example of intangible services is the feeling of motivation after hearing a motivational speaker. A product may be a good plus service too. In such a case it is both tangible as well as intangible for example the food that you eat in a restaurant is the tangible product, where as the feeling of eating in the luxurious atmosphere of the hotel is the intangible product.

Nowadays most product come in a dual package of good plus service and hence most products are both tangible as well as intangible. In fact a 'Product' means not just the physical product but includes all the services both before and after sales services, and the prestige that is felt upon the ownership of the product. A product is a bundle of all kinds of satisfaction both material and non material, ranging from economic utilities to socio-psychological satisfaction. It is thus a bundle of physical, service and symbolic particulars expected to give satisfaction or benefit to the consumer.

Definition of 'Product'

According to **Professor Harry L. Hanson** "*A product is the sum total of three things – THE INTRINSIC CHARACTERISTICS its materials and construction, its ability to perform – THE EXTRINSIC CHARACTERISTICS its packaging, brand or trade mark and THE INTANGIBLES associated with it*".

According to **Professor Phillip Kotler**, "*A product is made up of three parts TANGIBLE PRODUCT – materials and construction, EXTENDED PRODUCT PART services and GENERIC PRODUCT PART –the benefits*".

Product Characteristics

Anything to be called a 'Product' should have certain characteristics – both explicit and implicit. In order to have a clearcut understanding of the 'Product' concept, it is essential to understand these explicit and implicit characteristics of the product. Following is a brief outline of the explicit and implicit characteristics of a product as presented by Professor Sturdivant and his associates in their title "Managerial Analysis in Marketing".

Explicit Characteristics

Explicit product characteristics are those which are perceived almost uniformly by all observers. In other words there is not much disagreement amongst the buyers and sellers about the existence of these characteristics in the product. There is a common agreement amongst all as to the existence and nature of these characteristics. There are five such attributes. They are:

1. **Physical Configuration:** A product is a bundle of some physical material. It is made up of wood, plastic, glass, stone, metal etc. Every product has its own size, shape, colour, density, odour, texture, taste and a host of other such physical attributes. On the basis of its physical characteristics, it has an apparent function or a set of function to perform. For example a toothbrush is used to clean teeth. However an old one may be used to clean combs, jewellery, nooks and cranny's etc.

2. **Associated Services:** Products are sold with the common understanding that the seller will render associated services in case of each product. These are before and after sale services. Before sale services are its demonstration, credit facilities available and the 'after' sale services are its delivery, installation, making available spare parts, repair services and warrantees, both, express and implied.

3. **Package and Brand Name:** It is useful to consider package as part of the product, for it is sometimes difficult to separate a product into 'content' and 'package'. For example perfumes, deodorants, lipsticks etc. enjoy a greater demand because of their attractive package. Further the brand name is intrinsic to the product. A brand stands for the product. You do not need to name the product, you just name the brand. For example 'Colgate' means toothpaste, 'Ceat' means tyres, 'Lux' means soap, 'Savlon' means after shave lotion and so on.

4. **Product Mix:** This points out the relationship of the product to other products sold or made by the firm. That is, a given product is a part of a set of products offered for sale by a particular seller and has an impact on how the seller and the buyers consider it. The consumer does not think of the product in isolation as he knows that the producer makes other products too.

5. **Product Life cycle:** A product like a human being has a life cycle and at any point of time, a product can be located in some stage of its existence. The sales of a given product follows a characteristic pattern of increasing, at first slowly then at an increasing rate, then at a decreasing rate and finally absolute sales begin to decline. The time required for each of these stages varies widely among the products. The product life cycle is made up of four stages and each has its own implications for the producers as well as consumers. (Product Life Cycle is dealt with in detail at a later stage in this chapter.)

Implicit Characteristics

As discussed earlier, explicit characteristics are those on which there is near agreement amongst all about their existence and nature. When there is a disagreement amongst the consumers about the existence and nature of certain characteristics in a product, these disagreements form the intrinsic characteristics of the product. These disagreements exist because each individual sees the product in a some what different and therefore unique way. What is the perception of one person is not the same as that of another person. These different perceptions and disagreement points can be called as the intrinsic characteristics of a product. There are four such Features / Characteristics:

1. **Product Symbolism:** A product is a cluster of symbols. By virtue of its colour, shape size and function, it is a symbol. A different size of the product gives it a different meaning to different people. Similarly a different colour, or a different function and

so on. For example a gentleman wearing a white or a grey shirt get sloted into a traditional man image as compared to a gentleman wearing a red or rust coloured shirt. Thus a product is a sum total of the meaning it communicates when others look at it or use it. It may communicate a symbol of status, style economy, performance, achievement, boldness and so on.

2. **Communication Media:** Because a product is a bundle of symbols it is a bundle of communication also. Of course, what this communication is, it is determined by the consumer's personal interpretation of the symbols, mediated by his culture group, group influences and personality. Every product says something about itself. Every product is a story teller about: What it is, what it is used for, at what rate, by whom, where it is available, and so on. With every product there is information, given or hidden.

3. **The Product Perception:** Products are perceived or viewed in different ways by different consumers. Perception is a physiopsychological process. Perception begins with a cue of the environment that is received by a consumer. This cue sends a message to the brain. The brain compares this message with other stored messages in the brain, and perception occurs. For example when a cup of tea is placed in front of a consumer, the consumer smells the tea. The smell is the cue from the environment, which is received by the consumer. The brain records this smell and compares it with other stored smells and the consumer comes to the conclusion that the smell is of "Tata Tea" or "Lipton" or "Brook Bond" etc. In the same way instead of the smell, the cue from the environment can come from the taste, colour, texture etc. The perception of the consumer will help the producer to develop the relevant product. `Relevant Product' is the product that is perceived by the consumer as the seller intended him to perceive it, because it is relevant to the realized or aspired behavioural pattern of those people who comprise the market of the product.

4. **The Product Evaluation:** Truly speaking it is almost impossible to separate the perception of the product from its evaluation, both conceptually and operationally. Though theoretically separable, they occur simultaneously. Along with perception, evaluation implies the setting up of a set of criteria to determine expected satisfaction.

   It is comparing the 'efforts' involved and 'rewards' received by the consumer. Thus efforts may be the necessary search for the product, the price as it affects the consumer's pocket; the evaluation may be of rewards - functional, psychological that he gets in return. Here evaluation differs from individual to individual and from time to time in case of the same individual.

Thus every product has both implicit and explicit characteristics, and both these together make up the product.

Product Simplification, Diversification and Elimination

(A) Product Simplification and Diversification

A company usually deals in a variety of products. In fact no company can remain static as far as the production and marketing of its products is concerned. It has to always be on the lookout for new products. As products have a specific life span, old products go out of the market and they are replaced by new products. The various products that a company deals in are a part of its product mix. Sometimes the management of a company decides to add some products to its Product Mix; at other times it may decide to delete or discontinue the manufacture and marketing of a particular product. When a particular existing product is dropped from the product mix of the company it is known as Product Simplification or Product line Contraction. On the other hand, if a particular new product is added to the Product Mix it is known as product diversification.

Thus, Product Simplification and Product Diversification are totally opposite of each other. Basically, diversification can take place in two ways. Diversification of an existing product line and diversification by adding an additional product line. Diversification of an existing product line means adding another product to the existing product line. For e.g. Godrej company adding a washing machine to its existing product line of consumer durables. Whereas adding a new product line means starting the production and marketing of products in which the company was not previously dealing in. For e.g. a company not dealing in consumer non-durables commences production of consumer durable goods. When a company diversifies in an existing product line it is known as Diversification in depth. And when a company diversifies into a new product line it is known as Diversification in breadth.

Diversification by definition means adding on something new, it may be adding on a new product, a new market, new technologies, or even a new company to the existing line of the product mix.

Product Simplification and Product Diversification are major decisions that are taken by the management. Many sick or marginal products never die; they will continue to thrive in the product mix till they fade away. In this process they eat away the profits made by the other products. Not only this but if the same resources are used for other products the company will definitely be utilising the resources more profitably. In such a situation, the company may decide to give up the loss making products.

Sometimes, products are abandoned even while they are still profitable because the company may feel that the same resources used for another product may give a higher yield. Thus avoiding or stopping the production of a particular product is called Simplification. In spite of the advantages of product simplification, many managements do not like "Product Pressing Programmes". In spite of hesitation most management are always on the lookout for finding the weak products and adopting a gradual elimination of some products.

(B) Advantages of Product Simplification

1. **Reduction in Cost:** As simplification results in the discontinuation of certain products, the resources of this product are diverted to the production of some other product. Thus this other product is produced on a large scale and economies of scale are achieved. This reduces the cost of production. Further, supervision expenses are also reduced.

2. **Specialisation:** Simplification helps specialisation. This is because only a few products are produced and hence a company can have specialisation and standardisation for the manufacture of a few items.

3. **Skilled Personnel:** The company can make use of skilled personnel and hence better quality of products are produced.

4. **Increase in Profits:** As the resources of the firm are taken away from loss making products and utilised towards the manufacture of more profitable ones, definitely the company's profits will increase.

5. **Market Control:** As simplification results in lessening of the number of products of the firm, activities such as market analysis, consumer analysis and competition analysis can be extensively carried out. Thus, a greater control can be exercised over the market.

(C) Advantages of Product Diversification

Just as Simplification is carried out by a firm because it offers various advantages likewise there are various reasons why diversification has to be undertaken.

1. **New technological developments:** New technological developments make it necessary for the introduction of new products.

2. **New markets:** A company is constantly on the lookout for capturing new markets.

3. **Cashing in on the company's reputation:** Once a company has an established reputation in the market, any product introduced by the company automatically enjoys this reputation. Hence, a new product gains a quick acceptance by the consumers.

4. **Full utilisation of capacity:** A company may undertake expansion in order to utilise the existing capacity of the factory to the fullest possible extent.

5. **Utilisation of by-products:** Diversification may also take place in order to utilise the by-products of the manufacturing process. For e.g. the manufacture of sugar leads to a by-product called bagasse which is the raw material for the manufacture of liquor.

6. **Social change:** Social changes such as changes in the behaviour.

7. **Taste and fashion of consumers:** Taste of the consumers, demand, fashion, and style motivates the producer to diversify his products in order to meet the new demand.

8. **Industrial and economic policies of the government:** The policies of the government also control diversification. For e.g. the policy of the government to grant a 10 year tax concession to the software industry has promoted the expansion into this sector by many companies.

Diversification is possible only in the case of large companies which have multi-product and multi-markets. Such companies should have the required finance and organisation to support the expansion. As diversification helps to prevent recessionary trends in the industry, it is encouraged and is sometimes brought about through merger of one company with another.

Thus, simplification and diversification are two very important decisions which the management cannot avoid taking.

(D) Product Elimination

The process of withdrawal of a product is technically known as "Product Elimination". Thus there is a very thin line between simplification and elimination. Simplification is the dropping of a product from the product line or product mix of a firm. It is a method by which a fat and long product line is thinned out. Whereas, the process of withdrawal of a product from the market is known as "Product Elimination". When marginal or unprofitable products are to be eliminated a process is followed. The process is explained as follows:

1. **Selection of the products:** The first step would be the selection of the products which are to be considered for elimination.

2. **Collection and analysis of information:** After the products are identified, necessary information is to be collected and analysed. Factors which require analysis are deficiencies in the product, product life cycle, substitutes, price, profitability, inability of the product to satisfy the needs of the customers etc.

3. **Decision:** If after due analysis it is found out that the product can be modified to suit the needs of the consumers and it can be done profitably, then the product should be modified. However, if after a careful analysis the decision is reached that the particular product cannot be satisfactorily modified then a decision to eliminate it should be taken.

4.2 New Product Development Strategy

Introduction

The marketing, programme of any organisation revolves around the four P's of Marketing i.e. Product, Price, Physical distribution and Promotion. Out of all these four "PRODUCT" is the single most important component. It is the product policy and strategy that gives rise to the price policy, physical distribution systems and promotional strategy. If the product itself is not good then no amount of efficiency and expenditure on the other three components of the marketing mix will lead to successful marketing. It is the product that has to first be good and then wanted, needed and desired by the customers. Hence it is utmost important to plan and develop the right kind of product. Product planning and development is a continuous process and involves a good deal of deliberations on the following factors or elements.

1. **Research before Production:** Before arriving at a decision to introduce a new product extensive market research should be carried out. The company should know what kind of a product carrying, what kind of characteristics qualities, features and satisfying which particular needs in customers should be produced. Further, the company should also undertake research to find out the target customers for whom the product is being produced.

2. **Possibility of production method**: After deciding upon the development of a new product certain other decisions have also to be made. Whether the production process for the particular product are viable to be undertaken. Whether the required technology and raw material are available and whether the final product will satisfy the needs of the target customers.

3. **Modification of existing lines:** A study of the existing product lines should be made in order to ascertain whether a new product is really required or modifications in an existing product will meet the new requirements of the customers. If it is possible to modify an existing product then the extent of this possibility should be thoroughly explored.

4. **Elimination of a product:** Product planning also involves elimination of unprofitable and loss making products so that the resources can be used somewhere else.

5. **Improvements in existing products:** Product planning also includes improvements in the characteristics, features, quality, packing, labelling etc. of an existing product in keeping with the changing requirements of the customers as well as the policies of the competition.

6. **Price Determination:** Determining the price of the product is one of the main elements of the process of product planning. Should the prices be set on the basis of the prices charged by the competitors or on the basis of the cost of the product or on the basis of the forces of demand and supply is one of the important decisions to be taken

7. **Commercialisation of product:** Product planning also includes the commercialisation and sale of the product at a profit to the organisation and satisfaction to the customer. While undertaking product planning this aspect has also to be considered.

8. **Co-ordination:** Product planning also includes the co-ordination of various products so that the company can not only maintain but improve its competitive position in the market. This can be done by taking a periodic review about the various products in the market and taking decisions about which products to combine and which to eliminate.

Thus it is explicit from the study of the various elements of product planning that every decision right from the generation of idea about a new product to the elimination of a product from the product line is included in product planning.

4.3 Meaning and Definition of Product Planning

Planning is deciding in advance what is to be .done? when it is to be done? how it is to be done, and who is to do it. Product planning is the entire process of deciding what type of product to produce for which target audience, to satisfy which particular needs. If an existing product is not satisfying a target consumer then what type of modification it will require or after all possible modifications if it still fails to attract the attention of the consumer then product planning also includes the decision to withdraw such unprofitable or loss making products from the market.

According to **Karl H Tietjin**, Product Planning is *"The act of making out and supervising the search, screening, development and commercialisation of new products, the modifications of existing lines and discontinuation of marginal or unprofitable items"*. Thus product planning includes three major types of decisions:

1. Development and introduction of new products.
2. Modifications of existing products in keeping with the changing tastes and preferences of the target customers.
3. Elimination of unprofitable or obsolete products.

All the above decisions are influenced by various internal and external factors like company policy, goodwill of the company extent and type of competition faced, product image etc.

It is the Chief Executive of the company who is responsible for product planning. It is he who co- ordinates with the various departments and takes a final decision.

Organisation for New Product Development

An organisation is a group of people that come together for the achievement of a common objective. When this group comes together, the work has to be divided amongst these people in such a way that the person most suited to a particular job, gets that particular piece of work to perform. When the work is divided each individual is entrusted with the authority required to carry out the work and is also responsible for the execution of his piece of work. When the work is divided a relationship emerges amongst the various people working in the organisation. This relationship decides who is at what level in the organisation. Basically there are three levels in an organisation. The top level, the middle level and the lower level. At the top level of management the objectives are laid down, at the middle level they are executed and the lower level of management is basically supervisory work.

No organisation can spend its entire life time manufacturing and selling the same products. Products like human beings have a life span at the end of which they are deleted and disappear from the market. New products take their place. Hence, no organisation can remain a competitive one if it does not plan for new products.

While planning for new products the role of the top management and the organisation cannot be overlooked. It is the top management that lays down the objectives of the organisation, and hence the channels of communication between the top management and the Product or Development Manager should be clear, open and two ways. If the Development manager undertakes the development of a product, in which the top management is not interested, it will just lead to a waste of time, effort and money. Hence it is very important that the objectives of the top management are clearly communicated to the Product or Development Manager.

The Product manager does not operate alone. He has a team of workers working with him. It is the duty of the management to see that both the Product Manager and his team are recruited using the right and scientific process so that the right kind, and qualified people are appointed for the job. Work well begun is half done, and if the right people are selected the work of product planning and development will proceed smoothly. The top management has to also decide the budget to be allotted for Product Planning and development. There is no hard and fast method for deciding upon the budget. However the common practices are of setting a figure comparable with what the competition is setting, or by setting objectives for new product development work and then assessing each element of the objectives and planning and making the estimate.

The success of new product development lies in observing the following principles:
1. Clarity of thought on the part of the management.
2. Clear objectives and policies of the management.

3. The right attitude and patience of the top management.
4. Selection of the right kind of personnel to carry out the work of Product Planning and Development.
5. The allocation of the right budgetary amount for the work of Product Planning and Development.
6. A workable organisation structure.

When the work of development of a new product is undertaken an organisation can either assign the work to an existing manager or create a new department of product planning or set up a committee to take on the extra work. The way in which the extra work is handled will decide the type of organisation structure. Basically the product development activity can be handled by the following organisation structures:

1. **Assignment handled by Product or Development Manager:** Most companies do not wish to recruit new persons or transfer persons to new posts. They prefer to give the new assignments to the existing staff. However the existing present workload may not give the existing staff sufficient time for thinking and planning for new product development or they may not have sufficient knowledge, information and know how about the new work entrusted to them. They may also be ignorant about the procedures to be followed.

2. **Establishment of New Product Development department with a Product Manager at its helm:** The management can create a separate post of a Product Manager and recruit a new person to take charge of the post. This new post should be given the necessary authority so that the work can be effectively carried out. This new product manager can either head an existing group of people or a totally new department can be created to carry out this work. This new department should have the necessary infrastructure and facilities and would be responsible for the work of development right from the concept stage to the commercial or mass production stage for national launching.

3. **New Product teams or Committees:** Many companies have the policy of giving this responsibility to a committee or a group of people instead of an individual or a separate department. In such a case, a committee consisting of senior management persons from all areas such as production, purchase, marketing, design, finance, maintenance etc is formed. This committee or team is responsible for developing a new product within a specified time and budget. A chairman of the team is appointed who is responsible for co-ordinating the effort of all the members of the group. The work is divided and each member of the group is responsible for the work allotted to him. The channels of communication should be kept open and communication gaps should be avoided. It would be desirable to have the minutes of every meeting properly recorded and reports circulated to all concerned members.

4.4 Role of Product Manager

A product manager is a member of the middle-level management and shoulders the responsibility for the marketing of the product of the organisation or the marketing of a particular product line. A product manager is a specialist in the sense that he usually shoulders the complete responsibility for a particular product market. However he is also a generalists as he is expected to be conversant with all the elements of the marketing mix.

Each product or brand manager is provided with the required resources to perform the day to day marketing functions and decisions. A product managers role differs from organisation to organisation. However, his role can be divided into two parts:

1. **Shouldering the responsibility for the efficient marketing of existing products or product of the organisation:** A major portion of a product managers duties involves shouldering the marketing responsibilities for the efficient marketing and decision making for the existing product or products of the organisation.
2. **Taking an active lead in the planning for New Product:** A product or brand manager is also expected to assume an active role in the development of new products. As a product manager is supposed to have a complete knowledge of the buying process related to the products he handles, he is expected to come up with various ideas for development of new products. As far as development of new products is concerned he has to be in close contact with the top management and provide them with all relevant data and recommendations so that the decision to develop a particular new product can be made expediently.

The final "go/no go" decision is based on a number of interrelated factors like technical factors, economic factors, social and political factors that affect the commercial viability of the product. In this entire process the product manager has to perform a number of tasks.

(a) He has to supervise the decisions and co-ordinate each and every aspect.
(b) He gets expert advice and recommendations from the other departmental heads like sales, production, engineering' accounting and advertising.
(c) He has to ensure that the resources are allocated as per the priorities between the existing products and the new products.
(d) To prepare and get the budget approved for the development of the new product.
(e) To set up a steering committee to monitor the progress of the new product development.
(f) To maintain and manage a critical issues plan. This plan highlights those issues which could put the development of the product at a risk. Or it highlights those issues which if not taken care of can put the entire project at risk.
(g) To arrange a post launch evaluation meeting to ensure that the lessons learnt are taken into account in the development of future products.

Even though the product manager handles a very important portfolio, his job is full problems. The major problem confronting him is that his authority does not match the responsibilities he shoulders. Further he often has to perform trivial tasks like correspondence with customers and sales personnel. This task takes away quite a chunk of his attention and time. A product manager is constantly dividing his time and attention between existing products and new products. New products require a lot of entrepreneural talent and less of management talent. By giving the responsibility of new product development to a middle level manager one cannot expect many new product developments however product modifications are possible. However, these problems do not arise when the company establishes a separate new product development department with a product manager at its helm.

Steps of New Product Development Process

Basically, there are six logical stages or steps in the process of "New Product Development". They are:

1. Idea Generation,
2. Screening of New Products,
3. Business Analysis,
4. Product Development,
5. Test Marketing,
6. Commerialisation.

1. Idea Generation

The first step in New Product development is the generation of new ideas. For it is new ideas that give us new products. New ideas generally stem from needs. It is said that necessity is the mother of invention. First a partially fulfilled or unfulfilled need is located and then it is matched with an available technology. This is how ideas are generated. This need may be an apparent or latent one, new or old one, currently partly fulfilled or unfilled. Thus when an available technology is recognised to satisfy a particular need, a product idea is generated.

Though the basic input for the development of new products is ideas, all ideas are not converted into products. A large number of ideas are generated and then the best ones are chosen to be developed into new products. The larger the number of ideas the better it is as the more the number of ideas the more better the best ones will be. There are various sources four which new ideas can be tapped and they are as under:

The sources of new ideas: The sources of generation of new ideas can basically be divided into two:

(A) Internal Sources

(B) External Sources

(A) Internal Sources

These are in-company sources of product idea generation. They are as follows:

1. **Basic Research:** Almost all companies engage in some kind of basic or fundamental research. Research and development are often divided between the development of product ideas that have already passed the initial screening stages and research into areas of technology that offer the promise of the development of a totally new product.

2. **Manufacturing:** People who manufacture products often have ideas about the modifications and improvements that can be made. It is their constant involvement with and handling of the product that enables them to come up with various ideas for the improvements that can be made in the product.

3. **Sales People:** Sales people are the ones that are in constant contact with the customers. They are the ones who know which needs of the customers are being satisfied and which are not being satisfied. Thus, they are definitely in a position to give ideas regarding new products or modifications in existing products.

4. **Top Management:** Top executives play an important role in the generation of new ideas. Their ideas ought to be good as they know about the companies needs and resources. Further they are keen observers of the technological trends and competitors actions. If nothing else they should set an example. If they expect the rest of the organisation to generate new product ideas they should be doing so as well.

(B) External Sources

(i) **Secondary Sources of Information:** Ideas for new products can be procured from various business publications that publish lists of new products. Some business magazines devote an entire section to news related to new products. Clues about new product ventures can also be got from the list of available licences.

(ii) **Competitors:** Information about new products can be got by keeping tabs on the new product activities of the competitors. Of course it is not at all an easy job to get information about the new product activity of any organisation. However good inferences can be drawn on the basis of indirect evidence gained from salesmen, suppliers, and even customers.

(iii) Customers: Customers are a very good source of new ideas. When customers give information regarding problems in existing products, it usually leads to product improvements. Some educated customers write directly to the manufacturers with suggestions for product changes. Letters of complaints and complements are also the sources for new product ideas

(iv) Inventors: Certain people with a scientific bend of mind are always creating new products. Such inventors approach companies with new ideas for products. To make sure that the ideas received from this source are appropriately screened, and not lost due to early rejection, some companies identify such inventors and support them.

2. Screening of New Product Ideas

The first stage in new product development aims at increasing the number of product ideas. However every subsequent stage aims at reducing the number of ideas that were got in the first stage. Screening is the first stage in which the ideas are short listed. In fact it is the stage in which a majority of the ideas got in the first stage are eliminated. This is a very crucial stage for if a poor idea is allowed to pass through this stage it will lead to a lot of wasted efforts in terms of time and money till this poor idea is abandoned at a later stage. Hence this process of screening has to be carried out very carefully so as to ensure that only the worthy ideas are selected and all the non viable ideas are dropped at this stage itself.

3. Business Analysis

This is the third stage in the process of new product development. It involves an in-depth study of the "Economic" feasibility of the idea. An attempt is made to predict the economic consequences of the development, manufacture and marketing of this product on the company as a whole. In this stage an analysis is done in order to estimate the profitability of the development of the product idea. It is a rigorous and expensive activity that is carried out in order to drop out those ideas that do not conform to the conditions of business analysis.

Business analysis covers projections of future demand, sales, costs, investments and revenues. This is done so as to see whether the profit predictions of the product fits into the overall objectives of the firm or not. If it fits, then further development of the product idea is undertaken. If it does not fit then the idea is abandoned at this stage. The basic emphasis of this stage is on profits and profitability. However other considerations such as social responsibilities of the organisation are also considered. Ideas that satisfy the test of this stage pass on to the next stage.

4. Product Development

Until this stage the existence of the product is purely on paper only. This stage marks the first step of the product coming into actual existence. In this stage a prototype of the product is developed and a marketing campaign for the product is planned. During this stage the design of the product is formulated and a technically and commercially viable method of manufacture is developed.

In this stage a product idea that appears sound from the business point of view is handed over to the research and development department. This stage includes not only the development of the product itself but also the further development of the manufacturing, packing and distribution costs. Product development is a scientific task leading to the designing and development of a prototype working model on the one hand and a testing of the functioning of the product on the other hand.

This stage is very important because of the following:

(i) **It gives a concrete form:** It is in this stage that a concrete form is given to the product. Upto this stage the product was just an idea on paper.

(ii) **It speaks of investment:** This stage points out the technical difficulties that can be faced in the development and manufacture of the new product. It also points out the estimates of costs to be incurred in order to overcome these difficulties.

(iii) **It provides a definite answer:** This stage also points out in very definite terms whether the product idea can be translated into a technically and commercially feasible product. If not the company's investment upto now is lost.

5. **Test Marketing**

During the phase of product development the prototype of the product was placed in the hands of the customer for their evaluation, i.e. the customers were asked to comment upon or react to the product, its uses, packaging, advertising appeals etc. They were not asked to buy the product in a real market hence the need for the present stage of test marketing.

Test marketing is the production of the technically viable prototype on a small scale and marketing this product in a small selected market. Test marketing is the actual experiment of actual buying and selling of the product within a limited market, for a period that is hoped to be long enough to indicate its probable success on a large scale and on an indefinite basis. In this experiment the market place is used as a laboratory. Test marketing is the stage in which the entire product and marketing programme is tried out for the first time in a small number of well chosen and authentic sales environment.

Test marketing is undertaken for the following reasons:
1. To improve the knowledge of potential product sales.
2. To Pre-test alternative marketing plans.
3. To predict product failures.
4. To know the reaction of competitors.

Test marketing may not be undertaken by all enterprises for all the products. The enterprises which are confident about their products and marketing strategies may drop test marketing. Test marketing is more commonly carried out for consumer products than for industrial products. However when test marketing is carried out the following procedure is usually carried out.

Procedure for Test Marketing

1. **Selection of the cities:** The first step in test marketing is to determine the cities or markets in which the test marketing is to be done. While deciding upon this, two factors have to be taken into consideration: (a) Cost of testing (b) Representativeness. The markets chosen should be such that it represents all types of customers and their behaviour. Further it should be one in which the cost of testing can be within the limits.

   An ideal market with representation from all types of customers and fitting with the cost budgets should be chosen.

2. **The length of test run:** The duration of the test run basically depends upon three factors: (a) the average repurchase period (b) competition (c) cost.

   - **The average repurchase period:** Where the average repurchase period is long the duration of the test marketing will be long and where the average repurchase period is short the test marketing will be for a shorter period.
   - **Competition:** The length of the test run depends to a great extent on the existence of competition. If there is severe competition then the length of the test run cannot be too small as enough time has to be given so that the right results are drawn. Similarly too long a test period will give the competition enough time to come out with an improved product.
   - **Cost:** The cost of the test run is one of the deciding factors for test duration. The longer the period of test the higher is the cost and vice versa.

3. **Collection of necessary information:** The next step in test market is to collect the necessary information so that unbiased results can be procured from this information. Exactly what information is to be collected should be decided in advance. Basically the information to be collected is related to sales and profitability.

4. **The action to be taken:** Depending upon the information got further action is to be taken. If the sales are excellent a decision to go ahead with the commercial production of the product may be taken. If the sales are fair a decision to modify the product and undertake another test run may be taken and if the sales are poor the decision to abandon the product may be the right decision.

6. **Commercialisation**

Those products that pass the test marketing stage successfully are ripe or commercialisation the last stage. By now the company is quite confident about the future of the product. The products profits look good in relation to the risks and costs involved. Commercialisation is the actual introduction of the product into the market, with all the related decisions and committing of resources. Commercialisation is to implement the decision taken at the earlier stages and committing the resources to implement the launch of the new product into the market.

The product is not generally introduced in all the markets at the same time. It is introduced in the prime markets first and then in the secondary markets.

4.5 Product Life Cycle

Like human beings products also have a life span. The product like cycle begins when after going through the various stages of development it is introduced into the market for the first time on a commercial basis. After its introduction it passes through various stages till it is finally abandoned i.e. discontinued from the market. These stages taken together are known as "The product life cycle". The life cycle of a product comprises of four stages i.e. introduction, growth, maturity and decline. However it should be noted that this is purely a theoretical concept.

1. **Introduction Stage:**

During this stage the product is introduced into the market for the first time. As the product is new a lot of promotional expenditure has to be incurred in order to make the people aware about the characteristics and features of this new product. As the consumers are unaware about the availability of the product sales are slow to pick up, and profits are negligible. During this stage there is virtually no competition, as the product is yet to make its mark in the commercial world. This stage witnesses a large number of product failures and hence competitors are vary of entering the market at this stage. It is only when the product shows signs of promising profits that competition enters the scene.

This stage is marked by the following features:
1. High investment in promotional expenditure.
2. Limited sales and low profits.
3. Limited competition

2. **Growth Stage:**

After the introduction of the product, it gradually starts gaining acceptance with the customers and sales start increasing. As the sales pick up other competitors who were keenly watching the market come up with competing products. The sales keep rising and the market expands. Production increases. The number of distribution outlets increase. As this stage witnesses an increase in competition usually firms try to improve the quality of the products during this stage. Further a reduction in the price of the product is also done in order to increase the market share. During this stage even though the promotional expenditure is still high the promotion to sales ratio is lesser than the introduction stage as in this stage the sales are high.

This stage is characterised by the following:
1. Increase in competition.
2. Increased volume of sales.
3. Improvement in the quality of the product.
4. Price reduction.
5. Reduction in the promotional expenditure to sales ratio.

3. Maturity Stage:

As time passes the sales of the product stabilises and the growth slows down. At this point of time the product is said to have entered the maturity stage. During this stage the sales increase but at a diminishing rate. The maturity stage lasts much longer than any other stage. It is the most vital stage and all efforts must be made to prolong this stage. This stage can be divided into three parts:
1. Growth maturity
2. Stable maturity
3. Decaying maturity

1. During the growth maturity stage the sales start falling due to a saturation in the distribution system. There are no new areas of distribution to cover, nor any new and distinguished channel member available to push the sales.
2. During the stable maturity period the sales start falling because of a total saturation of market demand. All the potential buyers have tried the product. The purchase and replacement and repeat demand has already been consumed.
3. During the third stage of decaying maturity the market no longer accepts the product, as a new product has already taken its place. The sales thus start declining.

As this stage witnesses a gradual fall in the sales of the product the competition gets severe. All efforts are made to capture what is left of the market. In order to do this a lot of promotional expenditure is incurred. Because of this the weak competitors leave the market. The surviving competitors usually witness a promotional war with each trying to maximise his sale by luring the customers with attractive offers. A lot of efforts are made to modify the product and increase this stage. Some of the areas in which modifications are possible are product, market and marketing mix modifications.

This stage is characterised by the following features:
1. Increase in sales at a decreasing rate
2. Cut throat competition.
3. Exit of poor competitors.
4. New changes in the product.
5. Increase in promotional efforts.

4. Decline Stage:

During this stage the sales of the product starts falling. This is because the demand has been channelised elsewhere. The reasons for the fall in demand may be the introduction of a new and better substitute product, change in fashion, tastes and preferences of the customers, changes in technology etc. During this stage the sales fall to near zero level, and the product is gradually pushed out from the market. This stage is inevitable for most products. Usually companies decide upon a discontinuation of the product during this stage and withdraw from the market. One or two big companies remain in the market till the end in order to mop up the last bits of demand.

This stage is characterised by the following features:

1. A drastic reduction in sales.
2. Decline in profits.
3. Exit of the product from the market.

4.6 Price Mix

What is Price?

In all business and non-business transactions, the product or services offered to the consumer has some price depending upon the value of the product or service in a particular situation. Price is the only element of the marketing mix, which gives sales revenue. All other elements i.e. product, promotion and physical distribution (place) are a part of the cost.

It is not easy to define 'price'. Economists define 'price' as it's the exchange value of a product. To the consumer the price is an agreement between seller and buyer concerning what each is to receive. Price is the mechanism or device for translating into quantitative terms (rupees and paise) the perceived value of the product to the customer at a point of time.

Price can be defined as the amount charged for the product or service including any warranties or guarantees, delivery, discounts, services or other items that are part of the conditions of sale and are not paid for separately. To the buyer, price is a package of expectations and satisfactions. Thus, price must be equal to the total amount of benefit (physical, economic, social, ecological and psychological benefits.) Any change in the price will bring about a change in the satisfaction derived. To the ultimate consumer, the price he pays for a product or service represents a sacrifice of purchasing power. Prices paid by resellers are also sacrifices. To the consumer, 'price' is a product disfeature, i.e., a feature of which he disapproves. However to a seller, price, is a source of revenue and a main determinant of profit. To the seller it is a product feature most welcome.

Elements / Variables of Price Mix

There are a good many variables affecting the price of a product namely its nature, nature of the market, cost of manufacture, cost of marketing, sales policies and methods, channels of distribution and competitor's prices. The basic price variables relate to: The pricing policies, terms of credit, and resale price maintenance.

1. **The Pricing Policies and Strategies:** The pricing policies and strategies are the guidelines and the frames within which management adjusts pricing so as to match the market needs. Giving various types of discounts is one of the pricing policies used by companies to attract buyers or to meet competitive pressures.

   (a) **Discounts:** Discount is the price difference that reduces the quoted price so that the buyer pays much less than the quoted price. Discounts are reductions from the price list given by a seller to a buyer, who either gives up some marketing function or provides the function himself. Discounts are given to final consumers, customers or channel members for doing something or accepting less of something. In deciding the discount policies the marketer has to carefully find out exactly which function the buyer is giving up or providing when he gets each of the following discounts.

   (b) **Quantity Discount:** Quantity discounts are given to encourage customers to buy in larger amounts. This lets a seller get more of a buyer's business or shifts some of the storing function to the buyer or reduces shipping and selling costs, or all of these.

   (c) **Trade Discount:** Trade discount or functional discount is the deduction given from the quoted price because of the specific position enjoyed by the buyer in the channel of distribution. The aim is to compensate the channel members for the services rendered by them. Trade discount is a percentage deduction of the quoted price and differs from industry to industry, from company to company and from product to product.

   (d) **Cash Discount:** Cash discount is the deduction given from the invoice price granted to all those who clear their bills within the desired time limit.

   (e) **Seasonal Discount:** Seasonal discounts are discounts offered to encourage buyers to stock earlier than the present demand requires. If used by producers, this discount tends to shift the storing function further along the channel. It also tends to even out sales over the year and therefore permits year round operations.

2. **Terms of Credit:** The more the sales of a product, the more will be the production of that product. The larger the production, the more economies of scale the firm will be able to enjoy. It is the credit facility offered by various business houses that many

a times takes the demand to a level where economies of scale can be enjoyed. If credit is not offered then the size of the market would not increase, and thus economies of scale would not be enjoyed and thus production would not be worthwhile. It is credit sales that make production worthwhile.

Thus the expansion of modern businesses is built up on credit. Credit is the breath of modern marketing efforts. No firm can think of survival without offering credit facility. It is a means of sales promotion. Its significance is in its contribution to efficient selling. However, even though credit influences sales to a considerable extent it should be kept in mind that it is a financial matter and the credit obligation of the business house must be kept at a prudent level.

Of the total turnover of the business houses, the credit share ranges anywhere between 60-95%. The business houses grant credit to wholesalers and the wholesalers grant credit to retailers, who in turn grant credit to consumers. In case of direct selling, credit is granted to customers through hire purchase and installment purchase schemes. An organisation frames its policies regarding credit depending upon the nature of the product, its marketability, class of consumers, competitor's terms and consumer and credit facilities made available by financial institutions.

3. **Resale Price Maintenance:** Resale price maintenance is a practice whereby the manufacturer or distributor recommends the price and/or the profit margin at which the down line channel members will sell a product. It is a policy of establishing a minimum resale price below which a wholesaler or a retailer may not sell the manufacturers products. Resale price maintenance is designed to prevent excessive cost cutting by the intermediaries and the consequent reductions in their profit margins. Resale price maintenance maintains the prestige of the advertised brand and generates co-operation and merchandising support of dealers. Further, the consumers too are protected against over charging by the middlemen.

4.7 Need and Importance of Pricing

The importance of pricing as a function of marketing is brought out in the following points:

1. **Price is essential to marketing:** Price is a matter of great importance to both the buyer and the seller in the market place. In money economy without prices there can be no marketing. Price denotes the value of a product or service expressed in monetary terms. Only when a buyer and a seller agree on the price, does exchange and transfer of ownership take place.
2. **Price allocates recourses:** In a free market economy and to some extent in a controlled economy, the resources can be allocated and reallocated by the process of price reduction and price increase. Price is used as a weapon, to realise the goals of a planned economy, and to allocate resources towards sectors, which have priority from the planning point of view.

3. **Price determines the general standard of living:** Price influences consumer purchase decisions. It reflects the purchasing power of money and thus reflects the general standard of living. The lower the prices in an economy, the greater will be the purchasing power in the hands of the consumer and the higher will be the standard of living.

4. **Price regulates demand:** Price is the strongest 'P' of the four "Ps" of the marketing mix. The marketing manager can regulate the demand of a product by increasing or decreasing its price. To increase demand, reduce the price and to decrease demand increase the price. However as an instrument to control demand, price should be used by those who are familiar with the dangers involved in using price as a mechanism to control demand, as the damage done by improper pricing can ruin the effectiveness of a well-conceived marketing programme.

5. **Price is a competitive weapon:** Price is an important weapon to deal with competition. Any company whether it is selling high, medium or low priced products, has to decide as to whether its prices will be above, below or equal to the prices set by the competitors. This is a basic policy issue and affects the entire planning process.

6. **Price is a determinant of profitability:** Price influences the sales revenue of a product, which in turn determines the profitability of the firm. Price, thus is the basis of generating profits for the firm. A change in the price mix of the marketing mix can be made more easily than a change in any other element of the marketing mix. Thus price changes are used more frequently for defensive and offensive strategies of a firm. The impact of price rise and fall is reflected instantly in the rise and fall of the profitability of a product, all other variables remaining the same.

Thus price is a powerful marketing instrument. Every marketing plan involves a pricing decision. As such all marketing planners should make accurate and planned pricing decisions.

Objectives of Pricing

The pricing objectives can be divided into two:

1. **Short-Term Objectives**

Following can be the short-term objectives of the pricing policy adopted by an organisation:
- Meeting existing competition,
- Discouraging new competition,
- Securing key accounts,
- Recovering cash rapidly,
- Attracting new customers, distributors, agents,
- Using spare capacity,
- Trimming off overall demands.

2. Long-Term Objectives

The long-terms objectives of the pricing policy can be categorised as follows:

- Return on assets,
- Stabilising prices,
- Retaining target market share,
- Strategic pricing in different market,
- Keeping competition outside the market.

Depending upon the pricing objectives to be achieved, the organisation adopts a pricing method or strategy.

Factors Influencing Pricing / Factors Affecting Pricing Decisions

The marketing executive sets the product price between a lower and an upper limit. The upper limit is the highest value that the customer is likely to put on the product or service offered at a particular point in time. While the lower limit is the cost of manufacturing, promoting, distributing the product and also includes reasonable margins for the channel members. The actual price is fixed somewhere between these two extreme points. While setting the price, the marketing manager is influenced by many internal and external factors. The internal factors are the controllable ones and the external factors are the ones over which the marketing manager has no control. Let us here see each of these factors and how they influence the pricing of a product.

(A) Internal Factors Influencing Pricing

1. **Organisational Factors:** Organisational factors refer to the internal arrangement that a firm has for decision-making and its implementation. Normally in any firm, decision making for pricing occurs at two levels. One is the top-level management, which determines the basic price range for the product range with reference to various market segments. And the other is the lower level management that deals with the pricing decision. The price mechanism is the outcome of marketing and production specialists. Further they are greatly assisted by computers. Also pricing decisions may be centralised or decentralised. Thus the way in which an organisation is made up and functions, greatly influences the pricing decisions.

2. **Marketing Mix:** Price is an important component of the marketing mix. However while taking pricing decisions the other components namely product, promotion and physical distribution cannot be disregarded. Pricing decisions should not be taken in isolation but together with the total marketing strategy and should avoid conflict with the other elements of the marketing mix. Price changes will bring in the desired results only if they are properly combined with the other components of the marketing mix. Price changes that ignore the other elements of a marketing strategy have brought in disastrous results.

3. **Product Differentiation:** Product differentiation is the ability of the marketer to make his product distinct from others in the market. This difference is relevant to the consumers and may be real or imaginary. One product can be differentiated from another by use of package, design, size, colour, shape or an advertising theme. Thus toilet soap cakes are the same but can be differentiated by colour or smell. Thus a company can have different pricing for differentiated products. The fragrance of soap can be a point for differential pricing. Also the reputation of a firm can be a base for price differentiation.

4. **Product Cost:** Many of us think that costs determine the price of a product. That is price is cost plus profit. However production costs merely determine the existence of a business. It is demand and competition that determines the price. Precisely it is the market that determines the price and price that determines costs. However there is a close relationship between price and cost. It is the effort of every firm to cover all the costs so that the firm has a fair chance of making a profit. Though profit earning and maximisation are the goals of all pricing, it may not always be possible to do so.

5. **Product Life Cycle:** The pricing policy to be followed should be in keeping with the age of the product. What stage of the life cycle the product is in will decide the pricing policy to be followed. In the product introduction stage, the pricing policy to be followed is one of market penetration. That is the prices are kept at the lowest possible level. This builds goodwill. In the growth stage prices can be raised to the extent tolerated by the consumers. However abnormal rise is dangerous. In the product maturity stage, prices can be raised by following the policy of market skimming. (Market skimming means pricing at such a level that only the cream of society can afford to buy). However this should be done with utmost care as the competitors are in action. In the decline stage the prices are to be reduced to maintain the demand. Thus which stage of the life cycle the product is in, determines the pricing policy to be followed.

6. **Length of Channel of Distribution:** If the firm has a longer channel of distribution, the price to be paid by the consumer is bound to be higher than if there is a shorter channel. However this does not mean that the channel should be kept at the shortest possible level "so as to reduce the price to be paid by the ultimate consumer. But a sound channel management can bring about a reduction in the price of the product. Shortening the channel should be done by considering the merits of each individual case. Further there is a need for a coordinated functioning of all the channel members so that control over the internal operations, selling, advertising, and administrative costs can be maintained.

(B) External Factors Influencing Pricing

The pricing decisions of a firm are also affected by external uncontrollable factors, which are to be carefully analysed and interpreted. These factors are:

1. **Product Demand:** Demand is the single most important factor having a great impact on price, pricing policy and strategy followed by a firm. It is the nature and magnitude of demand that is most relevant to product pricing. The demand may be elastic, inelastic, perfectly elastic, or perfectly inelastic. The pricing decisions will vary depending upon the exact nature and the extent of elasticity.

   A perfect elastic condition brings about more than a proportionate increase in demand with a slight fall in the market price. Thus, a 5% fall in the price brings about say a 30% increase in demand. In case of elastic demand, normally called as unit elasticity, a 10% fall in the price would bring about a 10% increase in demand.

   In case the situation is that of perfect inelasticity, even a substantial fall in the price would not pull up the demand. Say a 25% fall in price will bring the demand up by 01%. However in case of inelasticity of demand the severity is reduced. Say 20% fall in price will bring up the demand by 05%. The conditions or magnitudes are not absolute but relative. It is the study of actual demand conditions that paves the way for price decisions and policies.

2. **Competition:** Knowing one's competitor is critical to successful marketing planning. The firm should constantly compare its products, prices, channels and promotion with those of the competitors. The company is supposed to know: who are its competitors, what their objectives are, what are their strengths and weaknesses, and what their reaction pattern is. A company's competitors include those who are seeking the same customers, or fulfilling same consumer needs, and making similar offers to them. A competitor's objectives, strengths and weaknesses go a long way towards making clear the possible moves and reactions of the rival companies to moves of the company like a price hike, or a price cut, or a promotion programme or introduction of a new product or grant of liberal credit facilities. The competitor's reactions or proactions are related to their philosophy of doing the business, their internal culture and beliefs. A firm's pricing policy thus depends upon the pricing and substitution policy of its competing firms.

3. **Economic Conditions:** The economic conditions prevailing in the country or region do have an impact on the firm's pricing policy. If the economic condition is good, generally the demand for the product is also high. However boom periods encourage the entrance of competition and this leads to keen competition. During periods of recession, price-cuttings are usually seen. Thus pricing decisions depend upon economic conditions.

4. **Government Regulations:** The governments of nations influence the pricing policies in a number of ways. The government happens to be the largest employer

and the biggest buyer in the economy. For e.g.: in defense industry, electronics industry, car industry, food grains etc. the government is the single largest buyer and thus influences prices. It also regulates the prices of the products and services that it makes available to the community like electricity, postal services, transport etc. Further we have various acts and laws in place for protecting the consumer from exploitation through unreasonable price hikes and artificial scarcity conditions by marketers. Thus marketers should consider all government regulations while drafting pricing policies and strategies.

5. **Ethical Considerations:** Business principles and ethics hardly go together. However, most business houses make a serious effort to maintain an image of themselves in the back-drop of ethical values. The most common problem faced by managers today is how high they can allow prices to move. The business principle says "Charge what the market can bear", however this is purely a business consideration. When seen from the ethical angle this price will be able to be met by only the rich class of consumers. The poor and people badly in need of the product or service will not be able to afford it. Thus ethical norms say that pricing should be such that the firm makes a reasonable profit, it maintains quality standards, time and place dimensions of supply. These conditions are sure to improve the company's image.

6. **Suppliers:** The pricing policy of a firm is also influenced by the price of the inputs to the manufacturing process as well as the pricing policy of the suppliers. Thus the price of a textile manufacturer will be influenced by the price of the cotton, which is a major input. Similarly the price of an automobile is bound to increase if the price of the parts like batteries, belts, spark plugs, windscreens, mudguards etc. move up. If the suppliers realise that their input is significant and cannot be substituted they may raise their prices to capitalise on this fact. Thus the pricing decisions of a firm are affected by the pricing decisions of the suppliers.

7. **The Buyer Behaviour:** Buyers here mean both industrial buyers and final consumers. The composition of these buyers and their behaviour has an impact on the pricing decisions of the firm. Generally, if the buyers are more in number and smaller in strength, less will be the impact on the company's pricing as they are too small to influence unless they are well organised. A few but large buyers can greatly influence the pricing decisions. Again the pricing policy to be followed would be different in case of industrial users and final users. The firm cannot have an identical pricing policy for different types of consumers.

Thus the decision makers for pricing decisions have to be aware of both the controllable and uncontrollable factors that have an impact on pricing, while drafting the pricing policies and strategies to be adopted.

4.8 Pricing Methods / Pricing Strategies

A company has a choice of various strategies and methods to choose from while resolving pricing issues. Some of them are as follows:

(A) Cost Oriented Pricing Strategy

Costs establish the base for the possible price range and there are two commonly used cost oriented pricing methods. They are (1) Cost Plus Pricing and (2) Target Return Pricing.

1. **Cost Plus Pricing or Mark-up Pricing:** This method is considered the best approach to pricing. It is based on the sellers per unit cost of the product plus an additional margin of profit. That means the following items are taken into account while determining the sales price. They are:
   - Cost of producing or acquiring the goods,
   - Cost of operating or selling expenses,
   - Interest, depreciation etc.,
   - Expected profit margin- or mark up.

   The expected profit margin or the mark up is usually decided as a percentage of the selling price. This pricing method is very popular in retail trade and wholesale trade.

   The mark up or percentage of profit varies from goods to goods. Very expensive premium products will have a mark up of around 30 - 40% where as expensive consumer goods will have a mark up of 20-30% and ordinary consumer goods will have a mark up of around 10 - 15%.

   The main drawback of cost plus pricing is that it does not take into account the current demand elasticity while setting the selling price. Any system that does not take into consideration the current demand elasticity while setting the price may not achieve maximum profits.

2. **Target Return Pricing or Target Pricing:** This is another very commonly used cost oriented method of pricing. Under this method, the firm establishes the price of the product with a profit that would give a predetermined target rate of return on its total cost at predetermined production levels and sales volume. The prices of many engineering products, high value consumer durable products, defence equipments and machinery are set using this method. Before setting the price using this method, the management must determine the fixed cost and the variable cost at various levels of production and determine the breakeven volume. Only then can the management decide the target profit-depending upon the rate of return.

   Target pricing has some basic flaws as it is based on a predetermined sales volume. Again target pricing does not take into consideration the importance of the demand function.

(B) Demand Oriented Pricing

The importance of demand cannot be ignored while taking pricing decisions. Under this pricing strategy the pricing is decided by the intensity of demand and the consumer's perception of the product price. Under this strategy there are two methods of pricing. They are: (1) Perceived Value Pricing and (2) Demand Differential Pricing.

1. **Perceived Value Pricing:** Perceived value pricing is based on the perceived value of the product and this is done with product positioning with the target market. The company decides the price of the product keeping the perceived value of the product by consumer's in mind.

   The essential thing in perceived value pricing is to make a realistic estimate of the market's perception of the value of the product. The manufacturers may overestimate the perceived value of the product and overprice the product thus affecting sales. Again, understanding the perceived value may reduce the profit. Market feedback would give the correct idea of the perceived value of the product, which could be useful for pricing the product suitably.

2. **Demand Differential Pricing:** This is another method of demand oriented pricing called the price discrimination method, in which a product or service is sold at two or more prices that do not reflect a proportional difference in marginal cost. Price discrimination may take one of the following forms:

   (a) **Customer basis:** In which one customer may pay one price for the product at one time and place and another may bargain to get a better discount and a lower price.

   (b) **Product form basis:** Different versions of the product are priced differently as consumers will see or visualise the products differently. A refrigerator with Sun mica top will be priced higher than a refrigerator with a plastic cover or plate.

   (c) **Place basis:** The same product may be priced differently in two different markets or with two different customers as they are separated geographically.

   (d) **Time basis:** Here, the product price is changing with time, like equity share prices, or petroleum, foreign currency, gold and premium products and a seasonal product may be priced differently during the course of the day or a week or a month. For price discrimination to be effective, following situations must prevail:

   - The market must be fragmented and demand intensity will vary from segment to segment.
   - There is very little possibility of a consumer in one segment purchasing a product at a lower price and selling it at a higher price in another segment.

- There will be uniformity of price by all sellers in one segment.
- The overhead cost to maintain the price discrimination should be excessive.
- Price discrimination should not demotivate consumers from buying the product.

(C) Competition Oriented Pricing

Many firms set their prices largely in relation to the prices of their competitors. Though no firm can afford to disregard cost and demand factors in pricing, firms using this pricing strategy pay major attention to positioning their prices in relation to the prices set by the competitors. Firms using this pricing strategy price their products either above the competition, below the competition or on par with the competition. When this form of pricing is adopted there is no relation between the cost demand and price. The firm may change its price just because the competition has done so, even though there is no change in its own cost and demand.

Thus the above strategies and methods are available for the pricing decision makers to choose from while finalising their pricing decisions.

4.9 Supply Chain Management

Introduction

Creating a customer is a major task of marketing. But delivering the goods to the customer so created is the most critical task. If the product is not available when and where the consumer wants it, it is sure to fail in the market. And it is this function, that of making available the product at the place that the consumer wants it, at the time that he wants, which is carried out by the physical distribution mix, or the place mix. Modern day marketing also calls this function as Supply Chain Management.

If you go to a Supermarket and pick up a few items of the shelf like shoes, clothes, accessories, jewellery, bags or electronic products and look at the labels, you will notice that they have been manufactured in China, Japan or Bangladesh. If manufactured in India, they have been manufactured in Gujarat, Punjab or any state of India. The ordinary tea leaves you use to make your tea every day comes from Darjeeling. Computers have been shipped out of South American Factories and wooden furniture in the various retail outlets and malls is from Malaysia and China.

Global markets are expanding beyond borders and this is what is re-defining the way demand and supplies are managed. Global companies are driven to source products from markets across continents, in order to keep the cost of manufacturing down. Every company in order to be competitive is forced to keep looking out to set up production centers at places where the cost of raw material and labour is cheap. In the competitive global environment, no company has the luxury of sourcing supplies through the internal or local market only. You have to explore to find the best and cheapest sources. Thus sourcing of raw materials and vendors to supply the right quality of material, the right quantity of goods, components and raw materials, at the right price requires a dynamic procurement strategy spanning across various areas, states and countries.

It is the norm today that companies expand beyond the borders not just of the city and state but also the country to source raw materials, components and parts for their production process. The finished goods so manufactured are then disbursed through a network of channels to the various parts of the world wherever the final customer is situated.

In simple language, managing all of the above activities in a synchronised fashion and to manage demand and supply on a global scale is Supply Chain Management.

Definition of Supply Chain

The supply chain starts at the source point of raw materials, components and parts. It follows all these materials through from the point of supply to the customer. This chain includes all suppliers for all parts of the final product. It encompasses all materials and information that moves up and down the chain.

Logistics is the portion of the supply chain that deals directly with the transportation and warehousing of goods and materials.

Definitions of Supply Chain Management

Supply chain management includes the management of material and information between its movement from source to final consumer. This includes all logistics, materials handling and purchasing. The goal of the management is to increase the efficiency of its function to the maximum extent and lower the cost to the ultimate extent so that the final output is either a lowered price for the end customer, or a higher profit for the organisation.

Supply Chain Management has been defined as *"the management of a network of all business processes and activities involving procurement of raw materials, manufacturing and distribution management of finished goods"*.

Another definition states that, *"Supply chain management is the flow of goods, services, information and money from the source of materials all the way to the consumer"*.

Supply Chain Management is also called the art of management of providing the Right Product, At the Right Time, Right Place and at the Right Cost to the Customer.

According to the **Council of Supply Chain Management Professionals**, *"Supply Chain Management encompasses the planning and management of all activities involved in sourcing* and procurement, conversion, and all Logistics Management Activities". Importantly, it also includes coordination and collaboration with channel partners, which can be suppliers, intermediaries, third party service providers, and customers.

Logistics: Logistics Management is that part of Supply Chain Management that plans, implements, and controls the efficient, effective forward and reverse flow and storage of goods, services, and related information between the point of origin and the point of consumption in order to meet customer requirements.

Importance of Supply Chain Management

It is said that, today, the supply chain management system is the back-bone of a business organisation. This statement itself shows how important a component of business, is the supply chain and its management. Whenever a product is introduced and advertised in the market, a demand for the product is created. It is at this point that the consumer enquires about the product in various available retail/wholesale outlets. At this point it is very essential that the entire market in the country and all the sales counters have the product, where the customer is able to buy and take delivery. If for any reason the product is not available at the right place and the right time, it can result in a drop in the customer's interest and customer demand. This can have a disastrous effect on the success of the product.

Thus a proper Transportation network design and management is of great importance, as a support to the sales and marketing strategy. In fact it can be said that without proper transportation network design and management, there is no way that the sales and marketing strategy can succeed. Thus it is an effective supply chain management that will ensure an effective Market Coverage and the availability of the right product at the right places across various locations in the country.

Another reason why supply chain management is important is because inventory control and inventory visibility are the two critical elements in any business operation. Inventory control and visibility have a direct impact on the cost of production and hence a direct impact on the profitability of the organisation. The lesser the capital locked up in inventory the more will be the profitability and vice versa. However visibility of inventory is also a factor that has to be considered. The two have to be balanced and the right or optimum inventory turnaround has to be established. Every company has a standard for inventory turnaround that is ideal or optimum for the particular business. Inventory turnaround is the number of times the inventory is sold and replaced during a particular period. This period is usually twelve months.

Today inventory or stock of finished goods is held at many distribution centers, wholesale and retail locations across the country. These may or may not be managed by the organisation itself. Some could be managed by third parties. Inventory could also be in the pipeline in transportation. Any loss of inventory anywhere in the supply chain will result in a loss. As such the effective control of inventory is an important factor of the supply chain management function.

Essential Purpose or Objectives of Supply Chain Management

"The goal of logistics and supply chain management is timely delivery, competitive pricing, mobility, and flexibility, together with innovative transportation services".

The basic objective of supply chain management is to ensure minimum cost and maximum efficiency in every aspect of handling of raw material, component parts and finished goods as they move from production centre to the final consumer. Effective supply chain bridges the following gaps that exist between the producer and the consumer:

Space Gap: This is the gap caused by the manufacturers and consumers being situated physically away from each other. Here supply chain moves the goods physically from the point of production to the point of distribution and fills the space gap. It is a supply chain management system that ensures that goods produced in one particular place are available for consumption to consumers at their right place

Time gaps: This is the gap that results because the manufacture of a product takes place at one point in time however it is required by the consumer at another point in time. Example - sugar is manufactured just after the harvest of sugarcane and beetroot. However sugar is demanded throughout the year. Thus the supply chain ensures that excess manufactured product is properly stored when not required and makes it available when required. It thus fulfills the time gap

Quantity gap: Quantity gap is the difference between the quantities produced and demanded. Certain products, in order to be profitable have to be manufactured in large quantities. However the demand is limited and spread over a period of time. For example a publisher cannot publish a small quantity of books. For the cost of production to be feasible, a particular number of copies of a particular book need to be published. However the sale is only of a copy per consumer. Thus this quantity gap too is taken care of by an effective supply chain management system.

Variety gap: Customers usually want a variety of products. The more the customers for a product the more variety is demanded. It is an effective supply chain management system that fills this variety gap and ensures a wide variety of goods for the customers. For example a stockist of consumer products or a retailer will keep soaps of various brands and manufacturers, thus ensuring a wide range of soaps for the consumer to choose from.

Information gap: It is the supply chain that bridges this gap. An information gap exists when either the supplier or the consumer does not have information about the other. That is the supplier lacks information about who or where is his consumer and the consumer lacks information about the various available options that are available to fulfil his product need. Here supply chain supplies the information and bridges this gap.

Scope of Supply Chain Management

Supply Chain Management includes, planning, design, control and implementation of all business processes related to procurement, manufacturing, distribution and sales order fulfillment functions of a business. Thus Supply Chain Management includes managing supply and demand, sourcing raw materials and parts, manufacturing and assembly, warehousing and inventory tracking, order entry and order management, distribution across all channels, and delivery to the customer. Due to its wide scope, supply chain management must address complex interdependencies, in effect creating an "extended enterprise" that reaches far beyond the factory doors.

All these activities involve multiple networks of vendors and service providers. These networks of suppliers and service providers have to be integrated and coordinated by the supply chain management experts in such a way that the raw material moves smoothly from various procurement points to the centers of production and the finished goods move smoothly from the centers of production to the various points of sale/ delivery to consumer, across the globe.

Logistics is the back bone on which the supply chains are driven. Logistics refers to the management of flow of goods and supplies involving information, data and documentation between two entities or points. Logistics plays an important role in the post procurement function of delivery of raw material and supplies from the supplier to the factory or production center and the dispatch of finished goods from the factory to the point of delivery to the customer.

When goods move from supplier to factory to point of sale they flow through a network of transportation by road, rail, ship or air. They may be stored in warehouses before being moved to forward locations. This entire activity involves various suppliers, agents and agencies including freight forwarders, packers, customs department, distributors and Logistics service providers etc.

Logistics therefore is an integral component of Supply Chain Management.

In many cases Supply chain is often referred to as Logistics and vice-versa. Though logistics and supply chain are intricately linked, both do not mean the same. Logistics is a sub component and extension of supply chain.

Market Logistics Decisions - Channel Structure

Market Logistics decisions basically pertain to all decisions affecting the transportation, movement and warehousing of raw material, supplies and finished goods as they move from source centres to production centres to the final consumers. Apart from this Market logistics decisions would also include the type of channel selected by the company. A company has a choice of various different channels. Some short, other long.

Companies today are looking at moving away from conventional supply chain system towards a supply chain network. What they are looking at is creating value networks by partnering with the various channel members. The choices for the creative and dynamic supply chain manager are many.

Here first let us study the various distribution intermediate available for the supply chain manager to make a choice from the base his market logistics decisions. Let us also study their characteristics as well as the various different types of distribution channels available.

4.10 Types of Distribution Intermediaries and their Characteristics

'Intermediaries' are the middlemen in the channel that take title to the goods and sell at a profit or do not take title to the goods but sell for a commission. These intermediaries could be individual businessmen and/or institutions/firms. The **American Marketing Association** has defined the term 'middlemen' as, *"one who specialises in performing operations of rendering services that are directly involved in the purchase and sale of goods in process of their flow from producers to the users"*.

Marketing intermediaries are the individuals and the organisations that perform various functions to connect the producers with the end-users. The individuals and institutions perform the functions of procurement, storage, packing, financing, transportation and counseling in linking the two ends. The important point to be noted is that these intermediaries perform these functions so efficiently and economically that it is impossible for either the producer or the consumer to do away with them.

Basically two types of middlemen are found in the distribution network of any organisation. They are Merchant middlemen and Agent middlemen. Merchant middlemen buy and sell goods on their own account at their own risk of loss. Examples of merchant middlemen are wholesalers and retailers. Agent middlemen are those that do not take the ownership title to the goods but actively negotiate the transfer of ownership from seller to buyer. Examples of agent middlemen are brokers, commission agents, factors, forwarding and clearing agents etc. Here let us see the various merchant and agent middlemen and their characteristics.

(I) Merchant Middlemen

1. Wholesalers

Wholesalers are individuals or business firms who act as the first outlet in distribution usually specialising in one or a group of allied product. Wholesalers sell the products primarily for resale or for industrial use. The wholesaler is a bulk purchaser with the object of resale to retailers or other traders after breaking down his 'bulk' in smaller quantities and, if necessary, repacking the smaller lots, into lots suitable for his customers, that is retailers. According to the **American Marketing Association** "wholesalers sell to retailers or other merchants and /or individual, institutional and commercial users but they do not sell in significant amounts to ultimate consumers". Thus wholesale trade is to do with marketing and selling goods to retailers, other traders, and/or to individuals - commercial and professional or other institutional users and not to the individual final consumer. Wholesalers perform a number of functions in the process of marketing of goods both for the producer and also for the retailer.

Wholesalers are of different types, and they can be classified into three broad categories as follows:

(a) **Full Function Wholesaler:** A Full Function Wholesaler buys the goods outright from the manufacturers and sells them to retailers or other traders. He assembles products from different sources in bulk, carries stock, sells in smaller lots, grants credit and renders valuable counsel and advice. He bears the risk of loss and offers a complete range of services to both manufacturer and retailers. Because of the wide range of functions performed by him and the services provided by him, he is known as full - line wholesaler.

(b) **Converter Wholesaler:** A converter is a full function wholesaler that buys products and sells them to the subsequent channel member after processing them. Thus a cotton textile converter wholesaler may purchase unbleached cotton textile and move it along the channel after bleaching it.

(c) **Drop Shipper Wholesaler:** A drop shipper is that wholesaler who neither stores the products nor delivers them to the buyer from his own stock, but books orders with the manufacturer, and directs the manufacturers to supply the goods directly to the retailer or the next channel member. However he has to take the delivery of the goods, in case the retailer/next channel member refuses to accept the same.

2. Retailers

The term retail implies sale for final consumption rather than for resale or for further processing. Thus a retailer is one who sells a wide variety of goods to final consumers. These goods are purchased from various sources and assembled at his premises, as per the requirements of the final consumer. A retailer is the last link in the channel of distribution. Professor **William Stanton** has defined retail trade as, *"Retailing includes all activities directly related to the sale of goods and services to the ultimate consumers for personal or business use"*. Thus retailer is that merchant intermediary who buys goods from preceding channel members and sells them to the final consumer in required quantities. Retailers can be classified in a number of ways. However the most practical and popular way is that of small scale and large retailers with further sub- classifications as under.

(A) Small Scale Retailers:

1. **Unit Stores:** Unit stores are the retail stores run on proprietary basis dealing in general stores or single-line stores such as drugs, clothes, grocery items, hard-wares, shoes, books, utensils etc. Single line stores are mostly called as speciality shops as they may specialise in one line only.
2. **Street Traders:** Street traders are the retailers who display their stock on foot-paths or the side-walks of busy spots of the cities and towns. The most prominent places are bus-stands, railway stations, parks and gardens, squares and so on. They deal in light goods in demand.
3. **Market Traders:** These retailers open their shops on fixed days or dates in specified areas. The time interval may be a week or a fortnight or a month. They do join fairs and festivals. They deal in general or special line stores. These retail outlets have fixed type of arrangements with built-in-flexibility.
4. **Hawkers and Peddlers:** This class of retailers have been there in all the centres from time immemorial. They do not have any fixed place of business. They carry the goods from one place to another on hand cart, selling the goods door to door. They keep on moving from locality to locality and business to business with the change in the seasons. Thus ice candy seller has a brisk business in summer and may change over to popcorn in rainy and winter seasons.
5. **Cheap jacks:** Cheap jack is a retailer who has a fixed place of business in a locality but goes on changing his place to exploit the market opportunities. Change of locality is quite common in case of these retailers. These deal in cheap varieties of ready garments, plastics, shoes and the like. However, the speed of change of locality is not as fast as that of hawkers and pedlars.
6. **Syndicate Stores:** It is an extension of the theory of mail order business on a small scale. Syndicate stores are known for widest varieties of goods in a product line. These retailers buy most of the unbranded varieties and try to sell under their names. These apply to readymade garments, toys, millinery items and so on.

(B) Large Scale Retailers:

1. Departmental stores:

The concept of departmental store is to provide all the goods and services under a single roof. In other words, it is a one stop shopping centre which is streamlined to get almost anything from Aspirin tablet to zip to Zodiac ties to soap. The goods are of wide variety of quality and price range.

A department store is a large retail establishment having in the same building countless departments each specialising in selling a particular item or line of products. It is an organisation of several shops under one central management.

Outstanding Features:

The main features of departmental stores are:
1. Central location in trading area.
2. Selling merchandise of many kinds with wide range of variety.
3. Emphasis on customer services.
4. Extensive use of advertising.
5. High cost of operation.
6. Application of division of labour and specialisation.

2. Chain stores:

Chain stores or multiple shops are an attempt to go nearer to consumers to residential areas using the principle of dispersion. This is another way of increasing business. Majority of the manufacturers resort to these chain or multiple shops. In India we have Bata, Planet M, Planet Fashion, Shoppers Stop, West Side and so on. We have high-way dabhas on the same lines.

A chain store consists of four or more stores which carry the same kind of merchandise, centrally owned and managed but located decentrally. These are the shops located all over the town, district, state or even entire nation dealing in same products. It is a system of branch shops operated under centralised management dealing in similar lines of goods.

Distinctive Features:

Chain store has certain specific features of its own. These are:

(a) **Cash and carry principles:** Chain stores work on cash and carry or terms cash. No credit or delivery services.

(b) **Limited items:** They deal in only one line; say readymade dresses, shoes, watches, sport, stationeries, and fast food and so on.

(c) **Standardised appearance, prices and products:** Each store located in any town or towns have same type of look, use of interiors, same goods, and same prices.

(d) **Centralised purchase and decentralised sale:** The purchase of all is made centrally in mass scale and are directed to each centre or branch throughout the network reaping economy.

(e) **Large and quick turnover:** The lines are limited and cash and carry lead to large sales and quick sales. This is an attribute in favour of management and ownership.

(f) **All goods are not suitable:** Any product cannot be sold under this style. They should possess certain qualities. These are those which can be sold quickly, products of daily use, standardized products and products that are portable.

3. **Mail Order Houses:**

We live in an age of self sufficiency and financial independence is becoming increasingly important. Mail order marketing is fast becoming one of the most popular and effective ways of selling goods and services to the general public. It is a unique form of business which gives freedom flexibility and financial independence to those who take it as a self employment means.

What is it?

Mail order business is done by post by retailing units engaged in carrying business through post or mail. The seller contacts the buyer through some media of advertising. Customers do not visit the seller's business premises nor do they make a personal examination of goods before they are bought. That is, the seller advertises his goods through press, sales literature or catalogues giving details. Of late T.V. advertising which is called as media marketing is an extension of the same. Goods or services like loans, insurance are sold via calls made to customers, also called telemarketing is common nowadays. Goods are ordered by post and delivered by V.P.P. or draft payment and sent through courier or post or other means of transport. From the customers' point of view it can be defined as "shopping by post". In other words of **Clark F.E.** "*a mail order house is that type of retail institution which solicits patronage by means of catalogues sent through mail and containing detailed description of merchandise offered by sale*". The unit running this business is called mail order house. Thus a mail order house is a retail trading unit doing business by mail wherein orders are received by post and goods are dispatched by post parcel or railway parcel and payments are made through post.

Outstanding features:

Mail order business has its unique features:
1. Dominant role of postal services.
2. Catalogues and sales literature.
3. Selected quality and standardised goods.
4. Payment in advance may be by demand draft, credit cards or V.P.P. order, money order.
5. Mailing list.
6. Multi-level marketing.

Features of goods suitable for mail order business:

All goods are not bought and sold through mail. The goods should possess certain features. These are:
1. High value with light weight.
2. Well known for their utility.
3. Fetching sufficiently high price to ensure gross profit.
4. They are durable.
5. Availability throughout the year.

4. Super Market:

A super market is a large retail store providing wider choice of consumer goods especially food and small articles of household requirements. In other words a super market is a self service food store with grocery and produce department. It carries a wide assortment of food, sundry drugs and items of hosiery and cosmetics. It specialises in food grain, groceries, fruit, meat, vegetables, medicines, drugs and so on. In other words supermarket is a "large cash and carry self-service retail store selling groceries, meat, fish, fruits and vegetables, dairy and bakery products and such other small articles of household requirement under one roof" e.g. Dorabji's.

Outstanding features:

The unique features of super market are:

1. **Dealing in basic needs under one roof:** The basic necessities of life are provided under one roof.
2. **Cash trading:** These super markets have no credit dealing. Hence, no bad debts.
3. **Self service:** No salesman is there and consumers are allowed to move from section to section with basket or trolleys as per their choice among wide range of varieties available.
4. **Packing services:** The super market deal with nicely packed product indicating price, weight, date of manufactured, date of expiry and other useful information likely to help in the safe and better use of products.
5. **Freedom of choice:** The consumers are at full liberty to choose their requirements from different sections dealing in a particular range or line of product.

5. Consumer Co-operative:

These are the retailers or stores owned by a group of consumers themselves on cooperative principles. It is an association of consumers to obtain their requirements by purchasing in bulk and selling through the stores to the member and non-member consumers. It believes in wholesale buying and retail selling at prices more reasonable than prevailing in the open market. Almost in all towns and cities in India, one comes across these consumers' cooperatives. The common name chosen is 'Apna Bazar' or 'Janta Bazar' or may be named after a locality.

II. Agent Middlemen

Agent middlemen are as important as merchant middlemen. Agent middlemen are those channel components who help in the transfer of goods from the hands of producers to the hands of ultimate users without acquiring the ownership of these goods; therefore, they do not assume any risk involved in marketing of goods; they operate for a commission and act on behalf of their principle. In other words, agent middlemen do not buy and sell the goods on their account but render a valuable service of bringing together the buyers and sellers or assume the role of striking a transaction for commission.

Types of Agent Middlemen

1. **Commission agent:** He buys and sells goods for his principal in return for a commission. He may or may not buy in his name but he does not assume any risk. He gets a fixed rate of commission for the business done. He has expert knowledge of all the commodities in which he is trading; he keeps close contacts with the producers and dealers on one hand and the market trends on the other. He procures goods as per the instructions of his principal; he gets orders and is responsible for arranging for packing, transport and delivery of goods including granting of credit and collecting the payments and the dues. He has the right to charge his principal for the costs of the goods purchased and the expenses incurred and his agreed share of commission, If he guarantees payment on goods sold on credit, he is eligible for extra commission called 'del credere' commission, over and above the normal commission.

2. **Brokers:** Broker is an agent who is employed to make bargains and contracts in matters of trade, commerce or navigation, between two parties for a compensation known as a brokerage. He is an independent agent who negotiates bargains or agreements between two or more parties for exchange. He brings together the intending buyer and the seller together. He does not take title to the goods and, hence, he does not take possession of goods. Brokers specialise in a particular branch of commerce. Thus, we have produce brokers, stock brokers, ship brokers, insurance brokers and so on. Brokers tender useful services to both the parties of exchange. First, they are bought into contact with one another. Secondly, they make actual arrangements for the delivery of goods. Thirdly, maintain extensive organisation to keep in touch with suppliers and customers. Fourthly, they give valuable advice to both the parties on the issues of marketing affecting their interests.

3. **Factors:** Factor is an agent employed to sell the goods or merchandise consigned or delivered to him by his principal for compensation. Thus, his major role is to sell the goods assigned to him under the instructions of the principal. Since selling is his sole responsibility, a factor has the power to sell the goods in his own name, and he can sell at such prices and times he thinks best. He can sell on credit: he can receive the payment and issue valid receipts on behalf of his principal; he has the lien on goods in his possession for the charges due to him and recovery of advance payments made. Thus, he takes possession of goods and sells in his own name for a commission. He finances his principal by making advance payment or immediate payment.

4. **Auctioneers:** There is some class of products where sale by auction takes place. The products like jewellery, tobacco, tea, automobiles, art pieces, land and buildings are more commonly sold by auction. Auctioneer is the legal agent of the seller till the goods are knocked down to the highest bidder. He is the intermediary between the buyer and the seller. His dealings are mostly on cash terms. He takes possession of goods and remits the sale proceeds to the seller after deducting his expenses and agreed commission. The auction is with 'reserve price' or 'without reserve price'. The first one implies that the bidder start with that minimum. Auction sale is always open to the public and, therefore, auctioneer is to give wide publicity as to the time and place of auction through newspapers, catalogues, posters, leaf-lets and the like. The advertisement gives the details of auction.

5. **Selling agents:** Selling agents are the intermediaries who are given the exclusive franchise only for a limited market segment. He performs the functions of an independent middlemen taking over all the selling activities of a producer. He negotiates sales of merchandise produced by his principal and has full authority and control over prices and the terms and conditions of the sale. Selling agents are to be differentiated from sole agents. The difference lies in terms of the restrictions imposed in regard to the territorial operations, products handled and the customers served. Sole agents are exclusive agents for whole, for substantially whole of the output without any territorial restrictions. Sole agents totally relieve the producers or manufacturers from the botheration of distribution.

6. **Forwarding and Clearing Agents:** Forwarding and clearing agents are the middlemen employed to collect, deliver and otherwise forward goods on behalf of others. Most of the manufacturing houses, with gradual expansion and growth of their business find it necessary and economical to employ the agents' middlemen to relieve them of the tedious tasks of collection, delivery and forwarding the goods to their destination. These agent middlemen have been indispensable in foreign trade. Forwarding agents receive goods from the exporters and arrange for the shipment of these goods to their destinations. Clearing agents receive goods from abroad on behalf of the importers at port of entry and arrange for their clearance. They have a professional touch and excellent operational efficiency.

4.11 Designing Distribution Channel / Factors Influencing Selection of Channel

It is very essential that the producer chooses the right channel as it involves long-term commitments to other firms with whom the marketer enters into a contract. A chosen channel cannot be terminated overnight and hence a lot of thought and analysis of a number of factors is done before the channel option is finalized. The factors influencing the choice of channel are:

1. **Product:** When deciding the channel to be adopted the first factor to be considered is the product category. A consumer product will require a different channel as compared to an industrial product. The channel of distribution for a consumer product will be a longer one, and that for an industrial product will be shorter. The other factors pertaining to product, which will have to be considered, are uses of the product, frequency of purchase, fashion, habits, perishability, level of service etc.

   If a product is perishable or fragile, a producer will prefer few and controlled levels of distribution. For perishable goods, speedy movement needs shorter channel or route of distribution. Similarly for durable and standardized goods a longer channel may be used. For technical products requiring special selling and servicing talents, the shortest channel may be used. Products of high unit value are sold directly by traveling sales force and not through middlemen. For e.g milk being a fast perishable item cannot have a long distribution chain. Vaccum cleaners, aquaguards were once upon a time sold door to door by individual salesman of companies for easy demonstrations and sale.

2. **Market:** The channel selected depends upon the nature and extent of the market. If the market size is large, we may have many channels. However if it is a small market direct selling will be more profitable. Similarly for consumer markets, the retailer is essential, whereas, in a business market, the retailer can be eliminated. For highly concentrated markets, direct selling is ideal. But where the market is widely scattered we may have more channels. The size and frequency of the customer's orders also influence the channel decision. If the ultimate buyers are numerous, the order is small, order frequency is great and the buyers insist on the right to choose from a wide variety of brands/ goods, the marketer must have three or more levels of distribution.

3. **Cost:** The most fundamental criteria for channel decision and channel choice is the economic criteria. Profit organisations are primarily interested in cost minimisation in distribution and assurance of reasonable profit margins. Thus the channel generating the largest sales volume at lower unit cost will be given priority. This will minimize cost.

4. **Channel used by rivals Competitors:** The channels used by rivals must be closely watched. Many a times it may be desirable to use the same channel as is being used by the rivals. However sometimes marketers deliberately avoid the channels that are being used by the rivals and chose the one that is not being used by the rivals. This is done to avoid competition. For example, if the rival firm is using the retail channel the marketer may decide to use door to door selling, where there is no competition.

5. **Marketing Environment:** The marketing environment can also influence the channel decision. During recession or depression, a shorter and cheaper channel is usually preferred. In times of prosperity, we have a wider choice of channel alternatives.

6. **Company:** The Company's size determines the size of the market, the size of its larger accounts and its ability to get cooperation from the middlemen. A big firm may have shorter channels. A company with substantial financial resources need not depend upon middlemen. It can afford to reduce the levels of distribution and have its own exclusive outlets. A financially weaker company has to depend upon the available middlemen. New companies have to rely upon available middlemen due to lack of experience and ability of management. A company desiring to have a better control on its products will use a shorter channel.

In short, the selection of the channel though it seems easy, is not so. The above factors taken together will influence the channel decision. Selecting the best channel will depend upon a balance of these factors and the relative importance which the management attaches to each of the factors in any particular set of circumstances. There is no `best' channel for all the manufacturers of a single class of products. Each management will have to take their own decisions depending upon their own unique situation and requirements.

Types of Marketing Channels

A marketing channel or a trade channel is the means through which goods move from the producer or the manufacturer to the ultimate consumer or industrial users. **Prof. W. Stanton** has defined it as *"it is the route taken by the title to the goods as they move from producer to the ultimate consumer or industrial user"*. Thus a marketing channel is a pipeline through which products flow on their way to the consumer. The manufacturer puts his products in the pipeline or the marketing channel and various marketing people move it along to the consumer at the other end of the channel. However the persons and institutions that render specialised services to bring about a change in the title of the goods such as banks, transportation agencies, insurance companies, and warehousing organisations are not included in the channel. The channel of distribution includes producers, wholesalers, retailers and agents and consumers or industrial users.

The most common routes used for bringing the products in the market from the producer to the consumer are as follows:

1. **Manufacturer – Consumer/User Channel (Direct Sale):** When this kind of a channel is adopted, the goods move from the manufacturer to the consumer without any kind of a middleman. Neither an agent, nor a merchant. Direct marketing is defined as an interactive system of marketing, which uses various media

of communication (one or more advertised media) to make a sale at any location or to secure a measurable response. A contact with customers at locations other than a retail store can be made through any communication medium-in person through sales force, by post (mail-order sale), by telephone, radio, television, newspapers, magazines and computers. Merchandise can be displayed and sold through vending machines.

A direct marketer is an organisation that uses personal selling, advertising, sales promotion, electronic media, vending machines etc. to promote and sell products directly to consumers or end users. Thus direct marketing is essentially any advertising activity, which creates and exploits a direct relationship between the marketer and the prospect or customer as an individual. Major direct marketing methods are: Mail order sale, telemarketing, marketing through electronic media (using television, radio, computers) and print media,Vending machines, in house marketing using sales force, and network marketing.

2. **Manufacturer – Retailer – Consumer:** This channel option is preferable when the buyers are large retailers like departmental stores, chain stores, supermarkets, shopping malls, big mail order houses or co-operative stores. This channel bypasses the wholesaler, and hence the manufacturer has to perform the functions of a wholesaler such as storage, insurance, financing of inventories, transportation etc. This channel is adopted when the products are perishable and speed in distribution is essential. Sometimes manufacturers want to have a better control over their products, they want to, know how their product is moving in the market and what is the reaction of the users to their products, and this is another reason why the wholesaler is eliminated and this channel is used. If the products are durable and subject to changes in fashion, the manufacturers prefer to eliminate the wholesaler to shorten the channel. Manufacturers use this channel for products like automobiles, appliances, men's, women's and children's clothing, shoes etc.

3. **Manufacturer – Wholesaler – Retailer – Consumer:** When this channel is adopted the goods move from the manufacturer to the wholesaler to the retailer and then to the final consumer. This is the most commonly used channel for marketing goods, and hence is known as the 'orthodox' channel of distribution. Nearly 50-60% of manufactured consumer goods are marketed using this channel. This channel is used for goods like groceries, drugs, tobacco products, hardware, dry goods etc; which have a low per unit price and the market for them is wide spread. In such a situation the services of both the wholesaler and the retailer are inevitable even if it adds to the cost.

4. **Manufacturer Agent – Wholesaler – Consumer:** Strictly speaking, the agent-middlemen are not included in the channel of distribution, for they do not take title to the goods. However, in actual practice, they play an important role in negotiating the purchase and sales of goods. It is because of this fact that they are included. This channel is nothing but the traditional 'orthodox' channel with the addition of one more middlemen in it. In this channel the manufacturer or producer uses the services of agent middlemen such as a sole selling agent, for the initial dispersion of the goods. This agent in turn may distribute to wholesalers who in turn sell to retailers. This additional middleman is used to relieve the manufacturer or producer from the worries of selling and helps him to concentrate on production on most efficient lines. This channel is used for products like imported goods, textiles. Oil products, etc. One large national sole selling agent can act as a distributor for many manufacturers. These agent middlemen operate at a wholesale level and are common in both marketing for manufactured goods as well as for agricultural goods.

5. **Manufacturer Agent – Retailer – Consumer:** This is another channel in which the wholesaler is bypassed. The agent performs the function of the wholesaler and acts as an intermediary between the retailers and the manufacturer.

6. **Manufacturer Wholesaler – Consumer/ User:** The retailer may be bypassed in the channel of distribution when there are large and institutional buyers like the government, business buyers, consumer co-operatives, hospitals, educational institutions, etc.

Thus there are six different channels for a manufacturer to choose from when deciding upon the distribution of his goods. Which channel he will choose depends upon a number of factors.

4.12 Promotion Mix: Meaning, Elements of Promotion Mix

Introduction

Promotion is marketing communication with an element of persuasion to accept ideas, products and services. Thus, persuasive communication is the heart of promotion, which is the fourth element of the marketing mix. Promotion is the process of communication to inform, persuade, remind and influence consumers or users in favour of the products and services of the organisation. Promotion has three specific purposes. It communicates marketing information to consumers, users and resellers. It persuades and convinces the buyer and influences his/her behaviour to take the desired action, and it acts as a powerful tool of competition providing the cutting edge for the entire marketing programme of a business organisation. Promotion is a non-price form of competition. Promotion has been defined as "the coordinated self initiated efforts to establish channels of information and persuasion to facilitate or foster the sale of goods or services, or the acceptance of ideas or points of view."

Elements/Scope of Promotion Mix

The promotion mix of any organisation includes four major ingredients/ elements. They are:

1. **Advertising:** The **American Marketing Association** has defined advertising as *"Any paid form of non-personal presentation and promotion of ideas, goods and services by an identified sponsor"*. Advertising is impersonal salesmanship for mass selling. It is a means of mass communication. It is salesmanship in print. It is an extremely attractive medium for the larger customer base. The purpose of advertising may also be to reassure employees or shareholders that a company is viable or successful. Advertisers often seek to generate increased consumption of their products or services through "branding," which involves associating a product name or image with certain qualities in the minds of consumers.

2. **Publicity:** Publicity is non-personal stimulation of demand for a product, service or a business unit by placing commercially significant news about it in a publication or obtaining favourable presentation of it upon radio, television, or stage that is not paid for by the sponsor. It is the deliberate attempt to manage the public's perception of a subject. Publicity is the act of attracting the media attention and gaining visibility with the public. In short it is giving out news and information about your product or services to prospective customers.

3. **Personal Selling:** In personal selling, people are used to sell products by way of face to face meeting with customers. In personal selling, a personal presentation of the product or service is made to the potential prospect by the sales person. Personal selling is the best means of verbal, face-to-face communication and presentation with the prospect for the purpose of making sales. There may be one or more prospects in the personal conversation. All presentations may not result in sales but this process will give rise to sales with some customers.

4. **Sales Promotion:** Sales promotion covers those marketing activities other than advertising, publicity and personal selling that stimulate consumer purchasing and dealer effectiveness. It includes various incentives and offers that encourage people to buy the product or service. Sales promotion activities also include displays, shows, exhibitions, demonstrations, and many other non-routine selling efforts at the point of purchase. Sales promotion tries to complement the other elements of promotion. Sales promotions can be directed at the customer, sales staff, or distribution channel members (such as retailers).

All the elements of the promotion mix together play the important role of communication channels between the marketer (the sender of the message) and the consumer (the receiver of the message). Promotion as an element of the marketing mix has three broad objectives:

1. Information
2. Persuading
3. Reminding.

The overall objective of promotion is to influence the buyer behaviour and predispositions (needs, attitudes, goals, beliefs, values and preferences) positively towards the products and services offered.

Significance of Promotion Mix

Promotion is the communication link between the seller and the buyer or consumer. It does not just provide information about the products and services, but it is an active attempt at influencing people to act by appealing to their emotions and thoughts. Thus, Promotion is not just the flow of information, but goes further to influencing and persuading people to action. This is just one side of the Promotion function, i.e. the communication side. There is another way of viewing the Promotion function; and that is from the marketing point of view.

Each organisation has marketing objectives and a marketing plan to achieve them. An organisation also identifies the segments of the market it intends to serve. In the process of achieving its marketing objectives, the organisation uses several marketing tools. In a study of marketing management, four variables are identified, which are well within the controllable limits of the individual organisation. They are popularly known as 4 P's - Product, Place, Price and Promotion. An ideal mix of these four variables is known as the ideal marketing mix to realize the set marketing objectives. This means that the right product should be developed and offered through a distribution network suitable to the organisation and the target market segment. The product should not be too costly and should be offered with a suitable promotion strategy. Under promotion, the marketer provides face-to-face communication with individuals or a group of buyers, as well as mass communication with a large audience by way of advertising. Thus Promotion is a major part of the marketing mix of any organisation.

Promotion as a part of the total marketing mix influences the sale of the product, as do the other variables of the mix. Together with the product or brand, price and channel of distribution, promotion attempts to achieve the marketing objectives. When a firm offers a prestigious product with a premium price, the promotional messages should reinforce the idea of the high quality and prestige of the product by associating it with prestigious people, places and events. Similarly, the Promotional message will be different depending upon the distribution strategy adopted by the firm. For e.g. an intensive distribution strategy will require a different form of Promotion to match it whereas a distribution strategy through selected or exclusive outlets will require an altogether different one.

All components of the promotion strategy should be complementary to each other. For example - advertising should be complementary to personal selling, which is another marketing tool primarily concerned with communication. In personal selling, communication is more effective, as it can be tailored to suit each individual prospect. Further in personal selling the sales message can be altered on the spot depending upon the response of the prospect. However, advertising supports personal selling and hence should be so designed that it is able to do this.

In short Promotion, being one of the marketing tools affects the sales of the firm. Right Promotion strategy is as essential as right product, right price and right distribution channel. Thus Promotion as a tool of marketing if planned and used properly will lead to the achievement of the marketing objectives. The achievement of marketing objectives will in turn lead to various consumer benefits as highlighted in another part of this chapter.

Factors affecting Market Promotion Mix / Factors Influencing Promotion Mix

The promotion mix of any organisation is a combination of the above four elements that is advertising, sales promotion, personal selling and publicity. How to blend all these four elements of the promotion mix, the amount to be allocated for the various forms of promotion, such decisions are influenced by the following factors:

1. **The Product:** The nature of the product determines the form of promotion undertaken by the marketer. Products like toys, toilet soap and cosmetics are effectively shown on television. Products targeting children will not use press advertisements as a means of promotion. Industrial and specialty goods are promoted through technical journals and through salesmen. Mass selling consumer goods are promoted through advertising, and sales promotion.

2. **The Buyer:** The promotion mix used by the marketer also depends upon the type and nature of the buyer. If the marketer has to provide realistic solutions to the problems of the buyers, they must know their customers, their needs, their desires, their attitudes, values, expectations and aspirations. Hence first the marketer must have an up to date information about who his buyer is and depending upon the characteristic and nature of his buyers the marketer decides upon that promotion mix which will most appeal to his class of buyer.

3. **The Company:** Every firm has a unique public image in the market. The firm's image must be closely associated with the promotional strategy so that its goodwill can be exploited. The image and reputation of the brand cannot be separated from the corporate image and reputation of them. In fact just as every child has a reflected reputation of his family (that is his birth right) so also every brand has a reflected corporate image of its company. Thus the promotional mix of a company should be so designed that it matches the corporate reputation, as well as it gains the maximum mileage from the corporate image.

4. **The Channel Choice:** The promotional strategy also depends upon the channel or the route through which the products flow from the firm to the consumer. And the choice of channel depends upon the promotional strategy used by the organisation. Basically there are two promotional strategies that are used. They are the 'push' strategy and the 'pull' strategy. When an organisation used the pull strategy, it undertakes advertising on a large scale. All the promotional efforts of the company are targeted directly towards the consumer. Due to this kind of intense mass communication, the consumers demand the product to such an extent that they literally pull the product from the retailers who in turn demand the product from the wholesalers, and the wholesalers on their part are forced by pressure of demand to stock the product. When this strategy is used, all channel members are forced to stock the product due to incessant demand and hence the dealer margins are lower in pull promotion. Personal salesmanship has a secondary role in pull promotion and the marketer relies on intensive distribution.

When the push strategy is adopted the producer directs all promotional efforts mainly on the middlemen that are the wholesalers and retailers. The product is pushed through the channel. Hence the flow of promotion and flow of goods move from the producer to the wholesaler and from the wholesaler to the retailer and from the retailer to the consumer. Industrial strategies are mostly the push type of strategies relying mostly on personal selling. In the push strategy personal selling expenses are considerable and dealer margins are also higher. In the push strategy marketers rely on selective distribution. Most consumer goods manufacturers generally employ a pushpull (combination) strategy to sell their products. The ratio of pull to push may differ according to the requirements of the market situation. Salesmen are used to push the goods through the marketing channel, while advertising and sales promotion pull the goods and support personal selling to accelerate sales. Thus all tools of promotion work together.

4.13 Advertising: Meaning, Definitions, Importance and Limitations of Advertising

Introduction

When a marketer or a firm has developed a product to satisfy market demand, there is a need for establishing contact with the target market so as to sell the product. Moreover, this has to be a mass contact as the marketer is interested in reaching out to a large number of people. Naturally the best way to reach this mass market is through mass communication, and advertising is one of the means of such mass communication along with other means such as publicity, sales promotion and public relations.

The term 'advertising' is derived from the Latin word 'advertere' which means 'to turn' the attention. Today all around us we see advertising turning the attention of every one towards a particular product, service or area. Advertising is a means of mass communication and has made mass selling possible. Advertising is a means of forceful mass communication, which promotes the sale of goods, services and ideas through information and persuasion. Here it should be noted that advertising only draws the public towards the particular product service or idea. Repeated sales will take place only if the consumer finds the product satisfactory. Thus advertising only helps in selling.

Definition of Advertising

The most widely accepted definition of advertising is the one given by the **'American Marketing Association'**, which is *"Advertising is any paid form of non-personal presentation of ideas, goods or services by an identified sponsor"*.

This definition highlights the following aspects of advertising:

1. **Any Form:** Advertising is any form of communication. It may be a symbol or sign, an illustration or an ad message in a magazine, or newspaper. It may be a commercial on television or radio, or a circular dispatched through the mail. Advertising can take any of these forms and others also.

2. **Paid form:** This means that advertising is a commercial transaction and has to be paid for.

3. **Non-personal:** This phrase in the definition excludes personal selling from within the scope of advertising. Advertising has to be non-personal, i.e. addressed to a mass audience. Thus person-to-person presentation is not advertising.

4. **Identified sponsor:** This means that the sponsor of the advertisement openly pays for it.

In other words advertising is a sales message directed at a mass audience, which seeks to sell goods, services and ideas on behalf of a paying sponsor through the use of persuasion.

In a nutshell, advertising is a mass communication process of persuading the prospects by convincing them to buy products or services with increased satisfaction to the consumers and profits to the sponsors.

Nature and Elements

Advertising is a mass communication of information intended to persuade buyers to buy products and with a view to maximising a company's profits. The elements of advertising are:

(i) It is a mass communication reaching a large group of consumers.

(ii) It makes mass production possible.

(iii) It is non-personal communication, for an actual person does not deliver it, nor is it addressed to a specific person.

(iv) It is a commercial communication because it is used to help assure the advertiser of a long business life with profitable sales.

(v) Advertising can be economical, for it reaches a large number of people.

(vi) The advertising communication is speedy, permitting an advertiser to speak to millions of buyers within a matter of a few minutes.

(vii) Advertising is identified communication. The advertiser signs his name on his advertisement for the purpose of publicizing his identity.

However it is important to note that advertising is not an exact science. The circumstance of each advertiser differs from others. He cannot predict with exact accuracy what will be the results of his present and future advertising efforts.

Advertising is not a game. But if it is done properly both the seller and the 'buyer tend to gain'.

Advertising is not a toy. Advertisers cannot afford to play with advertising. They realise that advertising funds come from sales revenue and must be used to increase sales revenue.

Advertisements should not be designed to deceive. Apart from ethics, the desire for repeated sales ensures a high degree of honesty in advertising.

Scope

Advertising consists of those activities by which visual or oral messages are addressed to a selected public for the purpose of informing and influencing them to buy products or services, or to act favourably towards ideas, persons, trade-marks or institutions featured. As contrasted with publicity and other forms of propaganda, advertising messages are identified with the advertiser either by signature or oral statement. Further, advertising is a commercial transaction and involves payments to be made to publishers, broadcasters or others whose media are employed.

The scope of advertising can be better understood by dividing all promotional activities into two: Activities included in advertising and activities excluded from advertising. Let us take up the first part.

1. **Activities included in advertising:** Advertising usually includes the following forms of messages: the messages carried in newspapers and magazines, on outdoor boards, on street cars, rickshaws, trains, posters and painted displays, in radio and television broadcasts, and in circulars of all kinds, whether distributed by mail or person, through trademen or by inserts in packages, dealer-help materials, window display and counter display materials and efforts, store signs, house organs when directed to dealers and consumers, motion pictures used for advertising and novelties bearing advertising messages or signature of the advertiser. Labels, tags and other literature accompanying merchandise are also deemed to be advertising.

2. **Activities excluded from advertising:** The activities excluded from advertising include the offering of premiums to stimulate the sale of products, the use of exhibitions and demonstrations at fairs, shows, and conventions; the use of samples, and the so called "publicity activities" involved in the sending out of news releases. Likewise totally excluded from the advertising activity is the activity of the personal selling force. The payment of advertising allowances that are not used for advertising; and the entertainment of customers.

Often these activities excluded from the scope of advertising are included in the advertising budgets, and directed by those in charge of advertising. Of many of these activities there is close room for argument whether they should be called as advertising or otherwise classified. They have been excluded from the scope of advertising for one reason or another. For example, exhibitions and demonstrations at fairs and shows are thought to be more closely related to personal selling than to advertising.

Origin And Growth of Advertising

Advertising, as we understand it today, was not used till about 200 years ago, as a business tool, it is not new. It has the longest history taking us back to the history of mankind and the human civilization. Though we fail to answer the question as to the exact age of advertising, it can be said that advertising began when man discovered the art of communication. Advertising by word of mouth is probably the earliest form of advertising, as man developed oral skills well before the development of reading and writing. The history of advertising can be studied by its progress through the centuries.

1. **Ancient times-up to the 5th Century**

    The use of advertising for the transmission of information dates back to ancient Greece and Rome. Criers and signs were used to carry information about goods and services well before the development of printing. During this time merchants used to identify their places of business with a symbol that told of their trade. Thus shop signs, as a means of identifying the place of business is a relic of this time. During these times the merchants also used "hired criers" or "barkers" to impress upon the customers the quality of their products.

2. **The Dark Age**

    The period from 465 AD to 800 AD is referred to as "The Dark Age". This is the period that starts with the downfall of the Roman Empire and ends with the coronation of Charlemagne. During this period due to the fall of the Roman Empire, business suffered a severe setback and commerce and trade routes were greatly diminished. Hence one does not hear much of advertising during this period. This does not mean that it dried up totally. Public barkers equipped with horns and bells were used to attract the attention of the public and hand executed signs and placards were used during this period too.

3. **The Middle Age**

    During the middle ages advertising signs were very extensively used. Criers for the taverns were so numerous in Paris in the 13th Century that they formed a union and were chartered by King Philip Augustus. The giving of free samples started during this era by these criers. Printing originated in China and the oldest book printed dates back to 868 AD. In 1438, Johann Gutenberg laid the foundation of modern education inventing a system of casting moveable type, in Germany and printed the famous Bible in 1456. This discovery, in the West was the first leap for advertising. New methods of advertising were now available like printed posters, hand-bills, pamphlets and newspapers.

4. **The 16th and 17th Century**

    This was the time when the printing technique was perfected, and newspapers introduced. The first newspapers were in the form of newsletters. The early advertisements in the newspapers were in the form of announcements. Importers of new products to England made these announcements. For e.g. the first advertisement offering coffee was made in a newspaper in England in 1652. Chocolates and tea were first introduced through newspaper ads in 1657 and 1658 respectively in England. The earlier advertisements in the newspapers were for books, marriage offers, new beverages and ads for travel. Initially advertising in newspapers was primarily "Pioneering advertising" in its nature. Competitive advertising came in much later in the 18th Century in England.

5. The 18th and 19th Century

This period witnessed the birth and blossoming of competitive advertising. Space selling came into existence. Around 1840, several people were selling space in newspapers in New York. Now there was no looking back. The age-old principle of 'Caveat Emptor' ruled the transactions. Advertising was not only competitive but also had an untruthful edge to it. That is why people did not totally believe the advertising messages given. Buyers were cautious and diligent in buying advertised goods. The 19th century was marked by a new trend of brand advertising. Magazines started catching the imagination of people by popularizing brands. This is the period during which Point of Purchase advertising became popular.

6. The 20th Century

The 20th Century saw the discovery of the radio, television and satellite communications. It has witnessed the world shrink into one global village. With this advertising has received a major boost as never before. New, different antivibrant advertisements are the order of the day. Advertisements can be viewed and heard across the length and breadth of the world. They can be heard on radio, seen and heard on T.V, Videos, computer C.D's, internet, as well as hoardings, newspapers, magazines etc. The era of information technology and mass communication has so developed that business without advertising is a virtual impossibility. Competitive advertisements and advertising wars are a regular feature of normal business life. The success and failure of a business is decided to a large extent by its advertising strategy.

Thus the advertising industry started with "barkers" and has culminated into a very powerful mass media of communication. It is an industry at the very core of all businesses, and something without which no business can exist.

Advertising as a Marketing Tool and its Significance for Consumer Welfare/Advertising and Marketing Mix

Advertising is the communication link between the seller and the buyer or consumer. It does not just provide information about the products and services, but it is an active attempt at influencing people to act by appealing to their emotions and thoughts. Thus advertising is not just the flow of information, but goes further to influencing and persuading people to action. This is just one side of the advertising function, i.e. the communication side. There is another way of viewing the advertising function; and that is from the marketing point of view.

Each organisation has marketing objectives and a marketing plan to achieve them. An organisation also identifies the segments of the market it intends to serve. In the process of achieving its marketing objectives, the organisation uses several marketing tools. In a study of marketing management, four variables are identified, which are well within the controllable limits of the individual organisation. They are popularly known as 4 P's - Product, Place, Price and Promotion. An ideal mix of these four variables is known as the ideal marketing mix to realize the set marketing objectives. This means that the right product should be developed and offered through a distribution network suitable to the organisation and the target market segment. The product should not be too costly and should be offered with a suitable promotion strategy. Under promotion, the marketer provides face-to-face communication with individuals or a group of buyers, as well as mass communication with a large audience by way of advertising. Thus advertising is a part of the marketing mix under the major variable of promotion.

Advertising as a part of the total marketing mix influences the sale of the product, as do the other variables of the mix. Together with the product or brand, price, channel of distribution and personal selling, advertising attempts to achieve the marketing objectives. When a firm offers a prestigious product with a premium price, advertising should reinforce the idea of the high quality and prestige of the product by associating it with prestigious people, places and events. Similarly the advertising message will be different depending upon the distribution strategy adopted by the firm. For e.g. an intensive distribution strategy will require a different form of advertising to match it whereas a distribution strategy through selected or exclusive outlets will require an altogether different one.

Advertising should be complementary to personal selling, which is another marketing tool primarily concerned with communication. In personal selling, communication is more effective, as it can be tailored to suit each individual prospect. Further in personal selling the sales message can be altered on the spot depending upon the response of the prospect. However, advertising supports personal selling and hence should be so designed that it is able to do this.

In short advertising, being one of the marketing tools affects the sales of the firm. Right advertising is as essential as right product, right price, right distribution channel and right personal selling. Thus advertising as a tool of marketing if planned and used properly will lead to the achievement of the marketing objectives. The achievement of marketing objectives will in turn lead to various consumer benefits as highlighted in another part of this chapter.

Role of Advertising in Modern Business/Benefits and Limitations of Advertising

Advertising deals with communication of messages from one person or a group to another. It is primarily a means by which sellers communicate with the prospective buyers regarding their goods and services. As such it is a basic tool of marketing – a method for stimulating demand.

The major economic problem in all countries is distribution. With production taking place on a large scale in anticipation of demand it becomes extremely important to see that the demand is created and that the goods are sold. Here advertising plays a very important role and every effort is to be made to see that it is effective.

In today's competitive business world the consumer is the king, and cannot be forced into buying products. He can only be persuaded to buy products and encouraged to buy more. When people fail to buy as much as our productive facilities require for a low cost mass production, the economic organisation may become unbalanced. When there is a large stock of unsold goods, production is decreased and workers are laid off. The period following a production cut-back is one of the depression and hardship for all. Thus a happy relation between production and consumption is essential to our economic stability. We must maintain a close balance between output and consumption. Advertising is one of the fundamental tools for a happy and durable relationship between production and consumption. Advertising has become an essential phase of modern marketing.

Advertising is not only an important requirement for a balance between production and distribution but benefits consumers, manufacturers, distributors and society at large. Let us here study its benefits and limitations.

Benefits of Advertising to the Consumer, Manufacturer, Salesman and Society

(A) Consumers and Advertising

The ultimate aim of all marketing efforts is to satisfy the needs of consumers by transferring the benefits of productive efficiency to the final users. Advertising as an important element in this process of transfer helps consumers in the following ways:

1. **Advertising adds perception utility to the product:** Advertising adds perception utility to the product just as manufacturing adds form utility, transportation adds place utility and warehousing adds time utility. Advertising influences the perception of the consumers about the product by pointing out the various benefits to be derived from its use. Thus it creates a desire in the mind of the consumers to purchase the product.

2. **Advertising helps the consumer in making the purchase decision:** Advertising through its various forms gives out useful information about the relative merits and features of the products and services in terms of price, quality, utility, quantity, durability, convenience of use etc. so as to guide the consumers to select a product or service of a particular sponsor. As advertising brings to the fore the various features of the various available products, the consumer can compare the merits of the various products and come to a purchase decision. Thus the process of decision making is made easier.

3. **Advertising ensures a better quality:** Advertising ensures that customers are drawn to the product at least for a trial order. However repeat orders are placed only due to the satisfaction received through the use of the product. Thus if the product is not good repeat sales will not take place and if the product proves to be good, it will imprint an image on the minds of the customers and earn a long-standing reputation for the manufacturing house. Such an image is possible by effective branding. Manufacturers are desirous not only of this image but of repeat sales and hence advertising ensures better quality products to the consumers.

4. **Goods at reasonable prices:** Advertising enables firms to sell goods on a mass scale. This has made it possible for producers to increase his production so as to earn economies of scale and thus he can offer goods at reasonable prices to consumers.

5. **Better standard of living:** Advertising reduces the prices of products and thus more and more products are affordable by a larger section of society today. Thus it increases the standard of living of the people. Further advertising creates a demand for new products and thus increases the standard of living of the masses.

6. **Time saved in shopping:** Advertising increases the knowledge of the consumers about the availability of the various brands in the market. He knows about the products and services of the different producers and as such it saves his time which would otherwise have been spent in locating, identifying and deciding about the products and services.

7. **Advertising contributes to consumer welfare:** Advertising helps consumers in a variety of ways. It tells him what to buy, how to buy, where to buy and why to buy. It also gives valuable price information. Advertising also promotes consumer welfare by encouraging competition, which leads to improvements in product quality and reduction in prices.

8. **Advertising makes consumers think:** Advertising makes consumers aware of many socially relevant causes like dowry, energy conservation, environmental pollution, child marriages, eye and blood donation etc. Advertising thus not only makes a consumer think, but acts as a friend, philosopher and guide to the consumers.

(B) Manufacturers and Advertising

Manufacturers, who make available their goods with the clear intention of disposing them at a profit to themselves and satisfaction to the customers, take full advantage of advertising as a major tool to popularize their products and services. Manufacturers spend a lot on advertising because it pays to do so. Advertising establishes a link between the manufacturer and the consumer. It is a form of mass communication. Through this form, the manufacturer makes his product offering known to the consumers. Advertising helps the manufacturer to get the following benefits.

1. **Advertising creates customers:** Even if the producer manufactures the best product he cannot sell it without advertising. Even though it is said that "A good wine needs no bush", information about the product should reach those interested in buying it. Thus it is advertising that informs the people about the product and creates a demand for it.

2. **Advertising increases the sales:** In a highly sensitive and competitive market, the profits of the firm can be maximised not only by reducing the costs but by increasing the sales. Sales of the firm can be multiplied by advertising. Thus advertising increases sales.

3. **Advertising helps the producer in informing the market about the changes in the product or service:** In our competitive system it is important for a manufacturer who has innovated a new product or service, to tell the public about the same quickly in order to reap the advantages right from the start before the competition can develop a similar product. Advertising helps the manufacturer to do this.

4. **Advertising controls product prices:** Through advertising, it is possible to control the prices of the products, specially the retail prices. Very often greedy retailers exploit needy consumers by charging higher prices. Advertising stops this exploitation by disclosing the maximum retail price of the product.

5. **Advertising acts as a salesman:** What a travelling salesman does for the manufacturer, advertising does at a lesser cost. Salesman have to be fed, paid a salary and provided with an expense account. Contrast this with the cost of selling through advertising. A national advertisement, once the original cost has been paid, may reach millions of prospects. There are no expense accounts and an advertisement carried by radio or television reaches into every remote corner of the country. Thus advertising not only acts as a salesman, but also reduces the selling cost of the manufacturer.

6. **Advertising widens the market:** Advertising is an important tool that can open the doors of national and international markets. Intensive advertising programmes conducted by a manufacturer gives him wider markets for his products.

(C) Salesman and Advertising

Sales of an organisation happen because of the active involvement of two functions. First the salesman makes sales happen through his direct personal efforts, and secondly advertising leads to sales through indirect efforts. Which of these two is more important cannot be said, as a company has to match the efforts of both these so as to achieve maximum sales. However, salesmen benefit from advertising in the following ways.

1. **Advertising creates a colourful background for the salesman:** A salesman is nothing less than an actor who by his skill and mastery over the art of selling, tries to win over the consumers for the products of his company. All his selling skills are more effective when they are performed against a good and colourful background. Advertising creates this background for the salesman and thus his job is made more effective.

2. **Advertising makes the salesman's job easier:** In the absence of advertising the salesman has to perform a double job. That of introducing the product to the consumer and then creating a need, want and desire in the mind of the consumer for the product. But because of advertising the customer is already aware about the product and to a certain extent need, want and desire have also been created. Thus the work of the salesman becomes much easier as advertising sells between the sales calls.

3. **Advertising instills confidence in the salesman:** Advertising creates an image and goodwill for the company, which in turn instills a feeling of pride amongst the salesmen that they are working for such an esteemed organisation. This feeling of pride instills in them self-confidence and makes them a dynamic and intrinsically motivated workforce.

(D) Society and Advertising

Advertising is not just a business activity that results in only profits and losses, but affects society at large. In fact every one in society tends to be affected by it. Following are some of the benefits of advertising that are reaped by the society at large.

1. **Advertising increases the standard of living of the society:** The standard of living of the society is conditioned by the amount of National Income and its distribution on the one hand, and the consumption pattern and the disposable income on the other hand. The generation of National Income is deeply influenced by advertising. This is because, effective and faithful advertising creates a demand, which in turns puts pressure on the wheels of production not only to produce more but also to produce better and cheaper products keeping an eye on the quality standards. Improvement in standard of living implies increased production, better production and cheaper production, thus making more and more people from the lower income brackets to enjoy the products they could not in the past.

2. **Advertising provides employment opportunities:** Advertising creates opportunities for gainful employment, both directly and indirectly. Directly employment opportunities are available in the various branches of this ever-growing field of advertising. This profession requires the services of various specialists and talented people like artists, painters, photographers, singers, musicians, executives, agents, researchers etc. Indirectly it stimulates the production of goods, which in turn creates employment opportunities.

3. **Advertising reflects and affects the culture of the society in which it operates:** Culture stands for the values of life and living. Each race has a different culture. Culture is always changing and is guided by the dynamics of the social, political and ethical dimensions of the people. Advertising simply reflects the culture of the people; it does not create it. It simply responds to the prevailing value system. The advertiser has to know very minutely the attitudes, beliefs and motives of the target audience. He then selects the appropriate, media, advertisement messages etc., advertisers are interested in a favourable response from the target audience, and this would be possible only when they offer, in the form of advertisements, products, and services that fit into the existing value system of the audience.

   Not only does advertising reflect the culture of the people, but it in its turn also affects the culture. It does not create culture but definitely is responsible for changes in culture. Advertising is a very dynamic and influential force. In fact, the current world is moving on the lever of advertising. With its educative value, provoking force and invoking tinge, it affects thoughts, gestures and behaviour of the people caught in the spotlight of advertising. Consumers' attitudes, habits, likes and dislikes, fashions, actions, in every walk of life are deeply influenced by advertising.

4. **Advertising provides information to the masses:** Advertising educates the public. Each advertisement is a piece of information because each advertising copy has a definite theme behind it. Advertisements carry messages to different sections of society. They carry the ideas, views and opinions of different people and thus provide information to the masses. It is through advertising that an employer fills the vacancies in his firm. An unemployed applies for a job, parents hunt for brides and bridegrooms, the govt. appeals to the public to pay their tax dues, various NGO's appeal to the public about various socially relevant causes, film producers speak of their films, cinema houses remind us of regular and special shows. Thus, advertising definitely informs the masses.

Limitations of Advertising
1. **Advertising cannot sell a bad product twice:** Advertising influences and persuades a consumer to try out the product. However, if the product is unable to satisfy the consumer, repeat sales will not take place. Thus advertising can persuade a consumer to try out a bad product, but fails to sell it twice.

2. **Advertising has a limited capacity to reach a selected audience:** The requirements of all consumers are not the same. This is why a single advertisement fails to meet the requirements of all consumers. Thus a cosmetic ad does not appeal to thousands of males while an ad of a shaving cream does not interest females. Further advertisements are at the mercy of the media with regard to timings and therefore, may not reach the audience when they are in a buying mood. This adds to the cost of advertising.

3. **Advertisements are rigid:** An advertisement message once set cannot be adjusted to the reactions of the consumers. Nor can an advertisement answer to the objections of the consumers to the product or service. The advertisement goes on as planned, irrespective of what the consumer thinks or says. Sometimes, the same advertisement is bombarded at the consumer so often that, it is a cause of irritation to the consumer. Change is the spice of life and human nature requires it. Thus this rigid nature of advertisement is a limiting factor in its effectiveness.

4. **Advertisements are not believable:** People do not completely believe the advertising message. They know that such a message is designed to influence them and they tend to discount any suspicious and exaggerated claims. The use of exaggerated claims by advertisers does not help to secure the much-desired confidence of the public. What is more important is that no advertiser speaks of the weaknesses of his product or service. He tries to show how his product or service is superior to other producer's products. Though there is truth in the advertisements, it is not the judicial truth but a commercial one. People take commercial truth with a pinch of salt.

5. **Advertising cannot conflict with the cultural values of society:** The advertiser has to know very minutely the attitudes, beliefs and motives of the target audience. He then selects the appropriate, media, advertisement messages, etc. Advertisers are interested in a favourable response from the target audience; and this would be possible only when they offer, in the form of advertisements, products and services that fit into the existing value system of the audience. Thus, advertising cannot conflict with the cultural values of the society.

6. **Advertising can persuade but cannot compel people to buy a product:** Advertising can persuade and positively influence the opinion of the people. However, it cannot force or compel people to buy.

7. **Advertising can be successful only when it is well co-ordinated with other elements of the marketing mix:** Advertising is just one element of the Promotional sub mix of the marketing mix. It cannot operate by itself. Advertising will lead to sales but repeat sales depends upon the Product. Similarly advertising will draw the

consumer to the shop, but it is the distribution system that ensures the availability of the product. Thus, advertising is effective only when it is well co-ordinated with the other elements of the marketing mix.

4.14 Types of Media: Outdoor, Indoor, Print, Press, Transit - Merits and Demerits, Concept of Media Mix, Recent Trends in Promotion

Advertising Media – Meaning, Types, Advantages and Limitations

The term media is plural for medium. In advertising terms medium is a channel of communication such as newspapers, magazines radio and television. A medium is a vehicle for carrying the sales message of an advertiser to the prospects. It is a vehicle by which advertisers convey their messages to a large group of prospects and thereby aid in closing the gap between the producer at one end and the consumer on the other.

Advertising media may be defined as "the physical means whereby a manufacturer of goods or utilities or a supplier of services tells the consumer about his product or service".

In the words of **Brennan**, *"The term media embraces each and every method that the advertiser has at his command to carry his message to the public"*.

Thus, advertising media is a vehicle or device that carries the message of the advertiser to the target consumer. There are various media that are available for an advertiser to choose from, to carry his particular advertising message. Here, let us discuss the various available media of advertising, their characteristics, advantages and disadvantages.

Classification and Characteristics of Different Media

Advertising media can be classified into the following four groups:

(A) Indoor Advertising Media
1. Press media
2. Radio media
3. Television media
4. Film media.
5. Internet Media

(B) Outdoor Advertising Media
1. Posters
2. Painted displays
3. Travelling displays
4. Electric signs
5. Sky-writing
6. Sandwichmen.

(C) Direct Advertising Media
1. Post cards
2. Envelop enclosures
3. Broad-sides
4. Booklets and catalogues
5. Sales letters
6. Gift-novelties
7. Store publications
8. Package inserts.

(D) Display Advertising Media
1. Displays
2. Showrooms
3. Exhibitions.

Let us now study the characteristics and advantages and disadvantages of each advertising media.

(A) Indoor Advertising Media

Indoor advertising, means using those media that reach the audience right inside their houses or indoors. These vehicles are newspaper, radio, television and film. Through these media the message reaches the audience indoors where it is cosy and the audience is in a comfortable and receptive mood. The audience is relaxed. Let us here study each of the indoor media.

1. Press media or Print media

Press or print media basically includes newspapers and magazines. Let us first consider newspaper media.

Newspapers: It is very hard to imagine a morning without a newspaper. Millions of people all over the world begin their mornings with a cup of tea and the newspaper. The newspaper is not just the carrier of news but also ideas, opinions, complaints and thoughts of the people. It enlightens as well as entertains. Of all the media it is considered as the back-bone of the advertising programme. This is because it has continued to remain the most powerful message carrier.

Merits of Newspaper Media

(a) **Local coverage:** Since newspapers are local, the advertisers can easily use them to reach a particular local market. Most newspapers contain maximum number of local advertisements. This is one of the major advantages as newspapers provide advertising in a geographically segmented market.

(b) **Lengthy and complex messages:** As newspapers can be scanned at the leisure of the reader, lengthy and complex messages can be released through this media.

(c) **It is comparatively cheap:** As compared to other media of advertising like television, Newspaper is a cheaper media.

(d) **Ease of release:** It is very easy to release an advertisement in the newspaper. A previously prepared advertisement can be released at the last minute to take advantage of some special marketing situation.

(e) **Wide reach:** Newspapers have a wide reach: Newspapers are read by virtually everybody. It reaches even the remotest corners of the country.

(f) **Trial Advertisements:** This media is good to conduct a trial advertisement run. This trial advertisement can be conducted on a small scale and on a regional basis at a relatively low cost.

Demerits of Newspaper Media

(a) **Short life span:** The biggest demerit of newspaper advertising is its short life span. Today's newspaper is tomorrow's wastepaper.

(b) **Chances of being unnoticed:** Newspapers are read basically to catch up on news and views. They are read in a hurry and the advertisements get skipped. Thus, an advertisement may go unnoticed if it is not strategically located.

(c) **Different rates:** Newspapers charge different rates for advertisements placed in different positions. The preferred positions often carry a higher rate. A majority of the newspaper advertisements are placed on an ROP basis, which means that the paper has the right to place the advertisements anywhere at its discretion. ROP means run of paper. Thus, the advertisement may get placed in a position which is not very eye catching.

(d) **Poor quality:** Newspapers are printed on coarse wood pulp paper known as newsprint. The quality of newspaper advertising is thus poor, as compared to magazine advertising.

Magazines

Magazines are periodicals that are published weekly, fort-nightly, monthly, quarterly and annually. Magazines are both specific interest magazines as well as general interest magazines. Further you also have both regional as well as national magazines.

Merits of Magazine Advertising

(a) **Longer life:** Magazines have a longer life as compared to newspapers. Further magazines are read at leisure and hence the advertisements have more chance of being noticed.

(b) **Visual display:** Magazines use good quality paper with a glossy finish. Further magazines advertisements have the advantage of colour and this makes them more visually appealing.

(c) **Selectivity:** As magazines usually have selective readership, a high degree of selectivity is provided to the advertiser through the use of this media. Advertisers can reach any market segment in terms of differing demographic variables like age, income, occupation, profession, sex and so on. It should also be noted that, magazines have a high degree of believability, acceptance and authority in their respective fields.

(d) **Geographical Flexibility:** Magazines have regional editions through which the advertiser can reach an audience in a particular geographical area. Thus, the advertisement message can be tailor-made to suit the culture, language and outlook of a particular kind of people.

Demerits of Magazine Advertising

(a) **Inflexibility:** Advertisements to be released in magazines, have to be submitted well in advance. In the case of some weekly magazines the space has to be bought and the advertisement copy submitted at least 8-10 weeks in advance, particularly in the case of colour advertisements. Once this date is over no changes in the advertisement copy is allowed and nor can the space bought be cancelled.

(b) **Waste in circulation:** Though magazines have regional editions, most of them have a national circulation. Thus, an advertisement that is released in a national magazine lacks geographical selectivity.

(c) **Costlier:** Advertisements in magazines are more costly than newspaper advertisements. This is because of the use of better quality paper, use of colours and mechanical preparations for advertisements.

(d) **Restricted frequency:** As magazines are usually published weekly, fortnightly, monthly, quarterly or annually the advertiser cannot communicate his message to the audience with any high degree of frequency. Magazines are "occasional ambassadors" that eat away frequency and immediacy.

2. **Radio Media**

Radio advertising can aptly be called as "word of mouth" advertising. It is a medium of mass communication that appeals to the ears through sound. It is a media that is virtually dead or dying in the urban areas. However, about 37% of the rural population still gets their information from the radio. Thus, it is an important media if the advertiser wants to reach the rural masses.

Advantages of Radio Media

(a) **Selectivity:** Radio is a selective vehicle of mass media in the sense that the advertiser can advertise in only those markets that he desires. He can select programmes, stations, time of the day and the type of listenership.

(b) **Instant medium that is flexible:** Radio is an instant medium. In the sense it does not require the paraphernalia of the camera and other things that is required for preparing television advertisements. In fact last minute alterations too can be easily done.

(c) **Human Touch:** The human voice is the most natural way in which people communicate. Radio communicates through the human voice and thus it is a personal medium that gives a human touch.

(d) **Mass Coverage:** Radio reaches almost all human beings except those that cannot hear. Further it is a mobile medium. It can easily be carried along and hence, can be heard anywhere and at any time, easily and comfortably.

(e) **Economy:** Radio advertising is cheaper as compared to other media like television or even prime hoardings.

Demerits of Radio Advertising

(a) **Lack of illustration:** Radio is one medium in which it is virtually impossible to show or even illustrate the product. The only way in which the product can be shown through this medium is through an oral description.

(b) **Message perishability:** Usually a person who listens to the radio does not do so with complete attention. In fact, work or play is usually undertaken and the radio makes up the background sound. In such a situation, the advertisement message may go unheard and perish away without any effective listening.

(c) **Limited time:** The time available for advertising is limited to a specific number of hours only. Once this time is sold, no more advertisements can be accommodated. This is not the case with the print media where extra pages can be added.

3. Television

In India the television was first commissioned in 1959 and commercial telecasting started only in 1976. It is an audio visual medium that provides a perfect synchronization of sound, light, motion, colour and immediacy.

Advantages of Television Advertising

(a) **It has a deep impact:** No other medium can compete with the television as far as effective presentation is concerned. It attracts attention immediately. Computer graphics have made it more effective than ever before. Through this medium the product is shown exactly as it is. It can be demonstrated. In fact it virtually replaces personal selling.

(b) **Mass communication media:** Like the radio, television too is a media of mass communication. Nearly the entire urban area and a great portion of rural India too enjoy television coverage. Every slum area in urban town boasts of a television. The poorest of the poor aspire for it. Thus, it reaches a maximum number of people every day in their houses.

(c) **Upper hand in distribution:** A television advertisement for a product or service is greatly appreciated by the merchants in the channel of distribution. They attach a certain amount of prestige towards handling products that are advertised on television. Thus, this medium helps the marketer in procuring the best distributors for distributing his products.

(d) **Life like presentation:** The most striking feature of television medium is its instantaneous transmission of sight, motion, sound and colour that is life like. Of all the media, television is the closest replicate of life. It presents the things and the events as they are and happen. Thus, it is the most believable medium. People tend to believe what they see.

(e) **Evocation of experience:** It stimulates the experience of using and owning the product, thus creating a desire for it.

(f) **Image building:** Television succeeds in building a powerful image of the company and its products. It can also project an image of the users rendering it excellent for life-style advertising.

Disadvantages of Television Advertising

(a) **It is time consuming:** It takes time to produce television commercials. This medium requires planning and deliberation. If it is not properly produced the television commercial may look crude. But once produced as per requirement they can be repeated over a long period of time.

(b) **Short life:** The television commercial has a short life. Once it is viewed and heard it is gone. It does not remain as a part of the household like the newspaper or magazine or the calendar. If the prospect misses the commercial at its exact time of presentation, the scene and message is lost and wasted as far as the prospect is concerned. It requires a repeated relay of advertisements to have an appreciable impact on the audience.

(c) **A costly medium:** Television is a costly medium. Not only is it costly to make a television advertisement, but the purchase of time on the television is also very expensive. This is one of the main factors that take television out of reach of the small advertiser. He cannot even think of purchasing a slot on television.

(d) **The clutter problem:** Television media suffers from the clutter problem. That is over crowding of too many commercials in a very short span of time. Both the advertisers and the viewers complain about this. The clutter reduces the effectiveness of the advertisements.

(e) **An immobile medium:** The television is an immobile medium. Radio can be listened to either in the car or while walking; on a picnic etc. Similarly, newspapers and magazines are read everywhere. However, television is to be viewed only at home.

4. **Film Advertising Media**

Film advertising is yet another medium of publicity characterized by sound, motion, colour, vision and timeliness. It is like a television run on the enlarged screen for a larger audience. This audio-visual medium has a wide range starting from an ordinary slide presentation to the advertising films screening. Screen advertisements are liked by people of all ages, sexes, professions, political affiliations, cultural heritage and income groups because of its magic of life size presentation of themes.

Advantages of Film Advertising

(a) **Film advertising ensures a captive audience:** People visit a cinema hall to see a movie of their choice. This choice ensures a higher degree of concentration as compared to viewing a television programme. Television cannot command as complete an attention, as commanded by the film media.

(b) **Film media is ideal for niche marketing:** Through this media the advertiser can be segment specific, market specific, right down to a particular district, city or even a theatre.

(c) **Advertising on cinema is economical:** The cost of screening an advertisement in a theatre is quite economical. However, the cost of making the advertising film is not so.

Disadvantages of Film Advertising

(a) **It is costly:** The cost of making an advertising film to be screened in cinema houses is expensive. However, the cost of making slides is not so.

(b) **Limited Coverage:** The coverage of film advertising is only limited to those few who visit the cinema hall in which these advertisements are released.

(c) **Resentment from viewers:** The viewers go to cinema houses for viewing a feature film and not an advertising film. The viewers view the advertisements to be a barrier in their entertainment and may resent it. This reduces the effectiveness of the advertisement message.

5. Internet Advertising

The internet is one of the latest media of advertising. It has a worldwide reach. People all over the world can access the internet. When a person accesses a particular web page, the advertisements released on that particular web page, is also viewed by him. Thus, the more popular a particular web page, the more in demand it is by advertisers. This is the reason why many a services are available for free on the internet. When the services are free, the viewership is more and, this increased accessing of a particular site, attracts advertisers.

Advertisements to be released on the internet are easy to prepare and a lot many courses on web page designing are available today. You also have many web page designers who compete with each other for the client's businesses. The cost of preparing an internet advertisement is much less as compared to the price paid for the preparation of a television advertisement or for the hire of a prime hoarding. Further, internet advertisements can result in immediate action as a person accessing the internet can make a direct on-line purchase. Thus, the effectiveness of the internet advertisement can be measured.

However, an advertisement on the internet has to compete with various other advertisements for the attention of the viewer. It also has to compete with the contents of the web page for which the viewer had originally accessed the internet. He definitely did not access it to view advertisements.

Thus, the internet advertisement has to be very attractive as the viewer is conscious of the time he is spending on the internet. This is because accessing the internet costs money and this has to be paid in terms of amount of time spent on the internet. Thus, in order to catch the attention of the viewer, advertisements on the internet are basically used as, vehicles that carry sales promotion messages. Thus, you will find most advertisements on the internet with words like FREE, 40% discount, MONEY BACK OFFER, in order to lure the viewer towards viewing it, and make immediate buying action. Sometimes, the internet advertisements take a lot of time to download, and hence, miss the attention of the viewer totally.

However, today is the era of the internet and information technology. People over the world are beginning to rely more and more on the internet due to its wide accessibility. In fact, its popularity is such that people are beginning to become internet addicts. Once used to it, you just cannot do without it. In other words, if you have a computer at home, today you can do away with the television as well as the music system. In the households of the future, the internet will be replacing the television and, hence, the importance of internet advertising is projected to occupy very 'dominant' place in the future.

Types of Internet Advertising

1. **Website Banner Advertisements:** Web Banner Advertising is a type of Internet Advertising whereby you pay another website 'X' amount to display an advertising

banner on their website for a certain length of time. The web banner links directly to your website, tempting visitors away from theirs and onto yours. Sometimes, advertising on another website in the form of a banner advertisement can yield a fairly good return. However, advertising on a website that has little or nothing to do with your target audience involves high levels of luck to convert any sales, producing little to no Return on Investment (ROI).

Stylishly done banner ad campaigns will continue to be the staple of internet advertising for the immediate future. Studies show that banners are terribly good at generating traffic through click-through and have a powerful branding effect. Matching site content to banner advertising subject can certainly increase their power. Selecting a banner to display based on the observed personal preferences and interests of a visitor are a hugely powerful sales tool. The potential for targeted banners is huge.

2. **Sponsorships :** If you 'sponsor' a section of a site you can integrate your advertising message and branding elements a bit more unobtrusively than you can with just a banner at the top. You might also be able to have your regular ads and have "these cool pages sponsored by ..." appear on the pages you're sponsoring. Thus, you may get more exposure and closer integration with content.

3. **Rich Media :** Right now, this term seems to mean a more-or-less normal-sized banner ad that uses Java, HTML or any other software to make the advertisement have drop-down boxes, wiggly bits, Sound on mouse-over, small games etc. Both visitors and sites like them because you don't have to actually leave the site to interact with the banner. Click through on such advertisements can be quite high.

4. **Text Link Exchanges and Paid Link Advertising:** In more recent times, link exchanges have become quite popular. The general idea is two likeminded websites exchange a contextually based link (text link), normally placed on a dedicated resources page which is linked from every page of the site. Webmasters will approach another website of a similar theme to ask if they would exchange a link. The link can provide traffic from one site to the other.

Link Popularity: Many of the largest search engines use link popularity in their complex ranking algorithms. The idea being, if a website is of good quality, other webmasters will link to it from their own site. Each web page has one vote, linking to another site is in effect casting that vote, if the page links to more than one site, the vote is diluted between each link. The other key part to conducting link exchanges is using keyword targeted descriptive text as the actual clickable part of the link (anchor text).

Purchasing text links works exactly the same way as above apart from the fact that you purchase the link rather than exchange, you don't have to provide a link back either. Purchasing links will often lead to a link displayed in a more prominent place. The price of purchasing links depends on a number of criteria, such as, the amount of traffic on the site and it's Google PageRank (PR) which is an indication of the weight a link would produce.

5. **Keyword Advertising:** This can be quite effective. What you do is pay a search engine, directory or site to have your ad or link to your site pop up first when someone does a search on the keywords you buy. When someone does a search using the word 'Scales', your matter comes up on top of the list and/or your banner ad is at the top of the page. The best searched words like 'Sex' and 'Air Transport ' are usually sold out or very expensive. The less-searched on words are cheaper but can also bring a very valuable targeted person to your site. By now, everyone's heard about the old misspelling trick. If someone else has already bought the keyword 'hamburger', you could probably buy slight misspellings like, 'hmburger' or 'hamburgr' cheap that would still get you good action.

6. **Coupon Deals:** Web Advertisements carrying digital coupons that give you special deals for ecommerce purchases or printable coupons provide the advertiser the opportunity to do all the wonderful and horrible things traditionally possible with coupons, but now you can do it on the Web. Airlines are using these to increase their air traffic.

7. **Pay per Click or Pay Per Sale:** Some sites sell space to advertisers. The advertisers have their banners or rich media advertisements on sites on which they have hired space. The advertiser pays the site only when someone clicks upon the banner or gets to the target site and buys something. Such advertisers pay a bit more to the site but the payment depends upon the number of clicks, or number of purchases, as the case may be. Such deals make people buying ads get a more secure return on their investment, Such deals are fine for the people buying the ads but do not tend to pay off well for the advertising sites, as some people will actually click on the ads and the site will lose them.

8. **Pop Ups and Pop Unders:** Pop Ups and Pop Unders are simply one of the forms of internet available. A Pop-Up displays an advertisement of a website in a new window when you visit another site, aPop Under inserts the advertisement under the page you are viewing so that when you close the window down, and you are presented with it.

If you use the internet you're bound to have come across Pop Ups before and probably are already sick to death of them. Most of the times, people see them loading up and they are unable to close the window before they've fully loaded. In recent times, Pop Ups have become much less popular, as they are being made redundant by most browsers and downloadable toolbars like, the Google toolbar and Microsoft IE, who are coming up with complete Pop Up blockers. However, these services are cheap and are sold mostly on the premise of people thinking well. It's only £ 10 for a thousand; I may as well give it a try.

Thus, these are some of the different ways in which a company can use the internet or web pages to advertise its products or services.

(B) Outdoor Advertising Media

Outdoor advertising is the oldest form of advertising. It is also known as 'position', 'Mural' or 'indirect' advertising. Outdoor advertising is literally out of door, i.e. it is out of the home or place of business. The importance of outdoor advertising can be gleaned from the fact that an ordinary human being spends one third of his time out of doors. The viewer has to incur no expenditure, nor has he to make any effort to see an outdoor advertisement. An outdoor advertising message is not bought to the viewer; it is the viewer who goes to the message, though they view it in the course of their other activities. Outdoor advertising media is made up of vehicles like posters, painted displays, hoardings, electric signs, travelling displays, sky writings and the like. A detailed explanation of various outdoor media vehicles is as follows:

1. **Posters:** A poster is a sheet of paper pasted on a wooden card or metal board depicting the advertising message. The poster advertising message should be simple, brief and attractive. Illustrations go a long way in increasing the effectiveness of posters. Mostly posters remain in position for a period of time say, several weeks. We therefore, say that they enjoy 24 hours exposure and a long life. Posters account for nearly 75% of all outdoor media vehicles. The success of a poster advertisement depends upon the designing of the poster as well as the site at which it is put up.

2. **Painted Displays:** Painted displays are painted bulletins and wall paintings. A painted bulletin is nothing but a metal sheet of a rectangular shape of a standard size erected at heights to command visibility from a distance. It is larger and elaborate form of outdoor advertising as compared to the poster. Painted displays are sometimes illuminated for the night traffic. The rentals for these sites are based on a period of one year. The advertiser may thus keep the same message for a period of one year or change it depending upon his requirement.

3. **Electric Signs/Neon Signs:** Electric signs and Neon signs are more popularly known as spectacular signs. These are large permanents signs that make use of elaborate light and action effects. These are a conspicuous vehicle of outdoor media and are designed to attract the public as they pass by. They are usually effective in places

that have a high nightlife. Electric signs are usually placed in high places so as to have a maximum rate of visibility. These signs are either authorized by the local administration or are put up on private buildings. Usually these signs are on a yearly contract.

4. **Travelling Displays/Transit Advertising :** Transit advertising stands for all types of advertising signs or displays used in trains, buses, cars, trams, autos and other such transportation vehicles and the terminals or the station from which they operate.

5. **Sky-writing:** The advertising industry has very creatively used the sky to advertise their goods and services. Sky writing is the kind of publicity where the message is spread across the sky in one form or the other. Usually sky writing takes the form of sky balloons, giant kites, and search lights. This is a novel medium and can catch the attention of the people. However, it has a short life, and is not very commonly used.

6. **Sandwich men:** This is the oldest and funniest medium of outdoor advertising. It is still popular in rural areas. Under this kind of advertising, the advertiser hires men. These men are called as sandwichmen because they are sandwiched between the posters both in the front and back. Further they are dressed in colourful and bright clothes, and shout slogans, thus attracting the public not just towards themselves but to the product and the advertiser.

Advantages of Outdoor Media

(a) The outdoor offers a long life.

(b) It offers geographic selectivity. Posters can be changed as often as required to keep up with the change in the advertising message to suit a particular segment in the market. This is one medium in which the advertiser has a choice of displaying a different message in every region and every locality.

(c) The advertiser can incorporate the names and addresses of his local dealers or agents at the bottom of the poster or painted display. These dealer imprint strips are called 'snipes'.

(d) This media offers an attractive display of the product trademark and slogan.

(e) This media attracts the attention of the people when they are out of doors. Thus, it results in influencing them when they are out shopping. Usually these posters and painted displays are strategically placed so as to have this effect.

Limitations of Outdoor Media

(a) Since the copy of this media has to be brief, this media merely supplements some other media.

(b) This media is non selective. In the sense, that the audience who get the exposure are people of all ages, sexes, educational and socio economic levels. There is no selectivity of a particular type of audience.

(c) This media when employed on a national basis is relatively expensive.

(d) It is difficult to measure the effectiveness of this media and getting reliable data on the number of people who actually see these advertisements, and is very difficult to estimate.

(C) Direct Advertising Media

There is a lot of confusion between the phrase 'direct advertising' and 'direct mail advertising'. Direct advertising is a very comprehensive phrase covering all forms of printed advertising delivered directly to prospective customer. Instead of using an indirect media like newspaper or television through which the prospect may or may not see the advertisement, through this media the prospect is directly approached. It may take various forms like pamphlets distributed to people on the road stuck under the wind screen of an automobile, handed over at the retail counter or it may be sent through the post. It is 'direct mail advertising' only if it reaches the customer through the post. However, if it reaches the customer in any other way it is 'direct advertising'. This is one of the oldest ways of reaching a prospect or customer. It is a direct approach to consumers. This direct approach may be through sales letters and circulars, or it may be through leaflets, folders and brochures.

The following are the different forms that a direct advertising can take:

1. **Post cards:** A post card is the most widely used form of direct advertising because of its high attention value and economy. It is designed to get direct and immediate attention of the recipient. It is used to carry brief messages.

2. **Envelop Enclosures:** The phrase 'envelop enclosure' is quite likely to mislead. By 'enclosure', we normally mean a paper that is enclosed or attached to the main letter. However, here it stands for the bunch of papers itself which is separately posted. It may be a circular or a stuffer or a folder.

    A 'circular' is a sheet of paper or sheets of papers printed on either one or both sides. Circular gives information about the product in colour or in black and white. They may or may not carry illustrations of the product.

    A 'stuffer' is an enclosure that is used as a means to deliver sales and goodwill messages. It is a vehicle used to amplify the sales literature by providing illustrations and detailed information of wide range of commodities of a single company or different manufacturers.

    A 'folder' is bigger than an ordinary card or a letter. It is folded in an impressive and convenient manner. It is very popularly known as adult leaflet or booklet without binding.

3. **Board sides:** Board-side is a large size advertising folder. Its striking features are its big size and illustrative display. These are also called as 'spectaculars in print' because they are excellent attention getters.

4. **Booklets and Catalogues :** Booklets are very small books consisting of not more than 8-10 pages fastened or stapled together to allow it to open as a book. A booklet is usually mailed in an envelope. It contains useful information answering the questions of prospective buyers about product features. However, it gives information about a limited number of products. Catalogues are quite similar to the book-let in physical make up. However, they are much larger and present information on a wide range of products of the business house. They also feature the prices of the products and give other conditions of purchase. They can be used as reference material too.

5. **Sales letters:** A sales letter is a silent ambassador of the firm. It first sells the name of the company and then its products. The success of a sales letter depends upon its appeal. The stationery used, the tone of the letter, the theme of the letter, all have their impact.

6. **Gift-novelties:** Gift advertising or specialty advertising is the medium that employs useful articles known as advertising specialties or gift novelties that are imprinted with the name and address and the sales message of the advertiser. These act as goodwill gifts or reminders. The advertiser hopes that the recipient is likely to be influenced favourably to buy in the future, if he is reminded of the company every time he looks at the gift. There are countless such items that can be presented like ball point pens, ash-trays, cigarette lighters, paper weights, calendars, drink stirrers etc.

7. **Store Publications:** A store publication is a house organ or bulletin or magazine published by the company mainly for the purpose of promoting goodwill and moulding the public opinion, though it has a sales tinge. These house organs are freely distributed to the dealers, customers, and employees. Though they are costly and have a high mortality rate, a well edited house organ can do a lot in getting customers, and dealers acquainted with the company's image, philosophy and progress.

8. **Package Inserts:** The phrase 'package inserts' is used in a broad sense to include packages, labels, and inserts. Though the package is a container that protects the contents and facilitates easy handling, it is a very effective means of carrying the message about the product. It acts as a medium of advertising. For better results, the advertising message on the package must be short, illustrative and giving product information and uses. 'Label' is a printed piece of paper giving the value of the product and its content, name of the product and producers and other such useful information. It is stuck or imprinted on the package. 'Package inserts' are printed matter that is inserted into the packages. They go only to those who purchase the

particular product. They provide a golden opportunity to the advertiser to pass on his message to the customers. Inserts give information regarding how best to use the product, as well as how to store and maintain it. This is also the most economical method of direct advertising.

Advantages of Direct Advertising Media:
(a) **High Selectivity:** Through the use of this media, the advertiser can select exactly which particular target audience he wishes to reach out to.
(b) **Personal Touch:** This media allows for a personal touch, especially sales letters. They can be directly addressed to the particular person.
(c) **Deep Impact:** The recipient receives these mailers at home, in a comfortable atmosphere. Further if they are addressed to him personally, they will have a deeper impact.
(d) **Measurement of effectiveness:** This is the only media in which some kind of definite measurement of the effectiveness of the message can be done. Depending upon the response received, the effectiveness of the advertising message can be measured.

Demerits of Direct Advertising Media:
(a) **Higher cost:** The cost per recipient works out to be much more than other mass media like newspapers, magazines, radio and television.
(b) **Low reader interest:** Much of the material sent through direct advertising finds itself in the dustbin.
(c) **Warrants special skill:** To be effective this media needs to be prepared very creatively. It has to attract the attention of the reader and hence requires special talents.

(D) Display Advertising Media

Display advertising media, in a broader sense is also known as P.O.P. i.e. point of purchase advertising. It is more a promotional medium than advertising. In recent times this medium is gaining more importance because of new trends in buying such as 'self-service'. The significance of display advertising lies in its ability to allow the prospects to experience the products before buying. It is also an effective dealer aid. It attracts customers to the shop and leads to impulse buying.

Display advertising is hinged on the concept of display. It has three dimensions namely displays, showrooms and showcases, and exhibitions. Let us take a brief look at all these.

1. **Displays:** Displays are of several types. There are window displays, counter displays, wall displays, shelf displays, overhead displays, floor displays, and jumble displays. Here, let us study the prominent ones namely window display and counter display.

    Window Display: The "display" of products in shop-windows so that passersby are attracted to enter the shop and buy the products, or at least be reminded of the products, is termed as "window display". Window display is an effective strategy for gaining the interests and attention of the passersby or 'window shoppers'. Attractive and innovative window displays attract and urge window shoppers to step into the shop. Today, the concept of window display has caught on so well in India that a new breed of designers specialising in the art of window display has emerged.

Counter Display: Counter display or interior display refers to all the arrangements that are made inside the shop. It refers to all kinds of internal showmanship in the garb of storage. It can be open, closed, and top of the counter, wall, architectural, ledge type and the like. It speaks of scientific and artistic arrangement of glass cupboards, fixtures, shelves, racks, show cases, stands and other supports.

2. **Showrooms:** Even today there are some customers who do not believe in purchase without inspection. In the case of industrial goods and consumer goods purchase after inspection is inevitable. Sometimes, demonstrations are also required prior to purchase. Showrooms basically accommodate the needs of such consumers. A showroom is a specially designed room used mainly for display, demonstration and after sale services. Two types of personnel namely technical and sales staff. A show room becomes the hub of activity of explaining the product features, merits, demonstrating and after sale services, particularly repairs and maintenance.

3. **Trade Shows, Exhibitions and Fairs:** Trade shows and exhibitions offer an excellent opportunity to manufacturers to display their products and to demonstrate their use and value. Manufacturers can buy display spaces or counters at reasonable rates- perhaps more reasonable than the exorbitant media rates for advertising. Many a times, trade associations too hold annual exhibitions and fairs. Now-a-days electronic fair, technology fairs, consumer products exhibitions have become quite common.

Thus, the above are the various media that are available for an advertiser to choose from in order to advertise his products. He may choose any combination of the various media mentioned above.

Points to Remember

- The basic task of Marketing involves the identification of the needs of the customer and then the manufacturing and marketing of a product or service that satisfies this need.
- The Marketing mix can be used by marketers as a tool to assist in defining the marketing strategy. Marketing Managers use this method to attempt to generate the optimal response in the target market by blending a number of marketing mix elements in an optimum way.
- The Marketing mix has four main sub mixes. They are:
  1. The Product Mix
  2. The Price Mix
  3. The Place Mix or Physical Distribution Mix
  4. The Promotion Mix.

1. **Price:** It is the mechanism or device for translating into quantitative terms (rupees and paise) the perceived value of the product to the customer at a point of time.
2. **Variables of price mix:**
   (a) The Pricing Policies: Discounts, Quantity discounts, Trade discounts, Cash discounts, Seasonal discount
   (b) Terms of Credit
   (c) Resale Price Maintenance
3. **Objectives of pricing:** The pricing objectives can be divided into two:
   (a) **Short-Term Objectives:** Following can be the short-term objectives of the pricing policy adopted by an organisation:
   - Meeting existing competition,
   - Discouraging new competition,
   - Securing key accounts,
   - Recovering cash rapidly,
   - Attracting new customers, distributors, agents,
   - Using spare capacity,
   - Trimming off overall demands.

   (b) **Long-Term Objectives:** The long-terms objectives of the pricing policy can be categorised as follows:
   - Return on assets,
   - Stabilising prices,
   - Retaining target market share,
   - Strategic pricing in different market,
   - Keeping competition outside the market.

   Depending upon the pricing objectives to be achieved, the organisation adopts a pricing method or strategy.
4. **Pricing Methods / Pricing Strategies:**
   (a) Cost Oriented Pricing Strategy
   (b) Demand Oriented Pricing
5. **Definition of logistics:** Logistics is the portion of the supply chain that deals directly with the transportation and warehousing of goods and materials.
6. **Definition of supply chain management:** Supply chain management includes the management of material and information between its movements from source to final consumer. This includes all logistics, materials handling and purchasing.
7. **Essential purpose or objective of supply chain management:** "The goal of logistics and supply chain management is timely delivery, competitive pricing, mobility, and flexibility, together with innovative transportation services".

8. **Definition of a market channel:** "it is the route taken by the title to the goods as they move from producer to the ultimate consumer or industrial user".
9. **Types of Distribution intermediaries:**
    (a) Merchant middleman
    (b) Agent Middlemen
10. **Types of Channels / Designing Distribution Channels:**
    (a) Manufacturer – Consumer/User Channel (Direct Sale)
    (b) Manufacturer – Retailer – Consumer
    (c) Manufacturer – Wholesaler – Retailer – Consumer
    (d) Manufacturer Agent – Wholesaler – Consumer
    (e) Manufacturer Agent – Retailer – Consumer
    (f) Manufacturer Wholesaler – Consumer/ User
11. **Factors influencing selection of channel:**
    (a) Product: If a product is perishable or fragile, a producer will prefer few and controlled levels of distribution
    (b) Market: If the market size is large, we may have many channels. However if it is a small market direct selling will be more profitable.
    (c) Cost: The most fundamental criteria for channel decision and channel choice is the economic criteria
    (d) Channel used by rivals Competitors: The channels used by rivals are closely watched.
    (e) Marketing Environment: During recession or depression, a shorter and cheaper channel is usually preferred.
    (f) Company: A big firm may have shorter channels. A company with substantial financial resources need not depend upon middlemen.
12. **Definition of Promotion:** Promotion has been defined as "the coordinated self initiated efforts to establish channels of information and persuasion to facilitate or foster the sale of goods or services, or the acceptance of ideas or points of view."
13. **Definition of sales promotion:** Sales Promotion includes those sales activities that supplement both personal Selling and Advertising and co ordinates them and helps to make them effective, such as, displays, shows and expositions, demonstrations and other non-recurrent selling efforts not in the ordinary routine".
14. **Elements of Promotion Mix:**
    (a) Advertising
    (b) Publicity
    (c) Personal selling
    (d) Sales promotion

15. **Objectives of Promotion:**
    (a) Information
    (b) Persuasion
    (c) Reminding
16. **Factors affecting promotion mix:**
    (a) Product
    (b) Buyer
    (c) Company
    (d) Channel choice
17. **Sales promotion techniques:**
    (A) Sales Promotion Techniques used to aid dealers:
    (a) Provision of Management Aid
    (b) Communicating Marketing Information
    (c) Training of Dealers
    (d) Furnish the Dealer with Sales literature and Display material
    (e) Attractive Terms of Sale
    (f) Dealer Contests:
    (B) Sales promotion techniques that influence the consumer:
    (a) Sales Promotion Letters
    (b) Catalogues
    (c) POP/Display
    (d) Demonstrations
    (e) Demonstrations at Retail Stores and Malls
    (f) Door to Door Demonstrations
    (g) Demonstrations to Key People
    (h) Trade Fairs and Exhibitions
    (i) Coupons, premiums, free offers, price-offs
18. **Definition of Advertising:** Advertising is a mass communication process of persuading the prospects by convincing them to buy products or services with increased satisfaction to the consumers and profits to the sponsors.
19. **Definition of Advertising Media:** The physical means whereby a manufacturer of goods or utilities or a supplier of services tells the consumer about his product or service.
20. **Classification of advertisement:**
    (a) Product-Related Advertising:
       (i) Pioneering Advertising
       (ii) Competitive Advertising
       (iii) Retentive Advertising
    (b) Institutional Advertising:
       (i) Public Relations Institutional Advertising
       (ii) Public Service Institutional Advertising
       (iii) Patronage institutional advertising

Questions for Discussion

1. Define Marketing Mix.
2. What is Marketing Mix? Explain the various Elements of Marketing Mix.
3. Explain the various stages of Product Life Cycle.
4. Explain the Elements of Price Mix.
5. Explain the Need and Importance of Price Mix.
6. Explain the Objectives of Pricing.
7. Explain the various factors influencing Pricing.
8. Describe the various methods of Pricing.
9. What are Departmental Stores?
10. Who is a Commission Agent?
11. Describe the various Types of Channels of Marketing.
12. Describe the various Factors affecting Selection of Channels of Distribution.
13. Explain the various categories of Merchant Middleman.
14. Explain the various categories of Agent Middleman.
15. Explain the various Elements of Promotion Mix.
16. Describe the various factors Influencing Promotion Mix.
17. Discuss the various Sales Promotion Techniques and Methods.
18. What are the different types of Internet Advertising?
19. What are the various outdoor Advertising Media Vehicles.
20. Write short notes on:
    (a) Merits and Demerits of Direct Advertising Media
    (b) Advantages of Television Advertising
    (c) Sales Promotion Technique used to aid dealers.
21. What are the different forms of Direct Advertising?

Questions from Previous Pune University Examinations

1. What is Marketing Mix? Explain Scope and Importance of Marketing Mix. **[April 2011]**
2. What is Marketing Channel? Explain Various Factors Influencing Channels of Distribution. **[April 2011]**
3. Explain Role of Advertising in Modern Business. **[Oct. 2010, April 2009, 2011]**
4. Define Product Life Cycle. Explain Various Stages of Product Life Cycle. **[Oct. 2011]**
5. What is Promotion Mix? Explain various factors influencing Promotion Mix. **[Oct. 2011]**
6. Define Pricing. Explain Various Methods of Pricing. **[April 2012]**

7. What do you mean by Promotion Mix? Explain the elements of Promotion Mix.
   [April 2012]
8. What is Product Life Cycle? Explain various stages in Product Life Cycle. **[Oct. 2012]**
9. State Advantages of Various Media of Advertising. **[Oct. 2012]**
10. What are the Elements of Marketing Mix? Discuss Utility of Marketing Mix.
    [April 2013]

11. Write Short Notes:
    - (A) Product Life Cycle. **[April 2009, 2010, 2011 & 2013]**
    - (B) Objectives of Pricing. **[April 2010, 2011]**
    - (C) Elements of Promotion Mix. **[April 2009, 2011]**
    - (D) Limitations of Advertising. **[Oct. 2011]**
    - (E) Elements of Price Mix. **[Oct. 2011]**
    - (F) Advertising Media. **[April 2012]**

    - (G) Place Mix. **[April 2010, Oct. 2012]**
    - (H) Product Simplification. **[Oct. 2012]**
    - (I) Factors Influencing Channels. **[April 2009]**
    - (J) Factors Influencing Promotion Mix. **[Oct. 2010]**
12. Explain Various Factors Influencing Pricing. **[April 2009, Oct. 2010]**
13. Explain Meaning and Importance of Marketing Mix. **[Oct. 2009]**
14. Explain Factors Influencing Channels of Distribution. **[Oct. 2009]**
15. What is Marketing Mix? Explain Scope and Utilities of Marketing Mix. **[April 2010]**
16. What is Marketing Mix? Explain Various Factors Affecting Mix. **[Oct. 2010]**
17. What do you understand by Marketing Mix? Discuss Elopement of Marketing Mix in Detail. **[April 2006]**
18. What are the 4 P's of Marketing? Why are they Important for a Marketing Managers?
    [April 2008]

■■■

Chapter 5...

Marketing Planning, Marketing Information System, Marketing Research

Contents ...

5.1 Marketing Planning
    5.1.1 Introduction - Meaning and Definition
    5.1.2 Scope of Marketing Planning
    5.1.3 Importance of Marketing Planning
    5.1.4 Components of Marketing Planning
    5.1.5 Steps in Marketing Planning / Marketing Process
    5.1.6 Essential Requirements of Marketing Planning
    5.1.7 Types of Marketing Plans
    5.1.8 Difficulties in Marketing Planning

5.2 Marketing Information System
    5.2.1 Concept, Meaning and Definition
    5.2.2 Components of Marketing Information System
    5.2.3 Features of Marketing Information System
    5.2.4 Importance of Marketing Information System

5.3 Marketing Research
    5.3.1 Introduction and Meaning
    5.3.2 Definition of Marketing Research
    5.3.3 Market Research and Marketing Research
    5.3.4 Objectives of Marketing Research
    5.3.5 Scope of Marketing Research
    5.3.6 Sources of Collecting Marketing Data
    5.3.7 Marketing Research Procedure, Types and Techniques of Marketing Research
    5.3.8 Importance of Marketing Research
    5.3.9 Limitations of Marketing Research
    5.3.10 Uses of Marketing Research in Management

- Points to Remember
- Questions for Discussion
- Questions from Previous Pune University Examinations

Learning Objectives ...

- To be able to Describe the Meaning, Scope, Importance and Essentials of Marketing Planning
- To be able to Discuss the Concept, Components and Importance of MIS
- To learn the Meaning and Scope of Marketing Research
- To understand the Use of Marketing Research in Management

5.1 Marketing Planning

5.1.1 Introduction – Meaning and Definition

Marketing planning is the starting point of any business activity. Planning is deciding at present what is to be done in the future. It involves not only anticipating the consequences of decisions but also predicts the events that are likely to affect the business.

The primary aim of Marketing Planning is to direct the company's marketing efforts and resources towards present marketing objectives like growth, survival, profit maximisation, service to customers etc. However the marketing activity and objectives are the deciding factors on which all other activities of a company are based. Thus the entire activity of a company is actually based on the premise of the marketing plan.

The success of any business activity is the outcome of the successful management of its market. A marketing plan is an instrument to implement the marketing concept. It is the document of the future course of action that spells out as to how the resources at the command of the firm are to be used to achieve the marketing goals. In simple words a marketing plan is a written document that specifies in detail the firm's marketing objectives and how marketing management will use the controllable marketing tools such as product design, pricing, channels of distribution and promotion to achieve these objectives. It is the central instrument for directing and co-ordinating the marketing efforts. A marketing plan is a blue print for marketing action. It is a written document containing strategies to achieve present goals.

According to **Malcolm H. B. McDonald**, *"Marketing Planning is a logical sequence of activities leading to the setting of marketing objectives and formulation of plans for achieving them."*

In the words of **Wendell R. Smith** *"Marketing Planning is the exercise of analysis and foresight to increase the effectiveness of marketing activities."*

In a nut shell any Marketing Planning is a managerial function that determines the future course of marketing action based on the analysis of past events so that the marketing objectives can be achieved. It is basically concerned with the allocation, development and future use of the marketing resources.

5.1.2 Scope of Marketing Planning

The scope of Marketing Planning in a company depends on the kind of orientation that the company has adopted. In a market-oriented company, Marketing Planning begins with the consumer needs and problems and covers all the components of the marketing mix. It covers marketing research, product planning and development, selling, distribution channels, advertising, sales promotion, pricing and physical distribution.

Within the broad framework of the company's marketing objectives and policies, plans for each component of the marketing mix are formulated and these are known as area plans or sub functional plans. Each area plan has its own objective, policies and programmes.

Once all the area plans are formulated they are integrated together and one master marketing plan is made which guides the marketing objectives of the company. However, while developing this master marketing plan not only are plans considered, but due attention is also given to the programmes of intermediaries operating in the company's indirect channel. This helps the company in developing its vertical marketing system. Thus the scope of marketing planning covers both: those operations that are controlled by a company's marketing department and also those controlled by the company's intermediaries, in so far as these are relevant to the company's products.

5.1.3 Importance of Marketing Planning

The importance of marketing planning lies in the fact that it brings definite benefits to both the marketing planners and the organisation. If activity is not preceded by planning then the actions taken will be disorganised and haphazard. Hence in order to have an orderly conduct of operations planning is definitely required. Apart from various other benefits the specific benefits which accrue from planning are as follows:

1. **Helps to foresee future developments:** Planning is the process of thinking before doing. When the marketing planners undertake planning they are naturally compelled to think. This results in them analysing the past and predicting the future. This in turn leads them to identify probable events of relevance to the firm with a reasonable degree of accuracy so that they can formulate the relevant course of action to be taken well in advance so as to meet the marketing needs.

2. **Makes possible knowing of opportunities and preparation for handling of threats:** While identifying future developments management planners undertake a scanning of the environment. This leads to both, locating the opportunities as well as identification of problem areas. This gives a chance to the management to consider the various areas of opportunities and threats well in advance so that best possible solutions can be formulated in time and as a result non-rational responses to unexpected events and happenings will be considerably reduced, and considered and well thought out actions will be taken.

3. **Focus on objectives:** When the marketing activities are planned, the marketing objective is the focus around which all the marketing policies, programmes, strategies, and procedures are built. As the marketing objectives serve as a measure of standard they will highlight all deviations whether good or bad. Thus timely corrective action will be possible and this will lead the company moving in the right direction that is towards the achievement of its objectives.

4. **It makes management by exception possible:** When marketing operations are planned the whole marketing programme is scheduled in terms of time and resources. This makes it possible for the marketing manager to delegate authority to his subordinates. He can thus concentrate on vital and important matters. This delegation and decentralisation brings in management by exception which in turn brings about the much desired efficiency in the organisation.

5. **Optimum utiltsation of resources:** When marketing operations are planned the time and resources available with the company are employed most economically and rationally. As a result there is optimum utilisation of resources and maximisation of the return on investment.

6. **Facilitates co-ordination:** Marketing Planning facilitates co-ordination both horizontally and vertically. This is because any person located at any level in the marketing organisation can come to know through the marketing plan what the other has been doing at what time period. As a result, the jobs are synchronised in terms of time and content, and the overall marketing operation is integrated for maximum market impact.

7. **Cost economy:** As marketing planning leads not only to optimum use of resources but also to integrated working, the cost of the entire marketing programme is considerably reduced. Thus planning actually results in economy in cost.

8. **Planning acts as a basis for control:** Planning is the basis for control. A plan lays down standard of marketing performances against which the management measures and evaluates the organisation's performance. All deviations can be noted and corrective actions can be taken. In fact the complete control exercise is rooted in marketing planning.

5.1.4 Components of Marketing Planning

A marketing plan is composed of three basic components. They are: Objectives, Policies and Programmes.

1. Objectives: The first component of a marketing plan is the marketing objective. The objective is the end towards which all marketing activities are directed. The marketing objectives usually answer the question where are we heading or what are we aiming at. In order to facilitate understanding, marketing objectives may be divided into three parts, namely basic objectives; goals and targets. The basic objectives define the long range fundamental purpose of the company's marketing operations. They are not bound by time, nor are they quantifiable. Some examples of basic objectives are given below:

- To develop and maintain product leadership;
- To win the loyalty and co-operation of dealers;
- To improve and strengthen the company's long range profit outlook.

The marketing objectives may also be expressed as goals and targets. The marketing goals and targets are specific and not vague or philosophical like the basic objectives. The marketing goals are statements of specific achievement standards whereas targets are the quantified expressions of these standards to be achieved within a given time frame. The basic marketing objectives, goals and targets are closely inter-related. The basic objectives shape goals which in turn shape targets.

2. Policies: Marketing policies are broad guidelines which guide the marketing personnel in decision-making. Policies are general statements or understandings which guide or direct the thinking and decision-making process of the subordinates. A policy limits the area of action. The examples of marketing policies include statements like the following:

- "We will be competitive in price but not be a price cutter"
- "Our after sale service will be most comprehensive".
- "Wholesaler-retailer channel of distribution will be the king-pin of our distribution system".

3. Programmes: A marketing programme is a sequence of pre-determined marketing actions made after taking into account the time and resources available. A programme has to be formulated within the limits of the policies of the organisation and it should be designed in such a manner that it achieves the marketing objectives. A marketing programme is made up of procedures, rules and budgets.

5.1.5 Steps in Marketing Planning / Marketing Process

Establishment of a plan for the firm's total marketing programme is a major task that the management has to undertake. Although the exact sequence of marketing planning varies from firm to firm, certain sequential steps are recognised. The process of marketing planning is a compendium of at least seven steps:

1. **Assessing Opportunities and Threats:** Analysis and interpretation of marketing opportunities and threats in the starting point. In the process of marketing planning Marketing opportunities are the marketing possibilities open to the firm and the threats represent the obstacles in the path of the company in achieving customer satisfaction. In this stage the marketing management of the company scans the business environment, both internal and external, to identify and understand the relevant factors which affect the marketing operations of the company.

This stage involves the following major steps:

- Developing a consumer profile by identifying the consumer needs and problems and determining their quantitative and qualitative character.
- Developing a corporate profile by identifying and assessing the corporate strengths and weaknesses in terms of physical, financial and manpower resources.
- Developing a market profile by identifying and assessing market forces like competitors, trade intermediaries, public authorities etc. which could have an affect on the marketing operations of the company.
- Measurement of the potential demand and forecasting of sales for the planning period.
- Assumptions about the economy, industry, government and technology.
- In short, the first step lays down the foundation on which the marketing plan is built.

2. **Establishing Marketing Objectives:** Having analysed and interpreted the marketing opportunities and problems, the next stage in the planning process is to establish the marketing objectives. Marketing objectives are made up of the basic objectives, goals and targets. Marketing objectives are the outcome of the interaction between the top management and the marketing manager because marketing objectives are shaped by the company's basic objectives. The marketing manager establishes the marketing goals and targets in the light of the broad company objective. The marketing goals and targets may be broadly divided as *financial* and *operating*. The **financial goals** are those which are expressed in financial terms and include return on investment, gross profit/sales, market value of shares, working capital ratio turnover ratio etc. On the other hand, **operating goals** are those *which are not expressed in financial terms and are not immediately and directly associated with profit*. These may be: balance between home and foreign sales, government or non-government sales, market share, utilisation of productive capacity etc. It is also important for the goals to be specific.

3. **Framing Marketing Strategies and Policies:** The marketing objectives provide essential inputs for the formulation of marketing policies and strategies. A policy is a broad guideline for thought and action whereas strategy is their interpretation and designing of competitive moves to face marketing pressures. Policies are largely influenced by the basic marketing objective(s) while strategy is influenced by goals and targets. While formulating strategies the following factors must be considered: moves of competitors, substitutability of marketing inputs, productivity of marketing inputs, input elasticity etc. so as to produce an action programmable to meet the special market pressures.

4. **Programming of Operations:** Based on the inputs of policies and strategies, the marketing management next develops action programmes in respect of each sub-function of marketing in terms of product or consumer groups and market segments with perspective of time and resources. In effect sub plans are to be prepared such as product mix plan, sales, force plan, advertising and sales promotion plan and so on. Programme is a major course of action that enables a manager to achieve his objectives within the frame of policy guidelines. These programmes for sub functions are based on procedures, rules, budgets and methods. They are designed to attain the functional objectives of the firm within the limits, of the firm's marketing policies and strategies.

   Such programming can be centralised or decentralised. In centralised programming the formulations of the programmes is done by the marketing manager and his associates at the top and these programmes are passed on to the lower levels to implement. Decentralised programming is contrary to centralised programming. In decentralised programming, the programming is done at the functional and sub-functional level within the broad frame work provided by the marketing manager. Both centralised and decentralised programming have their merits and demerits. Hence a company will have to make a choice after weighing the merits and demerits of each case.

5. **Developing Marketing Mix**: Whenever decentralised programming is followed, there is a need to integrate all sub-functional programmes so as to develop an integrated comprehensive master marketing plan. It involves evaluation of each sub-functional programme relative to others in terms of contribution to achievement of the marketing objectives and the requirements of the resource inputs. In accepting, rejecting, or modifying each programme while integrating them, the principle of differential advantage is always adhered to.

   This integration process leads to the development of the company's marketing mix in which each sub-function and its programme is adjusted with others in such a way that their interaction in the market produces maximum impact. For example, the advertising programme is adjusted in terms of media, content and timings that reinforces the working of the sales force and intermediaries to maximise consumer need satisfaction and price realisation on products.

   The preparation of the master plan is usually the responsibility of the top marketing management and involves deliberations, balancing and compromises. It involves co-ordination and adjustments with other functional plans such as production, finance, purchasing and personnel and plans of trade intermediaries and members of the company's vertical marketing system.

6. **Designing Resource Mobilisation Plan:** Once the master marketing plan is ready for implementation, the top management has to design a programme of resource mobilisation. A resource mobilisation plan shows the quantum, type and costs of resources to be used to implement the master plan. These resources can be of three types, physical, financial and manpower resources. The physical resources may be research paraphernalia, advertising development, materials handling, warehousing, selling kit and the like. The financial resources are the finance and credit needed to procure material and manpower resources and services from outside. The manpower resources refer to the number and the quality of men and women needed to implement the programmes. In essence, it is to plan, mobilise, organise and employ resources.

7. **Monitoring the Operations:** Once the above steps are carried out the master plan designed and resources mobilised should be used to achieve the marketing objectives. Once the activities begin to be carried out there should be constant feedback as to whether the activities are moving as per plan or not. Planning will be meaningless if control is not exercised on the activities to check whether the activities are moving as per the plan or not. Thus control is the counterside of planning. It is the ultimate step in planning. Through the control process the management receives information about the manner in which the marketing plan is being implemented.

5.1.6 Essential Requirements of Marketing Planning

The primary purpose of marketing planning is to increase managerial effectiveness. Planning is nothing but a systematic approach for the management to consider the possible alternatives it faces. In recent years, planning has become more formalised. There is a well-established procedure for management to follow for marketing planning. However a procedure that provides a technique should have the following characteristics or essentials.

1. **Planning should be simple:** The planning process or procedure should be simple. The planned programme works, only if the average manager is capable of using it in spite of the day to day work pressures that he has to face and in the absence of intensive training. In today's business world that is becoming more and more complex and competitive, it is very important that simplicity be maintained in planning. However simplicity should not be at the cost of producing results.

2. **Planning should be practical:** The planning process should be practical. It should be such that every manager at whatever level he may be benefits from it. If the benefits of planning accrue only to the top level managers then the lower level ones will extend only reluctant compliance and this will be followed by unwanted resentment. Thus it is very essential that planning be practical and beneficial to all. To make planning beneficial even to the average manager, the marketing manager should develop a practical process and should provide background information, training and technical assistance.

3. **Planning should be selective and adaptive:** The planning process must be so selective and adaptive that all the managers are covered. An eligibility to participate must not force the participants to use planning more than it is required especially in his area so that different areas of planning of each manager can be co-ordinated and consolidated.
4. **Planning should be flexible:** The planning process must be so flexible that it should be possible to change any portion of planning conveniently, with least cost, if anything happens warranting a change.
5. **Planning should be precise:** Future planning should be precise in terms of goals and objectives. In fact the future cannot be predicted with a high degree of accuracy, and the further into the future you try to predict the less accurate you are. However there are three ways of expressing expected results namely general, specific and dynamically quantified. The third is the best way as it is the way in which a precise statement is made so that the problem can be easily recognised. It facilitates quick and easy identification, detection and measurement of possible deviations.
6. **Planning should be based on reliable information:** For planning to be sound there is a requirement of reliable information on a continuous basis. The future estimate is neither a forecast nor a prediction but a temporary hypothesis regarding an important, probable future development that could not be predicted with accuracy. The planner needs to have continuous feedback of information so that he can revise the estimate whenever there is a significant deviation.
7. **Planning should be synthesising and synchronising:** The planning process should be such that it co-ordinates and integrates all types of plans and planning. In each functional area there should be perfect synchronisation and synthesisation of functions. If planning does not co-ordinate and integrate all the sub functions in each area the firm will have to pay a high price for time, effort, confusion, resistance, resentment and frustration.
8. **Planning should be motivating:** Planning in order to be effective needs the active participation of the managerial personnel. Planning will encourage people to participate provided they are motivated. Any properly designed planning process will motivate the personnel because, it will result in the following:
   - It gives the workers' a real sense of participating in the planning for their own future.
   - It relieves apprehension by converting the unknown to known.
   - It provides security as to their position in the organisation.
   - It develops pride amongst the personnel to be part of an organisation that knows where it is, where it wants to go and how to get there.
9. **Planning should be accompanied with the least amount of paper work:** An effective planning system is one which gets all the work done with the least amount of paper work. All planning should not be reduced in writing. In fact the

writing work can be reduced by following discussions and outlining, giving only the information that is required and avoiding duplicacy of information by providing common information from a common source

10. **Planning has to have a direction:** In order for the planning process to be most efficient a special director for planning should be appointed whose only job will be not to do planning but only to oversee how it is working and show it should work. He should be a planning specialist and should dedicate all his time only to ensure that successful and efficient planning takes place, and is properly implemented.

5.1.7 Types of Marketing Plans

Basically marketing plans are of two types: one which is based on the organisation structure and the other which is based on time. *Marketing plans which are based on organisation structure are known as structural plans.* Under this type of planning a separate plan is made for each function of management in the marketing area and then all these plans are integrated into a well-knit marketing plan. There can be separate plans for product groups, market segment, and customer groups finally synchronised into a single departmental marketing plan. Thus, there can be product mix plan - sales - force plan - advertising and sales promotion plan - distribution channel plan - pricing plan - marketing research plan - marketing organisation plan. However this type of planning faces one difficulty that of integrating the various functional plans into an integrated marketing plan.

Marketing plans based on time are known as time-span plans. The time span plans refer the short range and long range plans of the firm. A short range plan ranges between three months to twelve months. It is a projection for a short period twelve months at the most. Such a plan deals with routine issues like sales-force recruitment and training, maintenance of levels of inventory, advertising and sales-promotion issues. On the other hand long range plans are for a period of more than one year, and range right upto five to ten years. Long range plans deal with specific problems like planning for new products, developing new trade channels, entering new markets etc.

Whatever type of classification is undertaken, the results are usually the same.

5.1.8 Difficulties in Marketing Planning

The planning process described above is a logical and rational way of determining the future course of marketing action in any company. It analyses the past, considers the present and projects the future so as to facilitate the marketing management of a company. However the process of planning is not without its problems. Some of the major problems faced by a marketing planner are highlighted below.

1. **The problem of Accuracy in Projecting the Future:** One of the major problems in marketing planning is to accurately project the future on which the whole structure of planning is based. As far as projecting the future is concerned problems arise on two accounts. First and foremost there is a lack of reliable data and applicable tools

on whose basis sales and other marketing results are forecast. Secondly the market forces whose behaviour is to be predicted are very dynamic. In India reliable market information is not available and the facilities of procuring it are inadequate. As a result of this reliable and timely future predictions become difficult. This makes marketing planning problematic. However two alternatives have been suggested to overcome this problem. First the management may develop alternative sets of premises and alternative plans based on them so that major changes in future events may be readily reflected in action. And, second, management should be ready with detours in planning to allow for unforeseeable events. However, both the alternatives need flexibility of plan.

2. **Corporate Inflexibilities:** Another problem faced by a marketing planner is the inflexibilities built in the corporate working. Corporate inflexibilities refer to rigidities and resistance of persons and systems operating in the company with regard to the changes contemplated by the marketing plan. These may be both internal as well as external. Internal inflexibilities refer to the mental frame, attitudes, perceptions and behaviour of marketing and other personnel. The behaviour of the personnel may be so conditioned over a period of time that they may develop inflexibility and resist changes which a plan has envisaged. This is particularly so in old and established business houses. Similarly marketing systems policies, procedures, and rules tend to become so secure that there is an aversion to any change in them. Even investments made can act as impediments in marketing planning, e.g. the management may be very keen to recover the investment made in training of a particular salesman and may resist a marketing plan that writes off this training.

   Apart from internal inflexibilities, marketing planning is plagued by external inflexibilities also. External inflexibilities are rooted in the external environment of a company over which the marketing management has little or no control. These inflexibilities arise from the changes taking place in the culture and behaviour patterns of society, political climate, labour organisations and technological frame within which the organisation operates.

3. **Loss of Initiatives:** A closely knit comprehensive marketing plan stifles initiative because the participants are strictly tied to the set goals, targets, authorities and responsibilities. This discourages working with a free and open mind and therefore diminishes innovations in the marketing operations.

4. **The problem of Work Pressure:** One of the most important problems faced by marketing planners is that marketing personnel are so preoccupied with execution of marketing functions and solving day to day problems that they are not left with sufficient time and energy to think and plan marketing operations. Such job pressures are normally caused by enlarged span of control, non-delegation of authority, and reluctance to plan. It is a problem which encourages management by crisis and does not let planning take off the ground.

5. **The Cost of Planning:** In order to come up with an effective marketing plan the company has to spend in terms of time, money and talent. The specific and logical steps required in marketing planning, all consume a good deal of money time and talent. With all this the benefits of marketing planning are not available immediately. It has its own payoff period which is usually quite long. This discourages firms from undertaking marketing planning in the most systematic and scientific way. Inspite of the above problems the relevance of marketing planning cannot be denied and no company should attempt action without a plan.

5.2 Marketing Information System

5.2.1 Concept, Meaning and Definition

An Information system generates information from data. Data is in the form of raw material and it is subject to some manipulation to generate useful information. *If a system generates useful information for managerial use in planning, decision-making and control, it is called as a* "**Management Information System**".

An Information System is a man – machine system that produces information for use in managerial problem solving and decision-making. A full-fledged MIS provides for capturing of data at source with desirable accuracy and processing it to generate information in a usable form for managers.

The purpose of a Marketing Information System is to highlight a situation requiring a marketing manager's attention and action. The system collects data at source about every transaction in every area of activity and stores it for present or future use. The data items are processed and the information is either stored or communicated to the users.

A marketing information system is a management information system designed to support marketing decision-making.

A **Marketing Information System** (MIS) is *a set of procedures and methods designed to generate, analyse, disseminate, and store anticipated marketing decision information on a regular, continuous basis*. An information system can be used operationally and strategically for several aspects of marketing. A marketing information system can be used operationally, managerially, and strategically for several aspects of marketing.

Marketing Information System has been defined by various authors in various ways. Some of these definitions are as under:

According to **Phillip Kotler**, Marketing Information System is "*people, equipment, and procedures to gather, sort, analyse, evaluate, and distribute needed, timely, and accurate information to marketing decision makers.*"

According to **BusinessDictionary.com** A Marketing Information system is "*a system that analyses and assesses marketing information, gathered continuously from sources inside and outside an organisation*". Timely marketing information provides basis for decisions such as product development or improvement, pricing, packaging, distribution, media selection and promotion.

According to **Donald F Cox** and **Robert E Good** a Marketing Information System may be defined as *"a set of procedures and methods for the regular, planned collection, analysis, and presentation of information for use in making marketing decisions"*. This of course is a step beyond logistics systems, which handle inventory control, orders, and so forth."

5.2.2 Components of Marketing Information System

The basic components of any Information System are:

1. **Hardware:** This includes the Keyboard, Monitor, PCU, Mouse, Cable Connections etc that are used for collecting storing and analysing the data.

2. **Software:** This includes all programmes loaded onto the computer which are used for data collection, storage, analysis and communication.

3. **Database:** Database is a compilation of raw data from various areas of a Business. Thus a particular MIS could have a database of suppliers, customers, employees, retailers etc.

4. **Procedures:** This includes all procedures laid down for an efficient collection storage, analysis, communication and use of information.

5. **People:** This includes all people who help in gathering, processing, storing and communicating the information.

5.2.3 Features of Marketing Information System

Marketing Information System has a number of characteristic features. The purpose of MIS is to enhance marketing effectiveness through information support. For a Marketing Information System to be a sound source for decision-making, it should have the following features:

1. **MIS should be Marketing oriented/directed:** The MIS of an organisation should be so designed as to meet the information needs of the Marketing Department at all levels so that the marketing objectives are achieved.

2. **It should be Organisation Driven:** The Marketing Information System is a support function. Its purpose is to meet the marketing information needs of an organisation. As such the Marketing Information System should be so designed that its strategy is derived from the overall corporate strategy.

3. **It should be an Integrated System:** Marketing Information System views the organisations marketing information needs from a system's point of view. It should blend together databases of all subsystems of the marketing system and through information interchange integrates the overall marketing organisation.

4. **It should avoid redundancy in data storage:** As MIS is an integrated system, it should avoid unnecessary duplication and redundancy in data gathering and storage.

5. **It should be based on heavy planning:** As the design and implementation of MIS requires heavy investment, such a system should be designed and implemented only after heavy planning.

6. **There should be flexibility and ease of use:** The MIS should be flexible enough to accommodate new requirements. The system should be easy to operate so that not many computer skills are required on the part of the user to access information.

7. **Distributed systems:** Most organisations have their offices, sales outlets, etc geographically spread over a wide area. These offices work mostly independently of its headquarters. However information has to be routinely exchanged between these offices. In such cases the information system should be such as can meet the information processing requirements of the various constituents.

8. **Information as a resource:** Information is a resource. As such the MIS should be so designed that the information resources can be shared across offices and sales outlets and thus increasing the return from investment in information resources.

5.2.4 Importance of Marketing Information System

A Marketing Information System is important as it offers the following advantages or benefits:

1. **Aids in Recognising Trends:** A good marketing information system helps a marketing manager to recognise changing market trends. Trends are constantly changing and a marketing manager should be able to predict and respond to the changing trends. The changing trends may be in respect of prices, product design, packaging, promotion schemes, etc. A Marketing Information System helps managers to take effective marketing decisions in respect of prices, product designs, etc., in response to changing trends in the environment.

2. **Help managers to Recognise Change:** A sound marketing information system will point out the changing trends and thus aid a marketing organisation to change the product mix or to introduce a new line according to the changing market demand.

3. **Instant supply of required information:** Marketing is a dynamic function and a marketing organisation needs to respond quickly to the various changes taking place in the marketing environment. Here the Marketing Information System helps the marketing manager by supplying the required information in a quick and timely fashion, leading to effective decision-making.

4. **Quality of Decision-making:** Decisions have to be taken in every area of marketing by a marketing manager every day. A properly designed marketing information system promptly supplies reliable and relevant information. With the help of this information, the marketing manager can make the right decisions at the right time.

5. **Facilitates Marketing Planning and Control:** An effective Marketing Management System makes it possible for a marketing manager to effectively plan and control all marketing activities. Marketing planning with respect to product planning, price

planning and decisions, promotion and distribution is made more effective through the use of the Marketing Information System, as decisions related to all such aspects are taken on the basis of scientifically collected and analysed data and not in a vacuum.

6. **Provides Marketing Intelligence:** Marketing intelligence refers to information of the events that are happening in the external environment, i.e. changes in customer tastes, expectations, competitors strategies, government policies, international environment, etc. With the help of MIS specialists, it is possible to collect marketing intelligence which is vital to make effective marketing decisions.

7. **Integration of Information:** Large firms with widespread marketing departments can gather information which is scattered at many centers or and integrate it for effective decision-making. Such integration is possible if there is a centralised MIS.

8. **Tapping of business Opportunities:** An effective Marketing Information System helps a marketing manager in tapping, untapped markets. It thus makes available business opportunities to the Marketing Manager.

5.3 Marketing Research

5.3.1 Introduction and Meaning

In recent times the markets are flooded with products and services from a large number of companies. The buyers have become choosy while buying the products. Their buying decisions are affected by the opinions of their friends, their children and their better half. Moreover advertisements on television and in glossy magazines have also affected their decisions.

Hence in order to understand the needs of buyers and their behaviour, we have a tool; that of marketing research. It generates information for the decision-makers to design a suitable product, to develop it, to price it reasonably, to promote it and finally to distribute it for the convenience of the buyers. Hence it helps the decision-maker by providing him with correct and latest information for arriving at sound marketing decisions.

The management decision process has become more and more complex and this is more true for a firm's marketing management because it is located at the interface between a firm and the customer's of a firm. The changing characters of markets, unknown competitions, emergence of consumerism, changing production patterns, advanced technology and emergence of consumerism have given rise to the growing difficulties of making efficient marketing decisions. Hence marketing research has become an important component of the Marketing Information System to manage all areas of management in general and to marketing management in particular.

5.3.2 Definition of Marketing Research

The essential purpose of marketing research is to provide information, which will help in the identification of an opportunity or a problem situation, and to assist marketing managers in arriving at the best possible decisions when such situations are encountered.

To understand marketing research, the phrase 'Marketing' and 'Research' should be understood separately. **Marketing** is defined as *the managerial process by which products are matched with markets and through which the consumer is enabled to use or enjoy the product.* It is also related with need, wants and demands, products, value and satisfaction, exchange and transactions.

Research can be defined *as logical and systematised application of the fundamentals of science to be general and overall questions of a study and scientific technique, which provide precise tools in finding explanations to misconceived facts of social life.*

Hence the above two phrases explain that marketing research is required to solve specific problems, but it is more than that, since now it is considered an indispensable part of marketing information system which has been a continuous aspect of management

Against this background, one can say that marketing research is research relating to any problem in the area of marketing.

Marketing research is a social science research and is defined by different authors as follows:

1. *"Marketing research is the systematic, objective and exhaustive search for and study of the facts relevant to any problem in the field of marketing."*

    - American Marketing Association

2. *"Marketing research is the systematic recording and analysis of data about problems relating to marketing."*

    - American Marketing Association

3. *Marketing research is "the application of scientific method to the solution of marketing problems."*

    - Luck, Wales, Taylor

4. *"Marketing research is the gathering and analysis of information to assist management in making marketing decision. These decisions involve the manipulation of the firm's pricing, Production, distribution and product variables."*

    - Wentz

5. *"Marketing research is the application of scientific methods to the study of the factors that affect the buying decisions in a given market and the profitability of the business concerned."*

    - Glasser

Marketing research is an integral part of marketing information system. It is both a science and art. It is a science because there is systematic application of the principles of research. It is an art because it tells us how to solve day-to-day and specific problems of management, particularly problems of marketing management.

5.3.3 Market Research and Marketing Research

Many a times the terms Market Research and Marketing Research are used interchangeably. Both terms are an integral part of Marketing, however there is a definite difference between the two terms.

The basic difference between the two terms is the scope of each term. Market Research is a narrower concept as compared to Marketing Research.

The American Marketing Association defines "**Marketing Research**" as *"the systematic and objective identification, collection, analysis and dissemination of information for the purpose of improving decision-making related to the identification and solution of problems and opportunities in marketing."*

European Society for Opinion and Market Research (ESOMAR) defines "**Market Research**" as *"the systematic gathering and interpretation of information about individuals or organisations, using the statistical and analytical methods and techniques of the applied social sciences to gain insight or support decision-making."*

Market Research is any organised effort to collect information about markets or customers. Market Research will get you information about market trends (political, economic, social, technology, etc.), market players (e.g. direct and indirect competition), target market attributes, customer wants and needs, etc. **Marketing Research** pertains to information about research related to new products and product development, different modes of distribution, pricing, promotion research, advertising and public relations. In short it pertains to every aspect of the Marketing Process.

Marketing Research covers all four P's of Marketing. It covers every possible measure to identify and understand consumer preferences. Where as on the other hand, Market Research typically covers only one of the four P's i.e. place.

5.3.4 Objectives of Marketing Research

The following are the main objectives of marketing research:

(a) **Planning:** Marketing research is very useful in the formulation and evaluation of planning and its components, It helps the management of small and large scale firms to know their customers understand their needs by effectively taking planning and forecasting as a tools in their research activities.

(b) **Helps in reducing the cost:** Marketing research helps in minimising the costs in selling, advertising, promotion and distribution. The cost of distribution is reduced tremendously because research brings market closer to the consumers. The production cost per unit also decreases because of the different production patterns adopted.

(c) **Consumer behaviour:** Marketing research helps in studying the behavioural patterns of the consumers. The producer while producing the products keeps in his mind the needs and the tastes of the customers.

(d) **Innovative techniques in production:** Marketing research helps in finding out new techniques of production and the producer is in a better position to find out and compare his production results with the products of other companies. Research also helps in the discovery of supplementary lines of products. E.g. Bajaj Company has produced a wide variety of products both in automobiles and electricals in India.

(e) **Problem Solving:** The main objectives of marketing research are to solve the problems relating to the product, price, promotion, competition, advertisement and distribution of goods and services. The market researcher tries to bring alternative solutions to different problems. For instance, if he comes to know that a particular product is going out of fashion then he immediately discontinues that product line or diversifies that product lie.

(f) **Reduces Risks:** As the markets have expanded geographically there are various risks, hence the main objective of the market researcher would be to reduce such risks.

(g) **Survivals of the firm:** Marketing research is used for the survival of the firm. It helps in assessing the strengths and weaknesses of the firm and also analyse the firm's share of the markets and finally provides necessary information to the top management for proper decisions.

(h) **Growth of the firm:** It helps in the growth of the firm. Growth is possible if initiatives are taken to expand markets by introducing new varieties of products.

(i) **Introduction of new product:** Before introducing a new product in the market, the market researcher would find out the appropriate timing for introducing that product and also tries to find out suitable avenue and place and also the different methods to reach such markets.

(j) **Market orientation:** The objective of marketing research is to enable the firms to produce the goods and services acceptable to the customers. It sees that the goods and services must reach the market easily, quickly, cheaply and profitably. The right course of action to approach and sustain the market is possible with suitable marketing research.

5.3.5 Scope of Marketing Research

Marketing research is a comprehensive term with a very wide scope. Marketing research is used to find solutions for any problem of marketing. Different marketing managers with different objectives, feel the need for marketing research.

Marketing research can be quantitative or qualitative. Quantitative research generalises for the population on the basis of a sample study whereas qualitative research is diagnostic in nature. The scope of marketing research is wide and has application in all areas of the marketing mix such as,

(a) **Product research:** Product research consists of undertaking studies on new and potential product or improvement of present products or testing of the existing products. In product research the consumer's reactions to the products are analysed under product marketing research. The scope of this research varies from a new product to an existing product. Necessary changes must be made in the product line according to the changes in the market, which are revealed by the product marketing research.

(b) **Price research:** Pricing and establishing of price policies are the most important aspects in price research. It includes several forms of price analysis, marginal analysis and cost analysis.

(c) **Promotion research:** This research relates to personal selling advertising and publicity, sales promotion and public relations. In personal selling research, the research focuses on the sales organisation, sales effectiveness and sales compensation. In advertising, there is a media research and pre-testing and post-testing of the advertisements. For instance, which advertising media like television, radio, newspapers etc. would be more suitable for companies.

(d) **Distribution research:** This research undertakes activities such activities which helps to remove the gap between consumers and producers through retailers and wholesalers. The other components of distribution channel research are studies of dealer costs and profits, store audits, dealer relations and the industry pattern of distribution. The location research is also required to determine the most optimum location of distribution of products, this may range from local to national and international markets.

(e) **Policy research:** This research helps in deciding the marketing policy and inventory policy. It provides important data and information to predict future market conditions. The economic, social and political atmosphere is reviewed so that appropriate policies is adopted by the management.

(f) **Competition research:** In this research a study is being made to study the competitors' activities and also to study the company's competitive position in the market. The company undertakes intensive study of competitors, marketing practices and policies and also assesses its own strength and weaknesses.

(g) **Consumer Research:** All marketing decisions are ultimately geared towards consumers. Here the detailed studies of consumers and their behavioural pattern are undertaken. Who is the target audience? What do the customer's expect? What are their buying habits? Why do they behave like this? All these and related questions about consumers are answered by consumer research.

In conclusion, it can be said that marketing research is undertaken to guide managers in their analysis, planning implementation and control of programmes to satisfy customers and organisational goals. The need for market research is felt by marketing managers for different objectives, which ultimately decides the scope of marketing research. The scope of marketing research management covers all the market measurement studies, the competitive situation and the marketing mix studies.

5.3.6 Sources of Collecting Marketing Data

Data is generally classified as either primary data or secondary data.

(a) **Primary Data:** This data is collected by a researcher for the particular marketing research project currently being undertaken. This information has originated directly as a result of particular problem under investigation.

(b) **Secondary Data:** Data that already exists and may be used for an investigation but has not been collected for that specific purpose is called secondary data. It is usually cheaper to use this kind of data than to set up special investigations, but care must be taken to ensure that the data Is relevant, can be adjusted to the problem and is reliable.

There are basically three alternatives in collecting primary data:

1. Observation Method
2. Experiment Method
3. Survey Method

1. **Observation Method:** Observation is the process of recognising and recording the behaviour of the people. The observation may be natural i.e. just observing the consumers in a shop. In this method the consumers are not asked what brands they buy or what television programmes they watch but the researcher arranges to observe what type of products are bought and what programmes are watched. This method has certain advantage over other methods because it does not rely on the respondent's willingness to provide the desired data and moreover certain types of data can be collected only by observation. However the demerit of this method is that it is difficult to observe such things as awareness, beliefs, feelings etc.

2. **Experiment Method:** This method allows a maximum degree of control in comparison with other methods of collecting primary data. This method is also ranked as the best with respect to data accuracy but the disadvantage of this method is that it is costly and complex.

3. **Survey Method:** It is the most widely used technique in marketing research. In this method the information is recorded on a form known as questionnaire from persons who have believed to have the desired information. It is assumed that the respondents know the answers to the questions and have the authority to answer

these questions and are willing to co-operate in answering these questions in the best way. The survey method or the questionnaire method as is commonly known can have communication with the information in three different ways:

(a) **Through Mail or Post Office:** In this method an upto date mailing list is prepared. A copy of the questionnaire is mailed to the respondents asking the respondents to send prompt and accurate replies. A gift incentive is provided to ensure co-operation and get a quick return of the duly completed questionnaire.

(b) **Telephone Survey:** In metropolitan cities, and big urban areas, the respondent can be interviewed on the telephone. This method is very useful when the interviewer wants factual answers to certain questions. This method is quick and cheap, moreover large number of interviews in a short period can be undertaken. However in India this method has a limited scope because people in India are unwilling to give personal information on telephone.

(c) **Personal Interviews:** Here the selected sources are interviewed personally involving face-to-face communication with a free feedback of information. Personal contact is considered to be most important and is superior to the other two methods because it combines both features of getting information namely questioning and observation. This method involves long interviews responsible with complex questions and additional questions to secure more information. Accurate data is likely to be generated by this method.

Out of the two most important methods, field research is mainly used to collect primary data whereas desk research is used to collect secondary readymade data. Desk research is done indoors and is mainly done in libraries. The sources are trade publications, journals, books, directories, research reports etc. It is relatively less expensive, less time consuming and easy. Desk research is not preferable when data is obsolete and irrelevant.

The other research method is:

4. **Panel Research:** When a researcher interviews the same sample group, two or more times it is panel research. Panels are made up of respondents who regularly and routinely report their buying behaviour. They keep a diary of purchases, their shopping activities and on what advertisements they are influenced of any other item under research. This panel research offers three benefits. Firstly, the buyer behaviour can be easily related to the buyer characteristics. Secondly, changes in buyer behaviour can be related to changes in the marketing mix and thirdly, changes in buyer behaviour can be monitored over a period of time.

5.3.7 Marketing Research Procedure, Types and Techniques of Marketing Research

The marketing research process is a five-step application of the scientific method. The scientific method that includes

1. Definition of the problem
2. Situation analysis
3. Obtaining problem-Specific data
4. Interpretation of data
5. Problem solution

Step 1: Definition of the Problem

Defining the problem is the most important and often the most difficult step in the marketing research process. In this step, the objectives of the research must be clearly defined. The manager must think about what decisions need to be made and must clearly specify what information is really needed to make them. The manager and the researcher should both be involved so that both agree on the major objectives of the research.

The problem definition step sounds simple but it is not so. A manager may assume that all of the questionable areas are obvious or that the researcher really understands what information is needed, this is also not the case. Hence the important questions may be ignored while less important questions may be analysed in depth. It is also easy to fall into the trap of mistaking symptoms for the definition of the problem.

Sometimes the research priorities are very clear, for example when a manager only wants to know if the targeted households have tried a new product and what percent of them bought it a second time. But usually it is harder than this. The manager might also want to know why some didn't buy - or if they had even heard of the product. There is rarely any time and money to study everything. The manager may have to narrow things down. Developing a priority list that includes all the possible problem areas is sensible. The various items on the list may need to be considered more completely in the situation analysis step before final priorities can be set.

Step 2: Situation Analysis

When the marketing manager feels the real problem has begun to surface, a situation analysis is useful. A situation analysis is an informal study of what information is already available in the problem area. The situation analysis may help refine the problem definition and specify what additional information if any is needed.

The situation analysis usually involves informal talks with informed people. Informed people mean others in the firm, a few good gentlemen who have close contact with customers, or others knowledgeable about in the industry. In industrial marketing, where relationships with customers are close the customers themselves may be called; perhaps one of these people has already worked on the same problem, or knows about a useful source of relevant information. Their inputs may help to sharpen the problem definition, too.

The situation analysis is especially important if the researcher is a research specialist who doesn't know much about the management decisions to be made of if the marketing manager is dealing with unfamiliar areas. They must be sure they understand the problem area, including the nature of the target market, the marketing mix, competition, and other external factors. Otherwise, the researcher may rush ahead and make foolish mistakes or simply "discover" what is already known by management.

Step 3: Getting Problem-Specific Data

This stage of research calls for determining the type of information needed and the most efficient ways to gather this information. A researcher can gather secondary data, primary data or both. Secondary data consists of information that already exists somewhere, having been collected for another purpose.

Primary data consist of originally collected information for the specific purpose at hand. Primary research involves the collection of primary data by the marketing researcher or agents of the Marketing Researcher directly from respondents. Because these data may be collected first hand the process tends to be more costly and may be more time consuming than is the collection of secondary research data. However, the use of primary data is sometimes mandatory when secondary data are unavailable. The primary data are usually much more relevant to what is being researched because of the unique situation or problem, or the timing.

Secondary research depends on secondary data or data obtained from sources other than directly from respondents. In other words, the research has already been accomplished. Most researchers usually begin by examining published secondary research sources to see what data already exist that have been collected for some other problem or some other purpose. In some cases, the problem has already been researched in its entirety, and the data are timely and directly relevant and applicable to the problem at hand. In such a case, use of secondary research data could save the time and money of putting together and conducting a primary research project.

The Marketing Researcher has the following basic ways to gather Primary Data:
Observation Method

In the observation method, the data are collected by observing some action of the respondent. No interviews are involved, although an interview may be used as a follow-up to get additional information. For example, if customers are observed buying a drink in cans instead of bottles, they may be asked why they prefer that one form of packaging to the other.

Information may be gathered by personal or mechanical observation. In one form of personal observation, the researcher poses as a customer in a store. This technique is useful in getting information about the calibre of the salespeople, or in determining what brands they push. Mechanical observation is illustrated by an electric cord stretched across a highway to count the number of cars that pass during a certain time period.

Another example is a study on food prices, conducted on behalf of a local government. Observers were sent to a large sample of research food stores to obtain price data on every brand available in 65 categories of food products.

The observation method has several advantages.

1. It can be highly precise.
2. It usually removes all doubt about what the consumer does in a given situation.
3. The consumers are unaware that they are being observed, so presumably they act in the usual fashion.

The disadvantages are:

1. This technique reduces bias, but the possibility of bias is not completely eliminated as long as people are used as observers.
2. The technique is limited in its application. Observation tells what happened, but it cannot tell why.

Survey Method

Companies undertake surveys to learn about people's knowledge, beliefs, preferences, satisfaction, and so on, and to measure these magnitudes or importance in the population. The most common means of gathering primary marketing data is the survey method. It usually leads to a broader range of data than observation or experimentation methods do. Surveys are used to plan product designs, advertising copy, sales promotions, and other marketing activities.

In the survey method, the researcher gathers facts directly from a sample of respondents. The three principle kinds of surveys are the (a) telephone interview, (b) the mail questionnaire, and the (c) personal interview.

(a) **In a telephone survey,** a large number of interviews can be handled quickly at a comparatively low cost than either personal or mail surveys. By telephone the interviewer can talk with a number of family members during the same call and can clarify or elaborate on questions whenever necessary. This method is easy to administer, telephone survey may be timely. One disadvantage of the telephone survey is that interviews may be short. Lengthy interviews can be conducted satisfactorily over phone. Another limitation of the telephone is some people have unlisted numbers, so people do not have phones.

(b) **Mail questionnaires also have many merits:** Mail questionnaires can be presented in a more objective and controlled manner. It allows respondents to answer questions at their own pace. The haste and distraction of personal and telephone interviews can be avoided. Mailed questionnaires are more reasonable, short and the questions asked are very simple. The major disadvantage with mail questionnaires is the difficulty of obtaining returns.

(c) Personal Interview: When a long, complex questionnaire is used, a personal interview is most suitable. The personal interview provides an opportunity for the researcher to obtain complete answers and to judge the socioeconomic condition of the respondent. Interview bias may occur if the interviewer rewords the question so that the respondent provides anticipated responses. Respondent bias may occur, too, when the respondent relates to the interview what the Interview wants to hear. Personal interviewing is relatively expensive in terms of time and money.

Step 4: Interpretation of Data

The interpretation of marketing information is a significant nature of marketing research. The marketing information is properly interpreted and analysed. The information collected will have to be edited, coded, tabulated and analysed to interpret the facts and figures of the markets. One can see that getting a representative sample is very important. The most common method for getting a representative sample is random sampling, where each member of the population has the same chance of being included in the sample. Great care must be used to ensure that sampling is really random and not just haphazard.

The nature of the sample, and how it is selected, makes a big difference in how the results of a study can be interpreted. This should be considered as a part of planning data collection, to make sure that the final results can be interpreted with enough confidence so the marketing manager can use them in his planning.

Even if the sampling is carefully planned, it is also important to evaluate the quality of the research data itself. Besides sampling and validity problems, a marketing manager should consider whether the analysis of the data supports the conclusions drawn in the interpretation step. Sometimes the technical people pick the right statistical procedure and their calculations are exact but they offer a wrong interpretation because they don't understand the management problem. In one survey, two wheeler buyers were asked to rank five scooters in order from most preferred to least preferred. One scooter was ranked first by slightly more respondents than any other scooter, so the researcher reported it as the "most liked scooter". That interpretation however ignored the fact that most of the other respondents ranked the scooter last.

Step 5: Problem Solution

In the problem solution step, the results of the research are used in making marketing decisions. At the conclusion of the research process the marketing manager should be able to apply the research findings to marketing strategy planning. For instance, the mix of the four P's. If the research does not provide the necessary information, to help guide these decisions, the research money probably is wasted. It is to be noted that this step is the logical conclusion to the whole research process. In fact it is the reason for the earlier steps. This final step must be anticipated in every one of the preceding steps.

5.3.8 Importance of Marketing Research

It has been observed that marketing research concerns itself with every phase of marketing activity. It covers a very wide area and is a tool that pervades every marketing activity. Its need and importance can be judged from the following discussions:

1. **Helps in Decision-making:** Marketing research helps decision-making in the marketing area. It provides a logical basis for decisions. Such decisions are based on concrete data, tests, experiments and expert opinions.

2. **Management Planning:** Marketing research is used for management planning. Marketing management can access the resources that can be useful for the business. Short and long term planning can be effectively formulated with the help of marketing research. The research inputs are helpful to managers planning new market programmes and existing market expansion.

3. **Problem Solving:** Starting from problem identification to formulation of alternative solutions, and evaluating the alternatives in every area of marketing management, is the problem solving action of marketing research. Problem solving marketing research focuses on the short range and long range decisions that must be taken with respect to the elements of the marketing mix, i.e., product, price, place and promotion. It can help management bring about prompt adjustment and innovations in the above areas of marketing management.

4. **Large Scale Production:** It helps the manufacturers in taking suitable decisions for large-scale production by exploiting the resources available in the most optimum manner. It helps to explore, identify and locate markets to adopt intensive and extensive production techniques. Hence it helps the management to bring about change in product designs, to meet the changing marketing needs.

5. **Formulation of Product Strategy:** It helps to formulate a new business plan. The product strategy makes it possible to know how to have a right product mix and how to do strategic business unit analysis. It also helps to undertake product development strategy where new products are launched in current markets.

6. **Formulation of Market Strategy:** While formulating a new business plan the researcher can have market penetration strategy. In other words, he form can also think of developing new geographical market or market segments for current products. Marketing research helps us to determine market coverage strategies or positioning strategies. For instance the researcher can decide whether to market manual typewriters or electronic typewriters or both and whether these are to be sold to a limited class of customers with limited income or whether to be sold to elite customers to have selective specialisation so that it can lead to and attractive strategy or whether to have market specialisation which may be both the types of typewriters but for a limited class of customers.

7. **Marketing Research Improves Marketing Efforts:** Marketing research makes one realise the type of products that are in demand or are having potential demand. It makes pricing easier and reasonable for the products. It enables the firm to offer these products to the right customers, which ultimately improves sales performance and ultimately reduces the marketing costs.

8. **Distribution Channels:** The producers and distributors in the channel of distribution get a reasonable margin for their services. The misunderstandings between them can be removed at the evidence of the findings of the marketing research. Hence the producer reaches the final buyers through intermediate levels of distribution.

9. **Employment Opportunities:** The increased production, widespread distribution and sales promotion activities increases the employment opportunities in the country. Hence it helps the unemployed people to get themselves gainfully employed in the diversified economic activities which are available because of marketing research.

10. **National Income:** With the increase of production distribution and marketing activities the national income increases. The increased national income helps to increase the per capita income, which ultimately increases the purchasing power of the consumers.

11. **Non Profit Organisation:** Marketing research techniques are now extended to non-business organisations, the best example being the political parties and their candidates. Various social service organisations are becoming the clients of marketing research specialists.

5.3.9 Limitations of Marketing Research

Limitations of marketing research are as follows:

1. **Not an exact science:** Marketing research is not an exact science because it deals with human behaviour. And unlike the physical sciences it does not examine the various controllable and uncontrollable variables. However, sincere attempts are made to assess the scientifically and accurately, but there is always a possibility to arrive at wrong conclusions on account of improper use of techniques of analysis and interpretations.

2. **Time constraints:** Marketing research takes a long time in carrying out any research process. The collection of data, their analysis, and interpretations in fact take a very long time. Hence by the time the decision is implemented, the research report may prove to be outdated which may result in arriving at wrong conclusions.

3. **Wrong findings and conclusion:** The problems of marketing are complex and hence they are required to be studied in depth by the researchers. However due to insufficient time and techniques, the findings and conclusions are not proper and hence may lead to further problems.

4. **Not a proper tool of forecasting:** Marketing research cannot be used as a cent percent tool of forecasting because there are a number of complex marketing factors which act and interact and ultimately react to give a complex state of marketing. Hence latest techniques are necessary to be studied and used for arriving at logical solutions to such complex problems.

5. **Inefficient and less trained research staff:** Many companies feel that marketing research is not an important activity and hence they hire inexperienced research people who have not acquired formal training in research activities and hence the results are not proper. In fact market research is a function of great expertise as it involves human psychology and social character and therefore it is essential to have well trained and highly motivated staff to perform research activities.

6. **High cost of operation:** Marketing research is considered a luxury for the management as it involves high cost of operation. This is the reason why many companies do not adopt marketing research. Such companies believe in management expertise rather than conducting costly researches.

To sum up it can be said that marketing research cannot provide solutions to every business problem. It only offers accurate information, which can be used to arrive at a suitable decision to reduce problems. Research is not problem oriented, it involves too many techniques. The market research also suffers from samples or statistical errors and hence if these are eliminated, the results obtained from market research may prove a very useful tool of management decision. Marketing research has definite advantages if properly conducted and used in proper perspective.

5.3.10 Uses of Marketing Research in Management

Marketing Research is an Essential Management Tool. Marketing research as has already been covered consists of a plan that charts how relevant data is to be collected and analysed so that the results are useful and relevant for making marketing decisions. Once the research and the related analysis are complete, the results are communicated to the management. This provides management with in-depth information regarding crucial factors that have an impact on the target market and existing marketing mix. Marketing research allows management to make the changes necessary for better results through adopting a proactive approach.

Uses of Marketing Research in Management are enumerated below:

(a) To supply valuable data to the top management to formulate long-term marketing objectives and to set clearly defined strategies necessary to accomplish them.

(b) To design and develop marketing policies and strategies relating to product pricing, packaging, product line extension etc.

(c) To design and develop internal system to monitor, measure and evaluate performance of the marketing department.

(d) To supply data on competition, market trends, consumer behaviour etc., so as to make the marketing activity more effective.

(e) To assist in selecting suitable channel of distribution and finalise the rates of commission payable to agents and middlemen.

(f) To assist in making sales forecast more accurately and scientifically. This will enable the top management to find out present and potential demand correctly.

(g) To take decisions on allocation of resources among various products and activities.

(h) Research will help in identifying areas for expansion and test the market's readiness for a new product/service.

Points to Remember

- Marketing planning is the starting point of any business activity. Planning is deciding at present what is to be done in the future.
- The primary purpose of marketing planning is to increase managerial effectiveness. Planning is nothing but a systematic approach for the management to consider the possible alternatives it faces.
- Basically marketing plans are of two types: one which is based on the organisation structure and the other is based on time.
- Marketing plans which are based on organisation structure are known as structural plans. Marketing plans based on time are known as time-span plans.
- A **Marketing Information System** (MIS) is a set of procedures and methods designed to generate, analyse, disseminate, and store anticipated marketing decision information on a regular, continuous basis.
- **Marketing research** is the systematic, objective and exhaustive search for and study of the facts relevant to any problem in the field of marketing.
- Marketing research is a comprehensive term with a very wide scope. Marketing research is used to find solutions for any problem of marketing.
- Marketing research concerns itself with every phase of marketing activity. It covers a very wide area and is a tool that pervades every marketing activity.

Questions for Discussion

1. Write a note on the steps to be undertaken for marketing planning.
2. What are the essential requirements of marketing planning?
3. Give the importance and scope of marketing planning?
4. What are difficulties faced in marketing planning?
5. Define "Marketing Research". Give scope of marketing research.

6. Differentiate between Market Research and Marketing Research.
7. Give your views on the future of Marketing Research in India.
8. Write short notes on:
   (a) Types of Marketing Plans.
   (b) Components of Marketing Planning.
   (c) Objectives of Marketing Research.
   (d) Scope of Marketing Research.
   (e) Importance and Limitations of Marketing Research.
   (f) Present status of "Marketing Research" in India.

Questions from Previous Pune University Examinations

1. What is Marketing Planning. Explain essential requirements of Marketing Planning. **[Oct. 2010, April 2011]**
2. Define Marketing Research. Explain scope of Marketing Research. **[April 2011]**
3. What is Marketing Research? Explain scope of Marketing Research. **[Oct. 2012]**
4. Write Short Notes:
   (A) Components of Marketing Information System. **[April 2009, 2011, 2012]**
   (B) Scope of Marketing Research. **[Oct. 2011]**
   (C) Importance of Marketing Information System. **[Oct. 2011, April 2013]**
   (D) Marketing Research. **[April 2012]**
   (E) Marketing Planning. **[April 2006, 2012]**
   (F) Management's Use of Marketing Research. **[Oct. 2009]**
   (G) Marketing Information System. **[April 2010]**
5. What do you mean by 'Marketing Research'? Explain scope of Marketing Research. **[April 2009]**
6. What is Marketing Research? What role does it play in Effective Marketing? **[Oct. 2009]**
7. What is Marketing Research? Explain how Marketing Research in useful to Management? **[April 2010]**
8. What is Marketing Information System? Explain features and importance of Marketing Information System. **[Oct. 2010]**
9. What is Marketing Planning? Explain the steps involved in Marketing Planning Process with reference to any product. **[April 2008]**
10. What is Marketing Research? Explain its scope and importance. **[Oct. 2007]**

■■■

Case Studies

1. 'All Out' - Marketing a Mosquito Repellant: Making Waves

It is one of the contenders to become the Hindustan Lever Ltd. (HLL) of the next century."

Shunu Sen, Marketing Expert & CEO, Quadra Advisory, commenting on Karamchand Appliances Pvt. Ltd., in 2000

Karamchand Appliances Private Limited (KAPL) is perhaps not a familiar name for the average Indian consumer. However, KAPL's brand 'All Out' is very well-known. In fact, the name All Out is almost a generic name for Liquid Vaporizers (vaporizers), a segment of the ₹ 4 billion[1] (in 1999) mosquito repellant industry in India.

KAPL was almost solely responsible for creating this segment. Within a decade of its launch, All Out had converted a large number of customers into vaporizer users, and had also established itself as the market leader in the segment, with a 69 percent market share in 1999.

The success of KAPL is particularly noteworthy, considering the fact that it was a small family-owned company that managed to wrest market share from corporate giants such as Godrej Sara Lee Ltd. (GSLL) and Hindustan Lever Ltd. (HLL) with strong, established brands such as GoodKnight, Jet, Tortoise, Baygon and Mortein, amidst stiff competition.

Background Note

With over 255 species of mosquitoes - believed to be responsible for spreading diseases such as malaria and dengue fever India has a large and growing market for mosquito repellants. Many methods are used in households for dealing with the mosquito menace. In spite of the pervasiveness of the mosquito problem, the use of repellants in India is fairly low. It is estimated that only 16.4% of the households in all urban areas and 22.6% in the metros use mosquito repellants.

The figure for the rural areas is even lower, at only 6.9%. In terms of value, the mat segment was the largest (51%), followed by coils (21%) and vaporizers (7%). Coils were the first mosquito repellants to be introduced in the Indian market. The first brand of coils was Tortoise, launched by Bombay Chemicals Ltd. (BCL) in the 1970s. Until 1994, Tortoise remained the market leader in its segment, with a 67% market share.

Other significant players emerged over the years, offering products in many segments: Bayer with the brands Baygon Spray, Baygon Power Mats and Baygon Knockout; Balsara Hygiene with a repellant cream, Odomos; and Tainwala Chemicals with the Casper brand of mats and coils. Besides these large players, a number of local brands were also available across the country.

In the latter half of the 1990s, the market became much more competitive, with the entry of GSLL[2], Reckitt & Coleman (R&C, now Reckitt Benckiser) and HLL. GSLL launched an array of brands (all coils) one after the other - Jet Fighter (1997), GoodKnight Jumbo (1999) and GoodKnight Instant, GoodKnight Smokeless and Jet Jumbo (2000).

The company's other brands included Banish (mats), Hit (aerosols), Hit Lines (chalks), Mosfree (lotion) and Hexit (spray). The Jet brand was extended to coils and sprays.

R&C also launched its range of mats and coils - Mortein, Mortein King and Mortein Red - while HLL launched Raid and Attack. These new entrants resorted to heavy advertising and aggressive sales promotion tactics.

GSLL soon emerged as the market leader in the mats segment with a 68% share in May 2000. R&C quickly became the second largest player in the coils segment, next only to Tortoise.

While the other companies concentrated on the coils and mats markets, KAPL promoted the use of vaporizers. By the mid 1990s, vaporizers had attained a market share of 5 percent. This segment was almost completely dominated by KAPL, whose sales reached ₹ 253 million in 1996-97.

GSLL could no longer ignore this growing segment and launched its own vaporizer under the GoodKnight brand in 1996-97. GoodKnight soon acquired a 40% market share of the vaporizer market. However, this did not affect the sales of KAPL, as the launch of GoodKnight had led to a growth in the overall size of the vaporizer market.

Instead of eating into All Out's sales, GSLL ended up expanding the market. However, GoodKnight could not sustain its success, and by 1999, the brand's market share had gone down to 21% - a major portion of the 19% loss being taken up by All Out. Although the initial success of All Out was largely due to technological innovation and first-mover advantages, it was widely believed that what had kept the brand going was strong marketing.

This was corroborated when KAPL's promoters Anil, Bimal and Naveen Arya were given the 'Marketing Persons of the Year' award at the 2000 A&M awards[3]. A&M described KAPL as a 'sterling example of enterprise' and a 'tale for budding entrepreneurs and marketers of the new millennium.'

The Growth of All Out

The Arya brothers belonged to a Maharashtra-based family that was involved in the business of importing books. Reluctant to join the family business, the brothers shifted to Rajkot, Gujarat and joined a relative in making diesel engines for agricultural purposes. Before long, they became interested in the fast moving consumer goods business. Impressed by the success of a small mosquito repellant company in Rajkot, the brothers decided to venture into the business and set up KAPL.

KAPL decided to get the technology they needed to enter the market from Japanese manufacturers. Their decision was prompted by the fact that most of the modern mosquito repellants were developed in Japan. Having decided to launch mats, the brothers short-listed five Japanese companies and eventually zeroed in on Earth Chemical Co. Ltd. (Earth).

Established in 1892, Earth was part of the $ 8 billion Otsuka Group of Japan. Earth manufactured and sold industrial chemicals, pharmaceuticals, consumer products, agricultural chemicals and health foods.

After agreeing to a technical collaboration for mats, the Arya brothers happened to see a vaporizer being sold by Earth. The product consisted of a heating unit and a small container of chemicals, which had to be periodically replaced. It was reportedly doing extremely well in the Japanese market, as it was much more effective than mats. (The strength of mats reportedly weakened considerably after a few hours - vaporizers on the other hand could function consistently throughout the night).

However, Earth refused to transfer the technology for the manufacture of the vaporizer. After much lobbying and negotiations, a revenue sharing deal was finally signed, wherein KAPL agreed to invest in manufacturing the components of the product. KAPL began developing certain key components for the product at its factory at Baddi in Himachal Pradesh in 1989. Some items such as moulds were imported from Japan. KAPL then hired a research agency to come up with a brand name for their product.

The agency recommended the name 'Freedom.' 'Choo Mantar' (a Hindi phrase indicating the 'magical vanishing' of mosquitoes) was another possibility. However, KAPL rejected the agency's recommendations, and eventually settled on All Out, a name suggested by the youngest Arya brother, Naveen. Choo Mantar was dropped as it would not have made sense to non-Hindi speaking people and the brothers felt that All Out was better than Freedom.

To ensure that the packaging was of high quality, KAPL commissioned a well-known packaging unit in Hyderabad, Andhra Pradesh. However, due to delays in the supply of packing material, KAPL was forced to delay the launch of All Out by about six months. The product was finally launched in April 1990 in Mumbai. Sales were slow to pick up, as April was a lean month for the sales of mosquito repellants - mosquitoes being far more numerous during the rainy season.

KAPL hired Avenues, reportedly one of the best creative agencies in India, to handle the advertising for All Out. However, the company was not satisfied with the advertisements created by the agency, which had the baseline, 'All Out for modern mosquitoes.' Bimal said, "Six months down the line, we had holes in our pockets. They kept telling us to have patience as it takes time, but we lost patience."

The advertisement account was shifted to a bigger advertising firm, HTA, at the time of the product's launch in Delhi. HTA released a series of six advertisements, using humor to promote the product. However, the Arya brothers were not satisfied with HTA either. They felt that they were paying too much for the advertisements, without adequate results. Anil said, "Humorous and attention-grabbing they were, but the ads lost out on what the brand wanted to say."

KAPL then decided to handle the advertising for All Out on its own, surprising many industry watchers and drawing criticism from some ad agencies. However, the company surprised everybody with the launch of a campaign featuring an animated, jumping frog (actually an All Out vaporizer) eating mosquitoes, which proved to be immensely successful. The ad was based on similar advertisements made by Earth for the Japanese market. Later on, the advertisement included a man competing with All Out in a mosquito 'eating' competition and losing out. The short, funny advertisement cost KAPL just ₹ 50,000 to make. Over the next few years, KAPL continued with the same advertisement, with only minor modifications to suit the launch of new promotion schemes.

KAPL advertised on videocassettes of Hindi movies in a big way - a move criticized by many advertising agencies, as these were believed to be 'downmarket.' Explaining the rationale behind this decision, Anil said, "We went for video cassettes as they got duplicated 20 times in the grey market. And it cost a fraction of what it takes to advertise on TV."

KAPL also made use of the evening news program on FM Radio and test cricket commentary on the state-owned All India Radio (AIR) to communicate in a cost-effective manner. On television, KAPL preferred to sponsor news programs rather than costly and more conventional soaps or game shows such as the hugely popular Kaun Banega Crorepati.[4]

The company also pioneered the concept of sponsoring song/dance and fight sequences in movies on many satellite television channels (primarily) SitiCable and Doordarshan. All Out advertisements would appear before each song/dance and fight sequence in the movie. As Hindi movies typically featured 4-5 songs/dances, the viewers watched the All Out advertisement at least 4-5 times. This resulted in the brand attaining a very high mind-share among consumers.

While All Out had an overall share of voice (SOV[5]) of 31%, the nearest competitor GoodKnight had just 5% in 2000. KAPL priced the heating unit of the All Out vaporizer fairly high, to cover the cost of the relatively expensive components purchased from Matsushita Electronics. However, reacting to market sentiment, the company lowered its price over the years, aided in part by increased in-house manufacturing of components.

While All Out was priced at ₹ 225 when it was launched, the price was reduced to ₹ 135 for a cord model in 1994. In 1995, KAPL launched the 'Pluggy' (a small apparatus, in which the refill could be fitted and plugged in directly) for ₹ 90. In 1996, a twin pack (offering the Pluggy and a cord model) was launched for ₹ 135. In 1998, KAPL came out with a ₹ 99 pack consisting of the Pluggy and a refill. The deal, called the 'deadly offer' was backed by heavy advertising.

By then, it was clear that the company was treating the vaporizer as a loss leader, to promote the sale of its refill containers. The 'deadly exchange scheme' launched in 1999, gave customers the chance to exchange a mat machine of any make for a Pluggy for just ₹ 27. The response to this scheme was phenomenal with the company reportedly selling over half a million pieces in September 1999 alone.

Meanwhile, GSLL, which had launched its own vaporizer in 1996 under the GoodKnight brand, was struggling to maintain its market share in the segment after its initial success. GSLL launched a 60-night refill pack priced at ₹ 63, against All Out's 45-night pack at ₹ 54.

However, the move did not prove to be very successful and GSLL had to support the launch by introducing promotion schemes. After KAPL's 'deadly exchange scheme,' GoodKnight's share decreased by 9.3% in volume terms between September 1999 and February 2000.

GSLL then reduced the price of its vaporizer, but this too had little effect on sales. KAPL's distribution network consisted of around 120 distributors across the country. Of the 900,000 outlets across the country, that sold repellants, KAPL was available in only 18%.

As this was significantly lower than the 55% figure for R&C and 54% for GSSL, KAPL was working towards increasing its presence.

What Lies Ahead

According to industry reports, the Indian mosquito repellant market was expected to grow rapidly in the early 21st century. Analysts said that with improvement in literacy and health consciousness in rural areas, the use of mosquito repellants was expected to increase substantially in these areas.

As the per capita usage of repellants was very low in the country, there was considerable scope for the market to expand. However, increasing concern over the harmful effects of the chemicals in mosquito repellants on the health of human beings was expected to be hamper growth.

Allethrin, the chemical used in most of the repellants, was reported to be very dangerous, being potentially harmful to the eyes, skin, the respiratory tract and the nervous system. A study done on rats by the Industrial Toxicology Research Center[6] showed that the rats suffered brain, liver and kidney damage after prolonged exposure to liquid mosquito repellants.

Research in Sweden and the USA had also shown that long-term and persistent use of products containing Allethrin could cause brain cancer, blood cancer and deformity of fetuses.

There were also doubts about the efficacy of mosquito repellants. In 1998, studies conducted by the Malaria Research Center (MRC)[7] found that none of the leading brands provided 100% protection against mosquitoes. Also, in the 653 households surveyed in eight cities, 193 people complained of various health problems linked to mosquito repellants.

They suffered from breathing problems, headaches, eye irritation, skin rashes, suffocation, itching, bronchitis, cold and cough, asthma, nausea, throat and ear pain. Of the 286 doctors questioned, 50% reported cases of acute toxicity following the use of these repellants.

Though these problems concerned the industry as a whole, specific complaints against All Out had also begun to surface. All Out's advertisement in 2001, claiming that the brand had 'Extra MMR' had been severely criticized.

The Director of the Central Insecticide Laboratory (CIL)[8], Dr V Ragunathan said, "The advertisement was designed to sound as though MMR was a wonder substance that would eliminate the mosquito menace. In reality, the term is just an abbreviation for 'mosquito mortality rate'. If you look at the product and packaging, there is no mention of what exactly it contains. It contains a variant of a toxic compound called d-Allethrin, and 'Extra MMR' would only mean more toxic components."

All Out also faced criticism for some other aspects of its advertising strategy. Reports indicated that television viewers were unhappy about the brand's advertisements before every song, dance and fight sequence in all the films being telecast. Experts said that now that the brand was firmly established, repetitive advertising was not advisable, and could even prove counter productive.

KAPL's biggest competitors were large multi-product companies, with the financial muscle to introduce and sustain long and costly advertising and promotional campaigns. In spite of its success, KAPL remained essentially a single product company. With the product and the brand facing various problems, it was difficult to predict how long All Out would remain the leader in the vaporizer segment of mosquito repellants.

References:
1. 1999 figures. In October 2002, ₹ 48 equaled 1 US $
2. GSLL was incorporated in 1987 as Transelektra Domestic Products Private Limited. In 1994, India's leading business house, the Godrej Group acquired a 75% stake in the company, which was raised to 97.5% later on. In 1995, Sara Lee Mauritius Holding Limited (SLM), a Mauritius-based company, acquired a 40% stake in the company. The GoodKnight brand was acquired as a part of the Transelektra deal.
3. The A&M awards is an annual event that recognizes advertising and marketing excellence in India, conducted by the country's leading magazine, Advertising & Marketing (A&M). The awards are given based on the recommendations of a jury of eminent marketing professionals
4. One of the most successful programs on Indian television, Kaun Banega Crorepati was a quiz program aired on satellite television channel Star Plus. The advertising slots for the serial were reportedly sold at extremely high rates, as the program's viewership was very high.
5. Share of voice indicates the total percentage of mind-share that a brand possessed of the particular niche, market, or audience the company is targeting. The data is compiled by INTAM, a television audience measurement service of marketing research agency ORG-MARG.
6. An institution in Lucknow, Uttar Pradesh involved in conducting research in toxicology and hazardous chemicals.
7. MRC, based in New Delhi is involved in malaria research.
8. CIL was established by the Government of India under Section 16 of the Implementation of Insecticides Act, 1968. It functions as a referral laboratory for quality control of pesticides, besides carrying out pesticide residue analysis and investigations in medical toxicology.

Web Courtesy:
http://www.icmrindia.org/free%20resources/casestudies/ALL%20OUT%20_%20MARKETING%20A%20MOSQUITO%20REPELLANT1.htm

2. Amul's Diversification Strategy: A Pizza for ₹ 20!

"You've got to think big."

- **Verghese Kurien, Chairman, GCMMF, Commenting on Amul's diversification, 2001**

"This dairy, non-dairy thing is a producer's distinction."

- **B M Vyas, Managing Director, GCMMF, 2001**

In early 2001, Gujarat Cooperative Milk Marketing Federation (GCMMF)[1] planned to leverage its brand equity and distribution network to turn Amul[2] into India's biggest food brand. Verghese Kurien, Chairman of GCMMF, set a sales target of ₹ 10 bn by 2006 as against sales of ₹ 2.3 bn in 2001. In 2001, GCMMF entered the fast food market in India with the launch of vegetable pizzas under the brand name SnowCap in Ahmedabad, Gujarat. GCMMF was also planning to launch its pizzas in other western Indian cities like Mumbai, Surat, and Baroda.

Depending on the response in these cities, GCMMF would decide to introduce its pizzas in other cities in India. The pizzas were offered in four flavours: plain tomato-onion-capsicum, fruit pizza (pineapple-topped), mushroom and 'Jain pizzas' (pizzas without onion or garlic). GCMMF launched the pizzas in the ₹ 20-25 price range. The existing players in the pizza market, like Domino's, Pizza Hut and Nirula's offered pizzas at nothing less than ₹ 39. Analysts felt that GCMMF's move would force the existing players to reduce their prices in the long run.

GCMMF planned to open 3,000 pizza retail franchise outlets all over the country by 2005. The pizzas would be made at the retail outlets. The technical training and the recipe for the pizza would be provided by GCMMF. It would also negotiate with bulk suppliers of vegetables to get these at wholesale rates. These would be provided to the retailers.

The main cost component of the pizza is the mozarella cheese. GCMMF would offer the cheese at a bulk rate of ₹ 140 per kg, compared to the market price of ₹ 146 per kg, thus saving the retailers ₹ 6 per kg. GCMMF on its part would have a ready market for its cheese products.

Analysts felt that the supply of cheese products by GCMMF at a cheaper price would enable the retailers to price pizzas lower than that of the competitors. R S Khanna, General Manager-North zone, said that GCMMF intended to do to pizza what it had already done to ice cream. He said, "We want pizzas to become a mass consumption item. And as in the case of ice cream, we will force pizza manufacturers to slash prices. Eventually, this would expand the market for cheese."

Background

In 1996, B M Vyas, Managing Director, GCMMF, commissioned the Indian Market Research Bureau (IMRB) to conduct a consumer survey to identify the products consumers wanted from Amul. Based on the findings, Amul entered into the following areas: ice cream, curd, paneer[3], cheese, and condensed milk. In 1997, Amul launched ice creams after Hindustan Lever acquired Kwality, Milkfood and Dollops[4]. Positioned as the 'Real Ice-cream,' Amul Ice cream was one of the few milk-based ice creams in the market.

With GCMMF gradually expanding its distribution reach, Amul was all set to strengthen its share in the ice cream segment. In August 1999, Amul launched branded yoghurt in India for the first time, when it test marketed "Masti Dahi" in Ahmedabad first and then introduced it all over the country. "Masti Dahi" was plain yoghurt sold in plastic cups. Each 400 gm cup was priced at ₹ 12.

In January 2000, Amul re-entered[5] the carton milk market[6] with the launch of "Amul Taaza" in Mumbai. Amul Taaza was non-sweetened, plain, low fat milk. The product was positioned as a lifestyle as well as functional product. It was targeted at the upper middle class housewife who could use it for different occasions. Amul was targeting sales of about 0.1 mn litres per day. In November 2000, Amul decided to promote mozzarella cheese, which was used in pizza.

The growing demand for mozzarella cheese from pizza making companies like Pizza Hut and Domino's Pizza was expected to give Amul's cheese sale an additional push. In July 2001, Amul planned to enter the instant coffee market through a tie-up with Tata Coffee. GCMMF had a strong national distribution network while Tata Coffee had expertise in manufacturing and marketing coffee. As a part of the tie-up, Amul was to source the instant coffee from Tata Coffee and distribute it.

The domestic coffee market was estimated at ₹ 11bn, with the instant coffee segment being around ₹ 4.5bn. In August 2001, Amul decided to enter the ready-to-eat stuffed paratha,[7] cheeseburger, cheese and paneer pakoda[8], and cheese sandwich segments. The products were to be marketed under the SnowCap brand. The SnowCap brand would also include tomato sauce and ketchup.

Amul was also restructuring its chocolates business[9]. Seven of its brands that were withdrawn from the market were to be relaunched soon. Amul tied up with Campco, the cocoa and arecanuts farmers' cooperative in Karnataka and Kerala, for the supply of cocoa beans.[10] Amul marketed Milklairs, which was manufactured by Campco. This tie-up was expected to help Amul in the expansion of its chocolate business.

Why Diversify?

With the liberalization of the Indian economy in the early 1990s, and the subsequent entry of new players, there was a change in lifestyles and the food tastes of people. The new team that took over the management of the GCMMF in the mid-1990s hoped to take advantage of the change. The management adopted Total Quality Management (TQM) and set for itself higher benchmarks (in terms of growth). They also diversified the Amul portfolio, offering a range of food stuffs such as ketchup, jam, ice-cream, confectionaries, cheese, and shrikhand.[11]

According to some analysts, this diversification was probably not entirely demand-driven. Being a cooperative, GCMMF was compelled to buy all the milk that was produced in Gujarat. And with milk production having increased since the mid 1990s, GCMMF had to make use of additional milk, and hence the pressure to make and market more and more processed-milk products. Amul had to expand the consumption base of milk-based products in India. It planned to make its products (butter and cheese) a part of the regular diet in most households.

Amul launched its new products with the intention of increasing the offtake of its basic milk products, including cheese. This in turn was expected to increase the earnings of the farmers. The pizzas were expected to increase the sale of its cheese. The entry into the confectioneries market was another avenue for increasing milk consumption. This flurry of launches helped Amul broaden its appeal across all segments. Price was an advantage that Amul enjoyed over its competitors. Amul's products were priced 20-40 % less than those of its competitors.

Analysts felt that Amul could price its products low because of the economies of scale it enjoyed. Amul created two new distribution set-ups: a cold chain for ice-cream, and another for limited life fresh foods like curd. Expecting the demand for ready-to- eat foods to grow, Amul prepared to leverage the ice-cream cold chain for a new range of frozen foods, beginning with pizza. However, some analysts felt that as the pizza's would be made by the retailers, Amul would have little control over the quality of the pizzas. That was why Amul was marketing the pizzas under the brand name SnowCap.

Said S K Bhalla, Chief of Quality Control, "The product has received premature hype. Meeting consumer expectations will be a challenge, until we make the frozen pizza in our own facilities." According to some analysts, Amul's obsession with keeping down manpower costs and dealer commissions could be a weakness. In ice-creams for example, Amul's retail commission in Ahmedabad city was 17.5% which was 10% lower than what competitors offered.

They also pointed out that Amul might not have the financial muscle that multinationals had to achieve rapid growth. However, all said and done, Amul seemed to be all set to make steady progress in the coming years with its products having become quite popular in both rural and urban households. Said Vyas, "We've handled liberalisation and globalisation far better than our transnational rivals. It has made us fitter than ever."

References/Explanations:
1. GCMMF was India's largest food products marketing organisation based at Anand, Gujarat. GCMMF had annual sales of more than ₹ 22 bn in 2000-01. It is a state level apex body of milk cooperatives in Gujarat. GCMMF has 14 affiliated dairy plants with a total milk handling capacity of 6 mn litres per day and milk drying capacity of 450 Mt per day. With 12 milk processing units, each located at the district level, GCMMF has a membership of 2 mn farmers who belong to 10, 000 village dairy co-operative societies.
2. Amul is the mother brand of GCMMF
3. Paneer or cottage fresh cheese is made from low fat milk, without involving long, complicated procedures. It is rich in proteins.

4. In 1993, HLL acquired Dollops Icecream from Cadbury's India. In 1994, BBLIL launched the Wall's range of frozen desserts. By the end of the year, HLL entered into a strategic alliance with the Kwality group. In 1995, the Milkfood icecream marketing and distribution rights were acquired by HLL.

5. In 1983, Amul had introduced branded milk in 500-ml tetrahedron-shaped packs priced at ₹ 4.50 and one litre rectangular packs at ₹ 9. Amul felt that the tetrahedron pack was well ahead of its time, which was why it was not accepted in 1983. Moreover, the packaging was not convenient and it was difficult to store.

6. The three main players in the ₹ 360 bn packaged milk market are Amul, Nestle and Vijaya. The market is important to all three. Nestle is looking at a ₹ 1.50 bn business from milk alone by 2004. Amul Taaza is expected to be a ₹ 1 bn brand by 2001, and Vijaya could achieve ₹ 1.2 bn sales from packaged milk. Amul is investing ₹ 300 mn in two new factories in Andhra Pradesh and Maharashtra. Nestle is targeting the south as a potential big milk market. Nestle is setting up two more plants (amount invested yet to be revealed) in the southern region and is aggressive on the price front, pegging its Pure Milk brand at ₹ 20 a litre against Amul Taaza's ₹ 22.

7. A flat unleavened bread made from flour, water and clarified butter.

8. A deep-fried fritter made by dipping pieces of vegetable, meat or shellfish in chickpea flour batter and generally eaten as a snack.

9. Amul's chocolate portfolio includes brands like Amul Bitter, Amul Premium, Amul Crisp, Amul Fruit & Nut, Amul Badam Bar, Amul Milk and Amul Crunch.

10. Amul followed a strategy of roping in cooperatives to aid growth around the country. Amul ice cream is now manufactured in seven locations across the country. Pune Milk Cooperative and Akluj Dairy (near Baramati in Maharashtra) have been roped in to sell 0.2 mn litres of milk per day under the Amul brand name in Mumbai. In TamilNadu, Salem Dairy has signed up to produce milk and ghee under the Amul brand name.

11. A dessert made of curd, cardamom, saffron leaves and sugar

Web Courtesy : http://www.icmrindia.org/free%20resources/casestudies/amul1.htm

3. The Coke Pepsi Rivalry: Pepsi Vs. Coke

Our real competition is water, tea, nimbupani and Pepsi... in that order."

- Coke sources in 1996

"When you're No 2 and you're struggling, you have to be more innovative, work better, and be more resilient. If we became No 1, we would redefine the market so we became No 2! The fact is that our competition with the Coca-Cola company is the single most important reason we've accomplished what we have. And if they were honest, they would say the same thing."

- Pepsi sources in 1998

"Both companies did not really concentrate on the fundamentals of marketing like building strong brand equity in the market, and thus had to resort to such tactics to garner market shares."

- Business India in 1998

The cola wars had become a part of global folklore - something all of us took for granted. However, for the companies involved, it was a matter of 'fight or succumb.' Both print and electronic media served as battlefields, with the most bitter of the cola wars often seen in form of the comparative advertisements.

In the early 1970s, the US soft-drinks market was on the verge of maturity, and as the major players, Coke and Pepsi offered products that 'looked the same and tasted the same,' substantial market share growth seemed unlikely. However, Coke and Pepsi kept rejuvenating the market through product modifications and pricing/promotion/distribution tactics. As the competition was intense, the companies had to frequently implement strategic changes in order to gain competitive advantage. The only way to do this, apart from introducing cosmetic product innovations, was to fight it out in the marketplace. This modus operandi was followed in the Indian markets as well with Coke and Pepsi resorting to more innovative tactics to generate consumer interest.

In essence, the companies were trying to increase the whole market pie, as the market-shares war seemed to get nowhere. This was because both the companies came out with contradictory market share figures as per surveys conducted by their respective agencies - ORG (Coke) and IMRB (Pepsi). For instance, in August 2000, Pepsi claimed to have increased its market share for the first five months of calendar year 2000 to 49% from 47.3%, while Coke claimed to have increased its share in the market to 57%, in the same period, from 55%.

Media reports claimed that the rivalry between Coke and Pepsi had ceased to generate sustained public interest, as it used to in the initial years of the cola brawls worldwide. They added that it was all just a lot of noise to hardsell a product that had no inherent merit.

Coke had entered the Indian soft drinks market way back in the 1970s. The company was the market leader till 1977, when it had to exit the country following policy changes regarding MNCs operating in India. Over the next few years, a host of local brands emerged such as Campa Cola, Thumps Up, Gold Spot and Limca etc. However, with the entry of Pepsi and Coke in the 1990s, almost the entire market went under their control.

Making billions from selling carbonated/colored/sweetened water for over 100 years, Coke and Pepsi had emerged as truly global brands. Coke was born 11 years before Pepsi in 1887 and, a century later it still maintained its lead in the global cola market. Pepsi, having always been number two, kept trying harder and harder to beat Coke at its own game. In this never-ending duel, there was always a new battlefront opening up somewhere. In India the battle was more intense, as India was one of the very few areas where Pepsi was the leader in the cola segment. Coke re-entered India in 1993 and soon entered into a deal with Parle, which had a 60% market share in the soft drinks segment with its brands Limca, Thums Up and Gold Spot.

Following this, Coke turned into the absolute market leader overnight. The company also acquired Cadbury Schweppes' soft drink brands Crush, Canada Dry and Sport Cola in early 1999.

Coke was mainly a franchisee-driven operation with the company supplying its soft drink concentrate to its bottlers around the world. Pepsi took the more capital-intensive route of owning and running its own bottling factories alongside those of its franchisees. Over half of Pepsi's sales were made by its own bottling units.

Though Pepsi had a lead over Coke, having come in before the era of economic liberalization in India, it had to spend the early years fighting the bureaucracy and Parle's Ramesh Chuahan every step of the way. Pepsi targeted the youth and seemed to have struck a right chord with the market. Its performance was praiseworthy, while Coke had to struggle to a certain extent to get its act right. In a span of 7 years of its operations in the county, Coke changed its CEO four times. Media reports about the troubles faced by Coke and the corrective measures it adopted were aplenty.

(I) BOTTLING

Bottling was the biggest area of conflict between Pepsi and Coke. This was because, bottling operations held the key to distribution, an extremely important feature for soft-drink marketing. As the wars intensified, both companies took pains to maintain good relationships with bottlers, in order to avoid defections to the other camp.

A major stumbling block for Coke was the conflict with its strategic bottling partner, Ramesh Chauhan of the Parle group of companies. Coke alleged that Chauhan had secretly manufactured Coke's concentrate. Chauhan, in turn, accused coke of backtracking on commitments to grant him bottling rights in Pune and Bangalore and threatened legal action. The matter almost reached the courts and the strategic alliance showed signs of coming apart. Industry observers commented that for a company like Coke that was so heavily franchisee driven, antagonizing its chief bottler was suicidal.

While all this was going on, Pepsi wasted no time in moving in for the kill. It made huge inroads in the north, particularly in Delhi where Chauhan had the franchise and also snapped up the opportunity to buy up Coke's bottler Pinakin Shah in Gujarat. Ironically, the Gujarat Bottling Company owned by Shah, also belonged in part to Chauhan for whom the sell-out was a strategic counter-move in his battle with Coke. Coke moved court and obtained an order enforcing its bottler's agreement with the Gujarat company, effectively freezing Pepsi's right to use the acquired capacity for a year. Later, Coke made a settlement of $10 million in exchange for Chauhan foregoing bottling rights in Pune and Bangalore.

Towards the end of 1997, bottling agreements between Coke and many of its bottlers were expiring. Coke began pressurizing its bottlers to sell out and threatened them that their bottling agreements would not be renewed. Media reports claimed that Coke's bottlers were not averse to joining hands with Pepsi. They said they would rather offer their services to Pepsi than selling out to Coke and discontinuing a profitable business. In November 1997,

Pepsi made a bid to gain from the feud between Coke and its franchised bottlers. It declared that it was ready to join hands with 'any disgruntled Coke bottler, provided the latter's operations enhanced Pepsi's market in areas where Coke was dominant.' Pepsi was even willing to shift to a franchisee-owned bottling system from its usual practice of focusing on company-owned bottling systems supplemented by a few franchisee-owned bottling companies, provided it found bottlers who would enhance both the quantity and quality, especially in areas where Coke had a substantial marketshare. Pepsi won over Goa Bottling Company, Coke's bottler in Goa and became the market leader in that city.

(II) ADVERTISING

When Coke re-entered India, it found Pepsi had already established itself in the soft drinks market. The global advertisement wars between the cola giants quickly spread to India as well. Internationally, Pepsi had always been seen as the more aggressive and offensive of the two, and its advertisements the world over were believed to be more popular than Coke's. It was rumored that at any given point of time, both the companies had their spies in the other camp. The advertising agencies of both the companies (Chaitra Leo Burnett for Coke and HTA for Pepsi) were also reported to have insiders in each other's offices who reported to their respective heads on a daily basis. Based on these inputs, the rival agency formulated its own plans. These hostilities kept the rivalry alive and healthy. However, the tussle took a serious turn at times with complaints to Advertising Standards Council of India, and threats of lawsuits.

While Pepsi always relied on advertisements featuring films stars, pop stars and cricket players, Coke had initially decided to focus on Indian culture and jingles based on Indian classical music. These were also supported by coke advertisements that were popular in the West.

Somehow, Coke's advertisements missed the Indian pulse by a wide margin. Pepsi soon came to be seen as a 'defender' who had humiliated the 'invader' with its superior creative strengths. When Coke bagged the official sponsorship rights to the 1997 Cricket World Cup, Pepsi created media history by unleashing one of the country's most successful advertisement campaigns - the 'Nothing Official About It' campaign . Pepsi took on Coke, even when the latter sponsored the replays of the matches, through the campaign, 'Uncork a Cola.' Media coverage of the war even hinted that the exclusion of Rahul Dravid (Pepsi's model) from the Indian team had something to do with the war. However, Coke had its revenge when it bagged the television sponsorship rights for the 1997 Pepsi Asia Cup. Consequently, Pepsi, in spite of having branded the event was not able to sponsor it.

The severe damage caused by the 'Nothing Official About It' campaign prompted Coke to shift its advertising account from McCann Erickson to Chaitra Leo Burnett in 1997. The 'Eat-Sleep-Drink' series of ads was born soon after. Pepsi responded with ads where cricket stars 'ate a bat' and 'slept on a batting pad' and 'drank only Pepsi.' To counter this, Coke released a print advertisement in March 1998, in which cricketers declared, 'Chalo Kha Liya!' Another Thums Up ad showed two apes copying Pepsi's Azhar and Ajay Jadeja, with the line,

'Don't be a bunder (monkey), Taste the thunder.' For once, it was Pepsi's turn to be at receiving end. A Pepsi official commented, "We're used to competitive advertising, but we don't make fun of the cricketers, just the ad." Though Pepsi decided against suing Coke, the ad vanished soon after the dissent was made public. Commenting on this, a Pepsi official said, "Pepsi is basically fun. It is irreverent and whacky. Our rival is serious and has a 'don't mess with me' attitude. We tend to get away with fun but they have not taken it nicely. They don't find it funny."

Coke then launched one of its first offensive ads, ridiculing Pepsi's ads featuring a monkey. 'Oye! Don't be a bunder! Taste the Thunder', the ad for Thums Up, went with the line, 'issued in the interest of the present generation by Thums Up.'

The 1998 Football World Cup was another event the cola majors fought over. Pepsi organized local or 'para' football matches in Calcutta and roped in Indian football celebrity Bhaichung Bhutia to endorse Pepsi. Pepsi claimed it was the first to start and popularize 'para' football at the local level. However, Coke claimed that it was the first and not Pepsi, to arrange such local games, which Coke referred to as 'pada.'

While Pepsi advertisements claimed, 'More football, More Pepsi,' Coke utilized the line, 'Eat football, Sleep football, Drink only Coca-Cola,' later replaced by 'Live football, dream football and drink only Coca-Cola.' Media reports termed Pepsi's promos as a 'me-too' effort to cash in on the World Cup craze, while Coke's activities were deemed to be in line with its commitment and long-term association with the game.

Coke's first offering in the lemon segment (not counting the acquired market leader brand Limca) came in the form of Sprite launched in early 1999. From the very beginning, Sprite went on the offensive with its tongue-in-cheek advertisements. The line 'Baki Sab Bakwas' (All the rest is nonsense) was clearly targeted at Pepsi's claims in its ads. The advertisement made fun of almost all the Pepsi and Mirinda advertisements launched during 1998. Pepsi termed this as Coke's folly, claiming it was giving Sprite a 'wrong positioning,' and that it was a case of an ant trying to fight a tiger.

Sprite received an encouraging response in the market, aided by the high-decibel promotions and pop music concerts held across the country. But Pepsi was confident that 7 Up would hold its own and its ads featuring film stars would work wonders for Mirinda Lemon in the lemon segment.

When Pepsi launched an advertisement featuring Sachin Tendulkar with a modified Hindi movie song, 'Sachin Ala Re,' Coke responded with an advertisement with the song, 'Coke Ala Re.' Following this, Pepsi moved the Advertising Standards Council of India and the Advertising Agencies Association of India, alleging plagarisation of its 'Sachin Ala Re' creation by Coke's advertising agency, Chaitra Leo Burnett, in its 'Coke Ala Re' commercial. The rivals were always engaged in the race to sign the most popular Bollywood and cricket celebrities for their advertisements. More often than not, the companies pitched arch-rivals in their respective fields against each other in the cola wars as well. (Refer Table I)

Table I: Celebrity Endorsers *

	Indian film industry	Cricket players
Coke	Karisma Kapoor, Hrithik Roshan, Twinkle Khanna, Rambha, Daler Mehndi, Aamir Khan, Aishwarya Rai. **	Robin Singh, Anil Kumble, Javgal Srinath.
Pepsi	Aamir Khan, Aishwarya Rai**, Akshay Kumar, Shahrukh Khan, Rani Mukherjee, Manisha Koirala, Kajol, Mahima Chaudhary, Madhavan, Amrish Puri, Govinda, Amitabh Bachchan.	Azharuddin, Sachin Tendulkar, Rahul Dravid, Sourav Ganguly.

* The list is not exhaustive.
**Aamir and Aishwarya had switched from Pepsi to Coke.

In October 2000, following Coke's 'Jo Chaaho Ho Jaaye' campaign, the brand's 'branded cut-through mark', reached an all-time high of 69.5% as against Pepsi's 26.2%. In terms of stochastic share, Coke had a 3% lead over Pepsi with a 25.5% share. Pepsi retaliated with a campaign making fun of Coke's advertisements. The advertisement had a mixed response amongst the masses with fans of both the celebrities defending their idols. In May 2000, Coke threatened to sue Pepsi over the advertisements that ridiculed its own commercials. Amidst wide media coverage, Pepsi eventually stopped airing the controversial advertisement. In February 2001, Coke went on the offensive with the 'Grow up to the Thums Up Challenge' campaign. Pepsi immediately issued a legal notice on Coke for using the 'Yeh Dil Maange More' phrase used in the commercial. Coke officials, however, declined to comment on the issue and the advertisement continued to be aired.

(III) PRODUCT LAUNCHES

Pepsi beat Coke in the Diet-Cola segment, as it managed to launch Diet Pepsi much before Coke could launch Diet Coke. After the Government gave clearance to the use of Aspertame and Acesulfame-K (potassium) in combination (ASK), for use in low-calorie soft drinks, Pepsi officials lost no time in rolling out Diet Pepsi at its Roha plant and sending it to retail outlets in Mumbai. Advertisements and press releases followed in quick succession. It was a major victory for Pepsi, as in certain parts of the world, Coke's Diet Coke sold more than Pepsi Cola itself. Brand visibility and taste being extremely important in the soft drink market, Pepsi was glad to have become the first-mover once again.

Coke claimed that Pepsi's one-upmanship was nothing to worry about as Coke already had a brand advantage. Diet Coke was readily available in the market through import channels, while Diet Pepsi was rarely seen.

Hence, Diet Coke has a brand advantage. Coke came up later with a high-profile launch of Diet Coke. However, as expected, diet drinks, as a percentage of the total cola demand, did not emerge as a major area of focus in the years to come. Though the price of the cans was reduced from ₹ 18 to ₹ 15 in July 2000, it failed to catch the fancy of the buyers. In

September 2000, both the companies again slashed the price of their diet cans by over 33% per cent to ₹ 10. Both the companies were losing ₹ 5-6 per can by selling it at ₹ 10, but expected the other products to absorb these losses. A Pepsi official said that the diet cola constituted only about 0.4% of the total market, hence its contribution to revenue was considered insignificant. However, both companies viewed this segment as having immense potential and the price-cuts were part of a long-term strategy.

Coke claimed that it was passing on the benefit of the 5% cut in excise duty to the consumer. Industry experts, however, believed that the price cut had more to do with piling up inventories. Diet drinks in cans had a rather short shelf life (about two months) and the cola majors were simply clearing stocks through this price cut. However, by 2001, the diet-cola war had almost died out with the segment posting extremely low growth rates.

(IV) POACHING

Pepsi and Coke fought the war on a new turf in the late 1990s. In May 1998, Pepsi filed a petition against Coke alleging that Coke had 'entered into a conspiracy' to disrupt its business operations. Coke was accused of luring away three of Pepsi's key sales personnel from Kanpur, going as far as to offer ₹ 10 lakh a year in pay and perks to one of them, almost five times what Pepsi was paying him. Sales personnel who were earning ₹ 48,000 per annum were offered ₹ 1.86 lakh a year. Many truck drivers in the Goa bottling plant who were getting ₹ 2,500 a month moved to Coke who gave them ₹ 10,000 a month. While new recruits in the soft drinks industry averaged a pay hike of between 40-60% Coke had offered 300-400%. Coke, in its reply filed with the Delhi High Court, strongly denied the allegations and also asked for the charges to be dropped since Pepsi had not quantified any damages. Pepsi claimed that this was causing immense damage as those employees who had switched over were carrying with them sensitive trade-related information. After some intense bickering, the issue died a natural death with Coke emerging the winner in another round of the battle.

Pepsi also claimed that its celebrity endorsers were lured into breaking their contracts with Pepsi, and Coke had tried to pressure the Board of Control for Cricket in India (BCCI) to break a sponsorship deal it had signed for the Pepsi Triangular Series. According to Pepsi's deal with BCCI, Pepsi had the first right of refusal to sponsor all cricket matches played in India where up to three teams participated. The BCCI, however, was reported to have tried to break this contract in favor of Coke. Pepsi went to court protesting against this and won. Pepsi also alleged that Coke's Marketing Director Sanjiv Gupta was to join Pepsi in 1997. But within days of his getting the appointment letter, Coke made a counter offer and successfully lured Gupta away.

Coke also turned its attention to Pepsi's stronghold - the retail outlets. Between 1996-98, Coke doubled its reach to a reported 5 lakh outlets, when Pepsi was present at only 3.5 lakh outlets. To reach out to smaller markets, interceptor units in the form of mobile vans were also launched by Coke in 1998 in Andhra Pradesh, Tamil Nadu and West Bengal. However, in its rush to beat Pepsi at the retail game, Coke seemed to have faltered on the service front.

For instance, many shops in Uttar Pradesh frequently ran out of stock and there was no servicing for Coke's coolers. Though Coke began servicing retail outlets on a daily basis like Pepsi, it had to wait for a while before it was able to match Pepsi's retailing strengths.

One of Coke's victories on the retail front was in the form of its tie up with Indian Oil to set up dispensing units at its petrol pumps. Pepsi responded by striking a deal with Bharat Petroleum, whose network was far smaller than Indian Oil's. Of the estimated 2,50,000 retail outlets in the country that sold soft drinks, Pepsi was stocked only at 2,00,000.

In the late 1990s, Pepsi and Coke kept trying to outdo each other in sponsoring music concerts by leading artists in order to reach out to youth. Pepsi also tied up with MTV to hold a series of pop concerts across the country. Coke on the other hand, tied-up with MTV's rival Channel V for a similar venture. There were frequent skirmishes regarding movie sponsorships and vending rights at leading cinema halls.

In May 1999, the companies were involved in a 'freebies war' - promotional schemes designed to help grow the overall cola market besides the usual market share enhancement. Coke was running as many as 12 volume-building, national-level consumer promotions, while Pepsi had 8 schemes for its brands. Coke's schemes ranged from crown exchanges to under the crown prizes, which included toys, cars, free travel, consumer durables etc. Pepsi had crown exchanges and under the crown prizes as well, it also offered free gifts like cards and tattoos. A huge outlay was involved in promoting these schemes, with frequent media splashes.

Is The Rivalry Healthy?

In a market where the product and tastes remained virtually indistinguishable and fairly constant, brand recognition was a crucial factor for the cola companies. The quest for better brand recognition was the guiding force for Coke and Pepsi to a large extent. Colorful images, lively words, beautiful people and places, interesting storylines, innovative/attractive packaging and catchy jingles have made sure that the cola wars, though often scoffed at, rarely go unnoticed. And that's what it has all been about till now. The management of both the companies had to constantly adapt to the changing attitudes and demands of their consumers or lose market share.

The wars seemed to have settled down into a pattern. Pepsi typically won a market, sustained itself for a few years, and then lost to a very determined Coke. In the earlier years, Coke was content with advertising its product to build a strategic positioning for its product. With Pepsi's offensive moves getting stronger and stronger, Coke had no option but to opt for the same modus operandi. Though the market share debates would not have any conclusions, it would be safe to infer that the cola wars were a major factor in keeping customer interest alive in the segment so far. However, in the late 1990s, questions were raised about the necessity and more importantly, about the efficacy of these wars. Answers for this would be too difficult to ascertain and too shaky to confirm.

Web Courtesy:

http://www.icmrindia.org/free%20resources/casestudies/Marketing%20freecasep7.htm

4. Haldiram's Group - Seeking the 'Right' Marketing Mix

"Our brand (Leher) is nowhere near the dominance of Haldiram's."

— Manu Anand, Managing Director of Frito-Lay India[1]

"It is far easier to sell something that the consumer is already accustomed to. The company (Haldiram's) caters to the Indian palate, which is its primary driver of success."

— Neeraj Garg, Associate, AT Kearney[2]

Introduction

Over a period spanning six and a half decades, the Haldiram's Group (Haldiram's) had emerged as a household name for ready-to-eat snack foods in India. It had come a long way since its relatively humble beginning in 1937 as a small time sweet shop in Bikaner, in the Rajasthan state of India. In 2001, the turnover of the Haldiram's was ₹ 4 billion.

The group had presence not only in India but in several countries all over the world. Till the early 1990s, Haldiram's comprised of three units, one each in Kolkata, Nagpur and New Delhi. The Agarwals family that owned Haldiram's were always conscious of the need to satisfy customers in order to grow their business.

The company offered a wide variety of traditional Indian sweets and snacks at competitive prices that appealed to people belonging to different age groups. Haldiram's had many 'firsts' to its credit. It was the first company in India to brand 'namkeens'. The group also pioneered new ways of packaging namkeens[3].

Its packaging techniques increased the shelf life of namkeens from less than a week to more than six months. It was also one of the first companies in India to open a restaurant in New Delhi offering traditional Indian snack food items such as "panipuri," "chatpapri," and so on, which catered to the needs of hygiene conscious non-resident Indians and other foreign customers. Since the very beginning, the brand 'Haldiram's' had been renowned for its quality products.

The company employed the best available technology in all its manufacturing facilities in India. Given the increasing popularity of Haldiram's products, the group planned to expand its operations. However, some analysts felt that Haldiram's still had to overcome some hurdles. The company faced tough competition not only from sweets and snack food vendors in the unorganized market but also from domestic and international competitors like SM Foods, Bakeman's Industries Ltd, Frito Lay India Ltd.(Frito Lay) and Britannia Industries Ltd.

Moreover, the group had to overcome internal problems as well. In the early 1990s, because of the conflict within the Agarwals family, Haldiram's witnessed an informal split between its three units as they started operating separately offering similar products and sharing the same brand name. In 1999, after a court verdict these units started operating as three different companies with clearly defined territories. This split had resulted in aggressive competition among themselves for a higher share of domestic and international markets.

Background Note

In 1937, Ganga Bishen Agarwal, (popularly known as Haldiram), opened a small sweet shop in Bikaner, a small district in Rajasthan. Bikaner had a large number of sweet shops selling sweets as well as namkeens. 'Bhujia sev,' a salty snack prepared by Ganga Bishen, was very popular among the residents of Bikaner and was also purchased by tourists coming to Bikaner. In 1941, the name 'Haldiram's Bhujiawala' was used for the first time.

In 1950, Prabhu Shankar Agarwal (Prabhu), along with his father Rameshwar Lal Agarwal (son of Ganga Bishen), expanded the business by establishing a small manufacturing unit for sweets and namkeens in Kolkata. The success of this unit motivated Prabhu to upgrade its machinery to improve the quality of its products. As demand for Haldiram's products increased, it was decided to scale up the company's manufacturing and distribution activities. In 1970, a large manufacturing unit was set up in Nagpur in the state of Maharashtra (India).

In 1983, a retail outlet was set up in New Delhi. The outlet became very popular not only among the Delhiites but also among tourists visiting Delhi. Haldiram's was able to achieve significant growth during the 1980s and 1990s. In 1992, a manufacturing unit with a retail outlet attached to it was set up in the outskirts of Delhi. A year later, Haldiram's syrups and crushes were successfully launched in the Indian market.

In 1995, a restaurant was opened in New Delhi. In 1997, realizing the potential of namkeens, the company set up a manufacturing unit in Delhi exclusively for making namkeens. To add potato products to its existing product portfolio, machinery was imported from the US. Haldiram's maintained high quality standards at every stage of the production process. All its food items were prepared and packaged in a very hygienic environment.

In the mid 1990s, Haldiram's added bakery items, dairy products, sharbats and ice creams to its portfolio. At the beginning of the 21st century, Haldiram's products reached millions of consumers not only in India, but also in several other countries, including the US, Canada, UK, UAE, Australia, New Zealand, Sri Lanka, Nepal, Japan and Thailand.

Analysts felt that the growing popularity of Haldiram's products could be attributed to its constant focus on all the elements of the marketing mix. An article posted on the website apeda.com[4] quoted some of the company's strengths, "To sustain in the competitive market, Haldiram's has endeavored stress on its product quality, packaging, shelf life, competitive price with a special emphasis on consumers satisfaction and its lingering taste is amongst the best available in the world."

The Marketing Mix

Products

Haldiram's offered a wide range of products to its customers. The product range included namkeens, sweets, sharbats[5], bakery items, dairy products, papad[6] and ice-creams. However, namkeens remained the main focus area for the group contributing close to 60% of its total revenues. By specializing in the manufacturing of namkeens, the company seemed to have created a niche market.

Haldiram's sought to customize its products to suit the tastes and preferences of customers from different parts of India. It launched products, which catered to the tastes of people belonging to specific regions. For example, it launched 'Murukkus,' a South Indian snack, and 'Chennai Mixture' for south Indian customers.

Similarly, Haldiram's launched 'Bhelpuri,' keeping in mind customers residing in western India. The company offered certain products such as 'Nazarana,' 'Panchratan,' and 'Premium' only during the festival season in gift packs. These measures helped Haldiram's compete effectively in a market that was flooded with a variety of snack items in different shapes, sizes and flavors.

Pricing

Haldiram's offered its products at competitive prices in order to penetrate the huge unorganized market of namkeens and sweets. The company's pricing strategy took into consideration the price conscious nature of consumers in India.

Haldiram's launched namkeens in small packets of 30 grams, priced as low as ₹ 5. The company also launched namkeens in five different packs with prices varying according to their weights. The prices also varied on the basis of the type of namkeens and the raw materials used to manufacture it. The cost of metallized packing[7] also had an impact on the price, especially in the case of snack foods. The company revised the prices of its products upwards only when there was a steep increase in the raw material costs or additional taxes were imposed.

Place

Haldiram's developed a strong distribution network to ensure the widest possible reach for its products in India as well as overseas. From the manufacturing unit, the company's finished goods were passed on to carrying and forwarding (C&F) agents. C&F agents passed on the products to distributors, who shipped them to retail outlets. While the Delhi unit of Haldiram's had 25 C&F agents and 700 distributors in India, the Nagpur unit had 25 C&F agents and 375 distributors.

Haldiram's also had 35 sole distributors in the international market. The Delhi and Nagpur units together catered to 0.6 million retail outlets in India. C&F agents received a commission of around 5%, while distributors earned margins ranging from 8% to 10%. The retail outlets earned margins ranging from 14% to 30%. At the retail outlet level, margins varied according to the weight of packs sold.

Retailers earned more margins ranging from 25% to 30% by selling 30 gms pouches (priced at ₹ 5) compared to the packs of higher weights. Apart from the exclusive showrooms owned by Haldiram's, the company offered its products through retail outlets such as supermarkets, sweet shops, provision stores, bakeries and ice cream parlors. The products were also available in public places such as railway stations and bus stations that accounted for a sizeable amount of its sales.

Haldiram's products enjoyed phenomenal goodwill and stockists competed with each other to stock its products. Moreover, sweet shops and bakeries stocked Haldiram's products despite the fact that the company's products were competing with their own products. Haldiram's also offered its products through the Internet. The company tied up with indiatimes.com, a website owned by the Times of India group[8] to sell its products over the Internet. Haldiram's products could be ordered through a host of other websites in India and abroad.

Giftstoindia.com, giftssmashhits.com, tohfatoindia.com and channelindia.com enabled people residing abroad to send Haldiram's gift packs to specified locations in India. Region-specific websites enabled people to send gifts to specified regions. These include indiamart.com (Delhi and surrounding areas), mumbaiflowersgifts.com (Mumbai), and chennaiflowersgifts.com (Chennai and other parts of Tamilnadu). These websites competed on issues such as delivery time, which varied between 48 hrs to one week, delivery charges (some websites offered free delivery of products) and value added services (like sending personal messages along with the gift packs).

Promotion

Haldiram's product promotion had been low key until competition intensified in the snack foods market. The company tied with 'Profile Advertising'[9] for promoting its products. Consequently, attractive posters, brochures and mailers were designed to enhance the visibility of the Haldiram's brand.

Different varieties of posters were designed to appeal to the masses. The punch line for Haldiram's products was, 'Always in good taste.' Advertisements depicting the entire range of Haldiram's sweets and namkeens were published in the print media (magazines and newspapers). These advertisements had captions such as 'millions of tongues can't go wrong,' 'What are you waiting for, Diwali?' and 'Keeping your taste buds on their toes.'

To increase the visibility of the Haldiram's brand, the company placed its hoardings in high traffic areas such as train stations and bus stations. Posters were designed for display on public transport vehicles such as buses, and hoardings, focused on individual products were developed. Captions such as 'yeh corn hain' (this is corn), 'chota samosa - big mazaa' (small samosa[10] big entertainment), 'yeh Kashmiri mix khoob jamega' (this namkeen item will gel well) and 'oozing with taste' (for Rasgoolas) promoted individual products.

For those customers who wanted to know more about Haldiram's products, special brochures were designed which described the products and gave information about the ingredients used to make it. Mailers were also sent to loyal customers and important corporate clients as a token of appreciation for their patronage. Packaging was an important aspect of Haldiram's product promotion.

Since namkeens were impulse purchase items, attractive packaging in different colors influenced purchases. Haldiram's used the latest technology (food items were packed in nitrogen filled pouches) to increase the shelf life of its products. While the normal shelf life of similar products was under a week, the shelf life of Haldiram's products was about six months. The company projected the shelf life of its products as its unique selling proposition.

Posters highlighting the shelf life of its products carried the caption 'six months on the shelf and six seconds in your mouth.' During festival season, Haldiram's products were sold in attractive looking special gift packs. The showrooms and retail outlets of Haldiram's gave importance to point of purchase (POP) displays. Haldiram's snacks were displayed on special racks, usually outside retail outlets. The showrooms had sign boards displaying mouth-watering delicacies with captions such as 'Chinese Delight,' Simply South,' 'The King of all Chats.'[11]

Posters containing a brief account of the history of Haldiram's, along with pictures of its products, were also on display at these showrooms. Haldiram's also diversified into the restaurant business to cash in on its brand image. The company established restaurants in Nagpur and Delhi.

The restaurant at Nagpur devised an innovative strategy to increase its business: It facilitated people who were traveling by train through Nagpur station to order food from places where stockists of Haldiram's Nagpur unit were located. The customers could order for lunch/dinner by sending a demand draft (DD) or cheque to the Nagpur unit or giving the same to specified local distributors belonging to the Nagpur unit.

Along with the DD/cheque, customers had to provide information such as the name of the train, its likely time of arrival at Nagpur, their names and coach and seat numbers. Haldiram's restaurants in Delhi also used innovative ways to attract customers. The restaurant located at Mathura road had special play area for children.

To cater to NRI's and foreign tourists, who hesitated to consume snack foods sold by the roadside vendors since it was not prepared in a hygienic manner, the Haldiram's restaurant located in South Delhi used specially purified water to make snack foods including pani puri and chat papri[12]. These promotional strategies helped Haldiram's to compete effectively with local restaurant chains such as Nathus, Bikanerwala and Agarwals and with western fast food chains such as McDonald's and Pizza Hut.

Positioning

The above initiatives helped Haldiram's to uniquely position its brand. Haldiram's also gained an edge over its competitors by minimizing promotion costs. Appreciating the company's efforts at building brand, an analyst said, "Haldiram once was just another sweet maker but it has moved into trained brands first by improving the product quality and packaging. Through its clever products and brilliant distribution it had moved into the star category of brands."[13]

Haldiram's earned recognition both in India and abroad. The Nagpur unit of Haldiram's was conferred the International Food Award by the Trofeo International Alimentacion of Barcelona[14], Spain for having maintained high standards in quality and hygiene, at its manufacturing unit. The Delhi unit was awarded the Keshalkar Memorial Award by the All India Food Preservers Association in the mid 1980s in recognition of its efforts for popularizing ethnic Indian foods in India and abroad.

In 1994, the unit was awarded the International Award for Food & Beverages by the Trade Leaders Club in Barcelona, Spain. The unit also received the Brand Equity Award[15] in 1998. Manoharlal Agarwal, who played a key role in the success of the Delhi unit, was included in the eighth edition of Distinguished Leadership by the Board of Registrars of The American Biographical Institute[16]. Haldiram's was also admitted as the member of Snack Food Association, US[17].

The Road Ahead

In the financial year 2001-2002, the combined turnover of all three units of Haldiram's was estimated at ₹ 4 billion. The company targeted a growth of 15% for the financial year 2002-2003. Analysts felt that, given the competition in the industry, Haldiram's needed to develop new initiatives achieve this growth.

The competition in the ready-to-eat snack foods market in India was intensifying. Frito Lay India Ltd. (Frito Lay), one of Haldiram's major competitors, was expanding its market share. Instead of directly competing with the market leader Haldiram's, the company launched innovative products in the market and backed them with heavy publicity.

Frito Lay's product range consisted of a mixture of traditional Indian and western flavors which appealed to younger and older generations. Its products included Leher Namkeens, Leher Kurkure (snack sticks), Lays (flavored Chips), Cheetos (snack balls), Uncle Chips and Nutyumz (nut snacks).

Frito-Lay was the first company to launch small 35 gm packs namkeens priced at ₹ 5 and also the first company in the organized sector to launch Aloo Bhujia[18]. Another competitor, SM Foods, introduced a range of innovative products. The company launched India's first non-wafer chips in 1988. SM offered products under two main brands - Peppy and Piknik.

Under Peppy, it had sub brands such as Cheese Balls, Ringos, Hi Protein Crispies, Potato Rackets, Hearts, Veggie Treat, Mixtures and Minerette. Under Piknik, it had Protein Pin, Junior and Corn Puffs. Haldiram's also faced tough competition from domestic players such as Britannia Industries Ltd., Bikanerwala Foods and ITC.

In addition, FMCG major HLL had also announced plans to enter the snack food market. Analysts felt that Haldiram's lagged behind competitors in offering snack foods targeted at children, who were always eager to try new flavors in every product category. They felt that the company concentrated too much on traditional Indian items such as Bhujia Sev and Moong Dal.

Haldiram's had in fact, taken steps to fill the gaps in its portfolio. Rajendra Agarwal, the owner of the Nagpur unit said, "We want to expand our market by introducing snacks that will appeal to younger people. There will be no growth in the traditional snacks category."[19] The unit planned to launch products such as flavored ready-to-eat popcorn and a product similar to Leher Kurkure.

Though Haldiram's had increased its focus on advertising and promotion in the last couple of years, still more initiatives in this direction were necessary. Frito Lay's expenditure on product promotion was much higher. With successful ad campaigns such as "control nahin hotha" (it is irresistible) for the Leher brand of namkeens, the company made sure that it attracted the attention of viewers.

According to media reports, Haldiram's lagged behind competitors in the area of customer service. A report in Deccan Herald that Prabhu Shankar Agarwal, the owner of the Kolkata unit, was arrested on charges of manhandling customers only reiterated this opinion. The report also mentioned that few of the company's restaurants did not possess the minimum requirements, such as sufficient seating arrangements and adequate parking lots.

Haldiram's also had to deal with problems created by spurious products. Some companies claiming to be close associates of the original Haldiram's of Bikaner used the Haldiram's brand name in their products. For example the 'Haldiram Madanlal' company claimed that its proprietor, Anil Kumar Agarwal, belonged to the Haldiram's family of Bikaner.

The manufacture of spurious products threatened to dilute the Haldiram's brand image apart from affecting the sales. According to some analysts, many of the problems facing Haldiram's arose due to an informal split between its three units in the early 1990s.

The split occurred when Prabhu Shankar Agarwal, who was heading the Kolkata unit of Haldiram's, filed a complaint in the court against the Delhi and Nagpur units, alleging breach of contract when they opened a sweet shop in New Delhi in 1991. This led to a bitter court battle for many years. The court delivered a final verdict in 1999, when Haldiram's units were formally split as three separate companies with specific business territories.

The consequences of the split were a matter of concern. Though on paper, the three companies had clearly defined boundaries within which they should operate, in practice, they did not stay within their boundaries. They penetrated each other's territories and competed among themselves for a larger share of the snacks market. Analysts felt that competitors would take advantage of this split.

Since the scope for increasing market share in India was limited, these companies began to compete aggressively in international markets. They used the internet, not only to market their products but also compete with each other. Each company claimed that its products were superior to those of the others in terms of quality.

For instance, an advertisement in 'haldiramusa.com', a web portal that sold the products of the Delhi company in the US, read, "Our items come specially packed from the Original Haldiram's of Delhi offering superior taste and superior quality, the only Haldiram approved by the US FDA (Food and Drug Administration). Try the Delhi stuff and you will never touch the Nagpur Haldiram packets that most grocery stores store." Analysts were of the opinion that the internal rivalry among its own companies may lead to dilution of Haldiram's brand equity.

References:

1. In an article "It's snack time folks!" dated June 15, 2002, posted on the website www.blonet.com.
2. In an article "It all snacks up" in Brand Equity, Economic Times dated December 11, 2002.
3. These are spicy snacks made of chickpea flour, processed rice and roasted nuts. 'Namkeens' are very popular in India, especially among people from the northern part of the country. Around fifty varieties of namkeens are available in India.
4. Agriculture and Processed Foods Export Development Authority (APEDA) is an autonomous institution, which provides financial, logistics related and promotional assistance to exporters of processed food items from India. Through its website apeda.com, it enables exporters to give a brief account of the company and their products.
5. Juice concentrates offered in different flavors.
6. A flat, thin, dried roll of kneaded floor mixed with spicy ingredients. It has a reasonably long shelf life, can be toasted or fried in oil and served as a snack or taken along with food.
7. Packing where in Aluminum was used which helps in preserving the freshness of the products being packed.
8. The Times of India group is owned by Bennett, Coleman & Company Ltd. It is India's leading publishers of newspapers and magazines catering to a wide cross section of customers. The newspapers published by the group include Times of India, Economic Times, Nav Bharat Times and Sandhya Times (Hindi). The magazines published include Femina and Filmfare. Times FM, a music channel owned by the group, broadcasts programs in five cities in India.
9. An advertising agency based in India.
10. Triangle shaped pastry dough stuffed with spicy potatoes and deep-fried.
11. A traditional Indian snack food item prepared by deep frying potato in oil and mixing it with spices and other vegetables.

12. Snack items that are prepared with a spicy, water-based sauce. These snacks are commonly sold by roadside vendors.
13. In an article titled 'Brands and Bollywood,' on the website www.indiainfoline.com.
14. It is an international organization in the food processing industry.
15. An award given by "Brand Equity," a publication of the Times of India Group, to companies that are successful in their respective fields.
16. Based in the US, the American Biographical Institute is a publisher of biographical reference works collected from all over the world.
17. An international trade association of the snack food industry, representing snack food manufacturers and suppliers.
18. Paste of mashed potatoes and gram flour, fried and added with salt and spices.
19. In an article 'It All Snacks Up' in Brand Equity, Economic Times dated December 11, 2002.

Web Courtesy: http://www.icmrindia.org/free%20resources/casestudies/haldiram1.htm

5. Kellogg's Indian Experience: A Failed Launch

In April 1995, Kellogg India Ltd. (Kellogg) received unsettling reports of a gradual drop in sales from its distributors in Mumbai. There was a 25% decline in countrywide sales since March1995, the month Kellogg products had been made available nationally.

Kellogg was the wholly-owned Indian subsidiary of the Kellogg Company based in Battle Creek, Michigan. Kellogg Company was the world's leading producer of cereals and convenience foods, including cookies, crackers, cereal bars, frozen waffles, meat alternatives, piecrusts, and ice cream cones. Founded in 1906, Kellogg Company had manufacturing facilities in 19 countries and marketed its products in more than 160 countries. The company's turnover in 1999-00 was $ 7 billion. Kellogg Company had set up its 30th manufacturing facility in India, with a total investment of $ 30 million. The Indian market held great significance for the Kellogg Company because its US sales were stagnating and only regular price increases had helped boost the revenues in the 1990s.

Launched in September 1994, Kellogg's initial offerings in India included cornflakes, wheat flakes and Basmati rice flakes. Despite offering good quality products and being supported by the technical, managerial and financial resources of its parent, Kellogg's products failed in the Indian market. Even a high-profile launch backed by hectic media activity failed to make an impact in the marketplace. Meanwhile, negative media coverage regarding the products increased, as more and more consumers were reportedly rejecting the taste. There were complaints that the products were not available in many cities. According to analysts, out of every 100 packets sold, only two were being bought by regular customers; with the rest 98 being first-time buyers. Converting these experimenters into regular buyers had become a major problem for the company.

By September, 1995, sales had virtually stagnated. Marketing experts pointed out various mistakes that Kellogg had committed and it was being increasingly felt that the company would find it extremely difficult to sustain itself in the Indian market.

The Mistakes

Kellogg realized that it was going to be tough to get the Indian consumers to accept its products. Kellogg banked heavily on the quality of its crispy flakes. But pouring hot milk on the flakes made them soggy. Indians always boiled their milk unlike in the West and consumed it warm or lukewarm. They also liked to add sugar to their milk.

When Kellogg flakes were put in hot milk, they became soggy and did not taste good. If one tried having it with cold milk, it was not sweet enough because the sugar did not dissolve easily in cold milk. The rice and wheat versions did not do well. In fact, some consumers even referred to the rice flakes as rice corn flakes.

In early 1996, defending the company's products, Managing Director Avronsart said, "True, some people will not like the way it tastes in hot milk. And not all consumers will want to have it with cold milk. But over a period of time, we expect consumer habits to change. Kellogg is a past master at the art, having fought - and won - against croissant-and-coffee in France, biscuits in Italy and noodles in Korea."

A typical, average middle-class Indian family did not have breakfast on a regular basis like their Western counterparts. Those who did have breakfast, consumed milk, biscuits, bread, butter, jam or local food preparations like idlis, parathas etc. According to analysts, a major reason for Kellogg's failure was the fact that the taste of its products did not suit Indian breakfast habits. Kellogg sources were however quick to assert that the company was not trying to change these habits; the idea was only to launch its products on the health platform and make consumers see the benefit of this healthier alternative.

Avronsart remarked, "Kellogg India is not here to change breakfast eating habits. What the company proposes is to offer consumers around the world a healthy, nutritious, convenient and easy-to-prepare alternative in the breakfast eating habit. It was not just a question of providing a better alternative to traditional breakfast eating habits but also developing a taste for grain based foods in the morning."

Another mistake Kellogg committed was on the positioning front. The company's advertisements and promotions initially focussed only on the health aspects of the product. In doing this, Kellogg had moved away from its successful 'fun-and-taste' positioning adopted in the US. Analysts commented that this positioning had given the brand a 'health product' image, instead of the fun/health plank that the product stood on in other markets. (In the US for instance, Kellogg offered toys and other branded merchandise for children and had a Kellogg's fan club as well.) Another reason for the low demand was deemed to be the premium pricing adopted by the company.

At an average cost of ₹ 21 per 100 gm, Kellogg products were clearly priced way above the product of its main competitor, Mohun's Cornflakes (₹ 16.50 for 100 gm). Vinay Mohan, Managing Director, Mohan Rocky Springwater & Breweries, the makers of Mohun's cornflakes said, "Kellogg is able to cater only to the A-Class towns or the more affluent consumers whereas Mohun's caters to the mass market." Another small-time brand, Champion was selling at prices almost half of that of Kellogg. This gave the brand a premium image, making it seem unattainable for the average Indian consumer. According to one analyst, "When Kellogg tried a dollar-to-rupee pricing for its products, the company lost out on getting to the mass consumer." Even the customers at the higher end of the market failed to perceive any extra benefits in Kellogg's products. A Business Today report said that like other MNCs, Kellogg had fallen into a price trap, by assuming that there was a substantial latent niche market in India for premium products.

In most Third World countries pricing is believed to play a dominant role in the demand for any product. But Kellogg did not share this view. Avronsart said, "Research demonstrates that to be well accepted by consumers even the most nutritious product must taste good. Most consumers view quality as they view taste, but with a very high standard. We approach pricing on a case-to-case basis, always consistent with the total value delivered by each product." He also said, "Local brands are selling only on the price platform. We believe that we're demanding the right price for the value we offer. If the consumer wants quality, we believe he can afford the price." Thus, it was not surprising that the company went ahead with its plans of increasing the price of its products by an average of 28% during 1995-98. Before the product was made available nationally in March 1995, the demand from Mumbai had been very encouraging. Within a year of its launch in Mumbai, Kellogg had acquired a 53% market share. Following this, the company accelerated its national expansion plans and launched the product in 60 cities in a 15-month period. However, Kellogg was surprised to see the overall demand tapering off considerably. A Mumbai based Kellogg distributor explained, "Why should somebody sitting in Delhi be deprived of the product? So there was considerable movement from Mumbai to other parts of the country." As the product was officially launched countrywide, the company realized that the tremendous response from the Mumbai market was nothing but the 'disguised demand' from other places being routed through Mumbai.

Kellogg had also decided to focus only on the premium and middle-level retail stores. This was because the company believed that it could not maintain uniform quality of service if it offered its products at a larger number of shops. What Kellogg seemed to have overlooked was the fact that this decision put large sections of the Indian population out of its reach.

Disappointed with the poor performance, Kellogg decided to launch two of its highly successful brands - Chocos (September 1996) and Frosties (April 1997) in India. The company hoped to repeat the global success of these brands in the Indian market. Chocos were wheat scoops coated with chocolate, while Frosties had sugar frosting on individual flakes. The success of these variants took even Kellogg by surprise and sales picked up significantly. (It was even reported that Indian consumers were consuming the products as snacks.) This was followed by the launch of Chocos Breakfast Cereal Biscuits.

The success of Chocos and Frosties also led to Kellogg's decision to focus on totally indianising its flavors in the future. This resulted in the launch of the Mazza series in August 1998 - a crunchy, almond-shaped corn breakfast cereal in three local flavors - 'Mango Elaichi,' 'Coconut Kesar' and 'Rose.' Developed after a one-year extensive research to study consumer patterns in India, Mazaa was positioned as a tasty, nutritional breakfast cereal for families. Kellogg was careful not to repeat its earlier mistakes.

It did not position Mazza in the premium segment. The glossy cardboard packaging was replaced by pouches, which helped in bringing down the price substantially.

The decision to reduce prices seemed to be a step in the right direction. However, analysts remained skeptical about the success of the product in the Indian market. They pointed out that Kellogg did not have retail packs of different sizes to cater to the needs of different consumer groups. To counter this criticism, the company introduced packs of suitable sizes to suit Indian consumption patterns and purchasing power. Kellogg introduced the 500gm family pack, which brought down the price per kg by 20%. Also, Mazza was introduced in 60gm pouches, priced at ₹ 9.50.

Kellogg's advertising had not been very impressive in the initial years. Apart from 'Jago jaise bhi, lo Kellogg's hi,' the brand had no long-term baseline lines. Later, Kellogg attempted to indianise its campaigns instead of simply copying its international promotions. The rooster that was associated with the Kellogg brand the world over was missing from its advertisements in India. One of its campaigns depicted a cross section of individuals ranging from a yoga instructor to a kathakali dancer attributing their morning energy and fitness to Kellogg. The advertisement suggested that cornflakes could be taken with curds, honey, and banana.

In April 1997, Kellogg launched 'The Kellogg Breakfast Week,' a community-oriented initiative to generate awareness about the importance of breakfast. The program focussed on prevention of anemia and conducted a series of nutrition workshops activities for both individuals and families. The program was launched in Chennai, Delhi and Mumbai. The company tied up with the Indian Dietetic Association (IDA) to launch a nation-wide public-service initiative to raise awareness about iron deficiency problems. Nutritionists and dieticians from the country participated in a day-long symposium in Calcutta to deliberate on the causes and impact of anemia caused by iron deficiency. This program was in line with the company's global marketing strategy, which included nutrition promotion initiatives such as symposiums, educative programs and sponsorship of research.

Emphasizing Kellogg's commitment to nutrition education, Avronsart remarked, "Product modification, particularly the addition of iron fortification in breakfast cereals is how Kellogg responds to the nutritional needs of the consumers. In this spirit, Kellogg India is taking a major step to improve the nutritional status of consumers in the country, the specific opportunity being iron fortification for which we have undertaken major initiatives to promote the awareness of the importance of iron in the diet."

Kellogg also increased its focus on promotions that sought to induce people to try their product and targeted schools across the country for this. By mid-1995, the company had covered 60 schools in the metros. In March 1996, the company offered specially designed 50 gm packs free to shoppers at select retail stores in Delhi. This was followed by a house-to-house sampling exercise offering one-serving sachets to housewives in the city. The company also offered free pencil-boxes, water bottles, and lunch boxes with every pack. Plastic dispensers offering the product at discounted rates were also put up in petrol pumps, super markets, airports etc.

Kellogg identified distribution as another major area to address in order to increase its penetration in the market. In 1995, Kellogg had 30,000 outlets, which was increased to around 40,000 outlets by 1998. Avronsart said, "We have increased our reach only slightly, but we are now enlarging our coverage." Considering that it had just one plant in Taloja in Maharashtra, the company was considering plans to set up more manufacturing units.

Kellogg's also began working towards a better positioning plank for its products. The company's research showed that the average Indian consumer did not give much importance to the level of iron and vitamin intake, and looked at the quantity, rather than the quality, of the food consumed. Avronsart commented, "The Kellogg mandate is to develop awareness about nutrition. There is a lot of confusion between nourishment and nutrition. That is something that we have to handle." Kellogg thus worked towards changing the positioning of Chocos and Frosties - which were not positioned on the health platform but, instead, were projected as 'fun-filled' brands.

Kellogg then launched the Chocos biscuits, claiming that cereals being a 'narrow category,' the foray into biscuits would create wider awareness for the Kellogg brand. Biscuits being a mass market product requiring an intensive distribution network, Kellogg's decision to venture into this competitive and crowded market with stalwarts like Britannia, Parle and Bakeman, was seen as a bold move not only in India, but also globally. Avronsart said, "We are ready to develop any food based on grain and nutrition that will satisfy consumer needs."

The Results

In 1995, Kellogg had a 53% share of the ₹ 150 million breakfast cereal market, which had been growing at 4-5% per annum till then. By 2000, the market size was ₹ 600 million, and Kellogg's share had increased to 65%. Analysts claimed that Kellogg' entry was responsible for this growth. The company's improved prospects were clearly attributed to the shift in positioning, increased consumer promotions and an enhanced media budget. The effort to develop products specifically for the Indian market helped Kellogg make significant inroads into the Indian market.

However, Kellogg continued to have the image of a premium brand and its consumption was limited to a few well-off sections of the Indian market. The company had to face the fact that it would be really very difficult to change the eating habits of Indians. In 2000, Kellogg launched many new brands including Crispix Banana, Crispix Chocos, Froot Loops, Cocoa Frosties, Honey Crunch, All Bran and All Raisin. Kellogg also launched 'Krispies Treat,' an instant snack targeted at children. Priced on the lower side at ₹ 3 and ₹ 5, the product was positioned to compete against the products in the 'impulse snacks' category. According to some analysts, the introduction of new cereals and the launch of biscuits and snacks could be attributed to the fact that the company had been forced to look at alternate product categories to make up for the below-expectation performance of the breakfast cereal brands.

Kellogg sources however revealed that the company was in India with long-term plans and was not focusing on profits in the initial stages. In Mexico the company had to wait for two decades, and in France nine years, before it could significantly influence local palates. With just one rival in the organized sector (Mohan Meakins) and its changed tactics in place, what remained to be seen was how long it would take Kellogg to crack the Indian market.

Web Courtesy:

http://www.icmrindia.org/free%20resources/casestudies/Marketing%20freecasestudyp1.htm

6. Fairness Wars: Who's The Fairest of Them All?

"The saffron and milk combination in Fairever clicked with the people because they were familiar with the goodness of the products. And we changed the rules by introducing saffron which had never been used in fairness creams in the past."

- **C.K. Ranganathan, CEO & MD, CavinKare Ltd.**

"Fair & Lovely continues to grow in a healthy manner. Only two out of ten Indians use face creams. That means strong growth prospects for all brands."

- **A HLL Spokesperson**

In June 1999, the FMCG major Hindustan Lever Ltd. (HLL)[1] announced that it would offer 50% extra volume on its Fair & Lovely (F&L) fairness cream at the same price to the consumers.[2] This was seen by industry analysts as a combative initiative to prevent CavinKare's[3] Fairever from gaining popularity in retail markets. HLL's scheme led to increased sales of F&L and encouraged consumers to stay with F&L and not shift to the rival brand. In December 1999, Godrej Soaps[4] created a new product category - fairness soaps - by launching its FairGlow Fairness Soap.

The product was successful and reported sales of more than ₹ 700 million in the first year of its launch. Godrej extended the brand to fairness cream by launching FairGlow Fairness Cream in July 2000. By 2001, CavinKare's Fairever fairness cream, with the USP of 'a fairness cream with saffron' acquired a 15% share, and F&L's share fell from 93% (in 1998) to 76%. Within a year of its launch, Godrej's FairGlow cream became the third largest fairness cream brand, with a 4% share in the ₹ 6 billion fairness cream market in India.

The other players, including J.L. Morrison's Nivea Visage fairness cream and Emami Group's Emami Naturally Fair cream, had the remaining 5% share. Clearly, the fairness cream and soaps market was witnessing a fierce battle among the three major players - HLL, CavinKare, and Godrej - each trying to woo the consumer with their attractive schemes.

Background

In 1975, HLL launched its first fairness cream under the F&L brand. With the launch of F&L, the market, which was dominated by Ponds (Vanishing Cream and Cold Cream) and Lakme (Sunscreen Lotion), lost their dominant position. The dominance of HLL's F&L continued till 1998, when CavinKare launched its Fairever cream in direct competition with F&L.

Within six months of its launch, Fairever captured more than 6% of market share. The success of Fairever attracted other players. Every product in this segment was witnessing growth higher than the overall personal care product category growth. The fairness cream market was growing at 25% p.a., as compared to the overall cosmetic products market's growth of 15% p.a. In 2000, there were 7 main brands in the fairness product market across the country.

Fair (Ness) Wars

In 1998, CavinKare launched Fairever fairness cream. The company took care to stick to the herbal platform that its consumers had come to associate with all CavinKare products. Fairever seemed to be an instant success. Fairever's market share jumped from 1.23% in 1998 to 8.13% in 1999. The brand was expected to grow from ₹ 160 million 1999 to ₹ 560 million in 2000. Its success attracted many players, including Godrej (FairGlow) and Paras Chemicals (Freshia). Existing products like Emami Naturally Fair and F&L were promoted with renewed vigor.

In December 1999, Godrej launched FairGlow fairness soap and created a new product category. The soap claimed to remove blemishes to give the user a smooth and glowing complexion. FairGlow was positioned as a twin advantage soap - a clean fresh bath and the added benefit of fairness. In early 2000, Godrej Soaps launched Nikhar, which was based on the ancient Indian formula of milk, besan and turmeric.

Though Nikhar and FairGlow were positioned differently - Nikhar targeted fairness and FairGlow claimed to protect skin naturally - the objective of both was the same, get more of a stagnating market. In April 2000, HLL introduced Lux Skincare soap, positioned on the sunscreen platform. Priced at ₹ 14 for a 75gm cake, it was able to garner only a 0.5% share by 2000 end. In comparison, the mother brand Lux had a share of 14%.

Retailers claimed that sales for the Lux variant were poor as it promised only protection from ultraviolet rays. While this soap prevented one from growing darker, it did not promise to enhance the complexion. By 2000 end, F&L cream seemed to be losing ground not only to other creams but also to FairGlow soap. The switch from cream to soap was largely because soaps were perceived to be less harmful to the skin than cream.

HLL did not have a product in its soap portfolio for this segment, and this was where Godrej seemed to have gained. However, in 2001, HLL followed Godrej's footsteps and launched Fair & Lovely Fairness Soap. This intensified the competition. F&L's extension into soaps was in tune with HLL's strategy to develop and grow the premium segment of the market. Since the growth in the toilet soap market had slowed down, the industry felt that premium soaps would re-energise the market.

Sangeeta Pendurkar, Marketing Manager, HLL, said, "We are targeting the 50,000 tonne premium soaps market with F&L. We believe F&L soap will synergise with F&L cream as research reveals that the usage of both will deliver better fairness." Analysts felt that though FairGlow had the first mover advantage, F&L soap's growth potential could not be underestimated given the strong equity of the mother brand.

In 1999, HLL and CavinKare hiked the price of F&L and Fairever by ₹ 1 from ₹ 25 and ₹ 26 respectively. In 2000, Fairever was back to its original price to maintain price parity. Many stockists said that this was done to push the product against F&L. A stockist commented, "The company was trying out this price to compete with F&L and other new brands that have come in.

But we did not see higher sales due to this and the company reverted to its original price." F&L too followed suit. During 2000-01, while the fairness cream market was growing at an average of 15% Fairever's growth had slowed down. Analysts felt that this was mainly because Fairever was priced higher than competing products. Meanwhile, in January 2000, HLL filed a patent infringement suit for ₹ 100 million in the Kolkata High Court against CavinKare Ltd.

HLL alleged that CavinKare was using its patented F&L formula without its knowledge or permission. HLL obtained an ex-parte stay on CavinKare, but CavinKare got the stay vacated in a week's time. It also filed a patent revocation application in the Chennai High Court and defended the suit on the grounds that HLL's patent was not valid. CavinKare further claimed that the ingredients contained in the composition were 'prior art' and that the new patent was not an improvement of the earlier patent, which had expired in 1988. In September 2000, the companies suddenly opted for an out-of-court settlement.

CavinKare gave an undertaking to the court that the company would not "manufacture and/or market either by themselves or by their agents any fairness cream by using silicone compound in combination with other ingredients covered in patent no. 169917 of the plaintiff (HLL), namely Niacinamide, Parsol MCX, Parsol 1789, with effect from September 15, 2000." HLL also gave an undertaking that it would not interfere with the sale of the cream manufactured on or before September 15, 2000, lying with the wholesalers, re-distribution stockists, and retailers.

Promotional Wars

During 2000-01, with major players entering the market, the existing products were promoted with renewed vigor through price reductions, extra volumes, etc. Many products were marketed aggressively. While F&L advertisements projected fairness comparable to the moon's silvery glow, FairGlow offered the added benefit of a blemish-free complexion.

But Fairever, which sold at a higher price, did not initiate any promotional activities. B. Nandakumar, President (Marketing) CavinKare, explained, "We will not tailor our product to the competition. We'll do so for the consumer. Freebies are not the only way to garner sales." However, analysts believed that CavinKare did not undertake any promotional activities due to lack of financial muscle.

On February 14, 2000, as a part of its promotional activities, Godrej Soaps announced the 'Godrej FairGlow Friendship Funda'[5] in various colleges in Maharashtra. In August 2000, it launched the 'FairGlow Express,' the first branded local train in India, in Mumbai, in partnership with Western Railways. In December 2000, Godrej took its FairGlow brand to the web by launching www.fairglow.com. Later, it launched a unique online promotional scheme - 'the FairGlow Face of the Fortnight.'

Every fortnight, one winner was selected and showcased on the website. The winner also won prizes like perfume hampers, gold and pearl jewellery, holiday for two etc. In early 2001, Godrej Soaps also launched its FairGlow cream in an affordable sachet (pouch pack). The 9gm sachet was priced at ₹ 5, and claimed to give around 15-20 applications per pack. It was initially launched in South India, and was expected to enter other markets very soon.

The Wars Continue Unabated

In early 2001, three major players - HLL, CavinKare and Godrej - competed fiercely to penetrate the market further with their attractive schemes. A growing number of pharma and OTC drug companies like Emami, Ayurvedic Concepts, Paras etc. also entered this segment.

Companies were also facing competition from Amway, Avon, Modicare etc., which were into direct selling. The market was seeing a major convergence of product categories with the emergence of more and more variants to fill every conceivable niche. This heightened competition forced companies to increase their advertisement spends.

HLL re-launched F&L and quadrupled its advertising expenditure. CavinKare more than doubled its ad spends from ₹ 215 million in 1999 to ₹ 500 million in 2001. Godrej and Emami too planned to raise their ad spends. But even as ad spends increased, fakes entered the market.

Fair & Lovely's fakes were rampant with names like Pure & Lovely and Fare & Lovely. Fairever's copies were Four Ever, For Ever or Fare Ever. In early 2001, HLL launched Nutririch Fair & Lovely Fairness Reviving Lotion to protect its brand from any threat in the premium segment. The new product was claimed to be scientifically formulated to protect the skin from harmful ultraviolet rays and enhance natural fairness. The new formula, containing Triple UV Guard Sun protection system and the fairness ingredients Vitamin B3 and milk proteins, promised to restore and protect the natural skin colours from the sun's darkening effects.

The product was also claimed to contain Niacinamide making it the only patented formula fairness cream. It was targeted at women in the age group of 18-35 and was priced at a premium. A 50ml pack was priced at ₹ 38 and a 100ml pack at ₹ 68. HLL also launched 'Pears Naturals Fairness cream' at the same time. By mid 2001, the fairness concept was no longer restricted to creams and soaps, but had expanded to talcs also. Emami was test marketing a herbal fairness talc in the South.

The rapid expansion of the fairness business had two consequences: cutthroat competition and a flurry of copycats. Every company - from the market leader to the new entrants - was forced to rethink its marketing strategies, spend lavishly on advertisements, and even seek legal action against unfair claims. Even though there was no scientific backing for the manufacturer's claims that their products enhanced fairness, prevented darkening of skin, or removed blemishes, sales of fairness products continued to gallop.

Dr R.K. Pandhi, Head of the Department of Dermatology, AIIMS, Delhi, said, "I have never come across a medical study that substantiated such claims. No externally applied cream can change your skin colour. Indeed, the amount of melanin in an individual's skin cannot be reduced by applying fairness creams, bathing with sun-blocking soaps or using fairness talc." In 2001, the organised market of branded fairness cream products was worth about ₹ 6 billion. The unbranded and fakes market was estimated to be ₹ 1.5 billion. The market was big and the potential was even bigger. In India, beauty seemed to be associated with fairness more than with anything else. With such an attitude firmly entrenched in the minds of millions of people, the fairness products market would see fair days ahead.

References:

1. HLL, a 51.6% subsidiary of Unilever Plc, was the largest FMCG company in India, with a turnover of ₹ 114 billion in 2000. The company's business ranged from personal and household care products to foods, beverages, specialty chemicals and animal feeds.
2. Initially HLL offered ₹ 5 off on F&L. This was followed by 20% extra volume for the same price, which was later increased to 50% extra volume.
3. In 1983, C.K. Ranganathan (Ranganathan) established Chik India, with an investment of ₹ 15000. Chik India was later renamed Beauty Cosmetics, and then went public in 1991. In 1998, the company was renamed CavinKare Ltd.
4. Godrej Soaps' major product lines were toilet soaps and detergents, industrial chemicals, cosmetics and men's toiletries. It had interests in several other businesses such as real estate, agro produce, etc through its subsidiaries. In April 2001, the consumer goods business of Godrej Soaps was demerged into a new company. The chemicals division remained with Godrej Soaps, with the new name, Godrej Industries.
5. 'Friendship Funda' was a system for delivering messages on Valentine's Day. About 50,000 cards were distributed so students could write their Valentine's Day love messages. Special mailboxes for collecting these cards were spread out over 50 different campuses. The cards were collected, sorted, and handed over to the addressees.

Web Courtesy:
http://www.icmrindia.org/free%20resources/casestudies/Fairness%20Wars1.htm

Activities and Projects

1. Ask students to form groups. Each group is to list down the different kinds of Marketing activity that they come across in their day to day life. The class will then discuss why each of these activities is a Marketing activity.
2. Divide students into groups. Allot one Marketing Concept/ Philosophy to each group. Ask each group to perform a role play bringing out the particular philosophy/ Concept of Marketing given to them. When the group performs, the other groups should be asked to identify the philosophy/ concept so depicted.
3. Divide students into groups of six. Each group is a Marketing unit and has to decide on a new product that its wants to manufacture and sell in the market. Each group has to write down which factor of the external environment will impact their organization and why.
4. Ask students to visit a supermarket or a mall. The student is supposed to unobtrusively observe the behaviour of five consumers when purchasing a particular product. Write a report on his/her observation and share it in class. (All five consumers should be observed when purchasing the same product).
5. Divide students into two groups. Ask each group to come up with one product that they will market. Ask them to identify the market segment for their product. Why did they identify a particular segment? Each group will present the reasons why they have chosen a particular segment/s to market their product.
6. Each student has to make a chart of the different bath soaps available in the market, together with their prices. On the basis of this information the student is to identify the pricing objective/pricing strategy
7. Different products are available in different sized packages. Make a list of the different sized packages and the difference in pricing. What conclusions can you draw?
8. Divide the class into groups. This text book gives you two different types of classification of products. Ask students to research and see if any other types of classifications of products exist. Each group is to make a presentation on its findings.
9. Divide the class into groups. Allot each group a particular product category. Ask each group to work out a distribution strategy for the particular product. Each group has to justify its strategy.
10. Ask students to visit one of the fast food joints in the organized sector. Example Mc Donald or Pizza Hut. Ask them to interview at least five consumers with the objective of finding out whether the consumers are aware of any existing sales Promotion scheme being offered. Also ask them how they came to know about the scheme.

11. Ask students to Study the advertisement of competing products. They are to present whether the advertisements are competitive or not.
12. The Pepsi and Coca Cola advertising war is famous. Identify other competing products that are at war through advertising strategy.
13. Ask students to study the promotional strategy of two products. Based on the promotional strategy the students have to identify how the company is positioning the brand in the mind of the consumer. This can be a group or individual activity.
14. Each student is to list down his/her marketing experience with reference to the use of mobile phone service. Positive and negative experiences should be shared.
15. Divide students into groups. Each group should list down various marketing activities. Each activity is to be divided into the product component and the service component.

www.ingramcontent.com/pod-product-compliance
Lightning Source LLC
Chambersburg PA
CBHW062133160426
43191CB00013B/2289